Text – Varieties – Translation

ZAA Studies

Language Literature Culture

Buchreihe zur
Zeitschrift für Anglistik und Amerikanistik
A Quarterly of Language, Literature and Culture

Herausgegeben von
Edited by

Helmbrecht Breinig (Erlangen-Nürnberg)
Brigitte Georgi-Findlay (Dresden)
Thomas Herbst (Erlangen-Nürnberg)
Ekkehard König (Berlin)
Barbara Korte (Tübingen)
Albrecht Neubert (Leipzig)
Gerhard Stilz (Tübingen)
Günter Walch (Berlin)

Band 5

Wolfgang Thiele / Albrecht Neubert /
Christian Todenhagen (eds.)

Text – Varieties – Translation

**STAUFFENBURG
VERLAG**

Die Deutsche Bibliothek – CIP-Einheitsaufnahme

ZAA studies : language, literature, culture ; Buchreihe zur Zeitschrift
für Anglistik und Amerikanistik. – Tübingen : Stauffenburg-Verl.,
Buchreihe ZAA Studies zu: Zeitschrift für Anglistik und Amerikanistik
ISSN 1434-0348

Bd. 5. Text – Varieties – Translation – 2001

Text – Varieties – Translation / Wolfgang Thiele ... (eds.). –
Tübingen: Stauffenburg-Verl., 2001
(ZAA Studies ; Bd. 5)
ISBN 3-86057-734-4

Printed with the support of the Institute for Applied Linguistics,
Kent State University, Kent, Ohio.

© 2001 · Stauffenburg Verlag Brigitte Narr GmbH
P.O. Box 25 25 · D-72015 Tübingen

Printed by Difo-Druck, Bamberg
Printed in Germany

ISSN 1434-0348
ISBN 3-86057-734-4

Table of contents

Preface

Text – Varieties – Translation brings together a wide range of papers concerned with problems reflecting theoretical as well as practically-oriented debates. The contributions have been written from different linguistic and adjacent angles and deal with specific questions of present-day English Studies, trying, more or less explicitly, to relate them to more basic topics of theoretical relevance. Their underlying theme, however, is the attempt to view the study of English through different lenses reflecting their objects in the light of textuality and variability with translation playing the part of a mediating agent.

On the one hand, the papers focus on aspects of English which have gained ground in scholarly discussions in recent years. On the other hand, the articles belong to well-established areas of philology. They represent approaches to the investigation of English and Englishes which have an important impact on 'traditional' sub-disciplines like the study of English literature, the history of English literature, English linguistics or English culture in the present and past. Though dealing with selected sub-problem of English Studies all papers are focused on being more than mere contributions to the traditional sub-disciplines because they go beyond the confines of narrow traditional areas. In looking at English literature and English culture, or viewing texts from the point of view of literature and language, or perceiving and investigating the close connections and interrelations between the English language and culture, English (text) linguistics and translating, etc., all articles aim at transcending accustomed viewing angles. This is more or less due to the fact that what used to be called philological phenomena cannot be adequately explained without recourse to theories and principles outside philological paradigms. Communicative concerns of using English, that is, its varieties, its textual representations, and its translational extensions transcend established frames of reference. The inclusion of methods and questions discussed and elaborated in psychology, semiotics, translatology and sociology are examples of this very general problem.

The volume includes papers which refer to two main areas of investigation, both of them contributing in their own special ways to elucidate the textbound varieties of English discourse, original and in translation.

The first area combines articles which endeavour to view the text or discourse in relation to one or more aspects of English culture, linguistics, literature and translation. In *Translations as 'varied' texts*, Albrecht Neubert clarifies relationships between the role of equivalence in translation studies and the overall theme 'text and variety'. Christoph Gutknecht and Lutz J. Rölle show that texts can never be translated 'as such' (i.e. as sequences of linguistic signs) but have to be processed by insisting on a hierarchy of *Translation factors*. Gottfried Graustein and Wolfgang Thiele discuss *Elements and relations again* with regard to textual relevance viewed from an actional angle. Christian Todenhagen explains the cognitive strategies involved in the interpretation of two versions of a radio commercial in *Point de capiton as textual metaphor*. Wolfgang Lörscher describes and categorizes *Nonverbal aspects of foreign language classroom discourse*. In *Texts with a view – Windows onto the world. Notes on the textuality of pictures* Hartmut Stöckl pursues a metaphoric application of textual categories to pictures. Horst W. Drescher's contribution *Literati, literature, language; or, Patterns of identity* is devoted to Scottish thinking, cultural identity and the literary tradition of the eighteenth-century generation representing Scottish Enlightenment. In *"Freedom is a noble thing" – Scottish independent rhetorics and the referendum of 11 September 1997* Joachim Schwend discusses Scotland's future in Europe by focusing on distinctive patterns of discourse.

The second part of the volume is concerned with several varieties of English exemplified by typical modes of representation. These contributions relate to aspects of language, culture, literature, and applied fields. Gerhard Leitner in *The Aboriginal contribution to mainstream Australian English. A corpus-based study* looks at the interaction of English with indigenous languages in Australia and explores the use of Aboriginal expressions and concepts in English. Norbert Schaffeld's article *Staging the rehearsals: theatrical patterns of the play within the play in contemporary British, Australian and Canadian metadrama* presents a comparative approach which tries to probe the diverse ways in which theatricalism can be employed. Clausdirk Pollner considers his paper *'Braw pearls' – The New Testament in Scots* as a contribution to the discussion of the role of the old Scottish national language as a written medium. In *The domains of the Lampeter Corpus as a window to Early Modern English social history* Josef Schmied analyses lexical variation and puts it into its sociocultural historical perspective. The volume is rounded off by *ESP from a linguistic and didactic point of view: some suggestions* by Manfred Markus, who gives a survey of the variable interests in, and the different approaches to, the use of texts representing English for Specific Purposes.

It is hoped that this collection will highlight some novel aspects characterizing work in progress and thus advance the discussion of interested scholars. As a result of its overarching theme *Text – Varieties – Translation* could perhaps help to open some new avenues of research.

The editors

Albrecht Neubert *(Leipzig)*

Translations as 'varied' texts

Translations in a study on language and text variation

In the course of a larger project attempting to clarify the role of *equivalence* in translation studies, I came to discover that this topic actually bore a number of striking relationships with the overall theme *text and variety*. Thus, the inclusion of *translation* in the title of this book has, I think, a deeper justification than just a lumping together of three concepts in order to cater to the various interests of our contributors.

It has become increasingly clear that translational equivalence, a concept of long standing but often put into doubt by scholars of translation (cf. Snell-Hornby 1986 for arguments), can not possibly survive as a linguistic term. There has actually never been a linguistic equivalence between source and target texts. Even literal renderings cannot help exhibiting deviations, i.e. between the **systems** of the source and the target languages. In the light of the systemic contrasts characterising adequate translations, the idea of equivalence, i.e. linguistic equivalence, has therefore been more and more discredited. Linguistics which had helped to procure a scholarly status for translation studies has evidently not been in a position to equally supply such a key concept for the categorial framework of the new discipline.

Though translating, on the face of it, is about 'rendering (items of) one language into (items of) another language', it is essentially much more than this. Translations are not primarily judged by how close individual words and structures, even sentences are to the original. They rather derive their quality from the way linguistic forms lend themselves to the textual set-up that allows them to function as a complex equivalent of an original in a new **communicative space**. And this space is determined, not by 'mere' linguistic correspondences (between source and target language) but by the particular discourse world in which the translation is meant to function.

Translations, therefore, stick to new textual coordinates that tend to **vary** from those of the originals. It is this principled sense that a translation is a **variety** of the original. In its character as a target text a translation varies the source text. The very concept of the dichotomy between **source and target texts (ST and TT)** is rooted in a framework of varieties. The TT stands for the ST. In the widest sense of the term *sameness* the two texts are about the same thing, which they vary in a particular way caused by the social context of translation.

Of course, translations are varied texts or textual variations of a particular kind. It is the aim of this paper (1) to describe how far translations are different from other variations and (2) to explain how the varieties concept as such can illuminate some of the crucial aspects of translation in general. Though these two considerations are closely linked, I shall try to deal with them one by one, concluding with a synthesis of the two. Concentrating on the 'varied nature' of all translated texts, I will demonstrate the usefulness of this variability hypothesis by applying it, first, to translation practice including translation teaching, and, secondly, to translation theory, or more modestly, to the present state of translation studies.

Translation vs. language variation

The first criterion differentiating translations from other language variants is, essentially, their **bilingual** or often **multilingual** nature. Whereas the competence of 'normal' language users guides them to, at least, understand most variants and to produce a fair number of variants of their native language, translators have to go beyond this since they have two competences at their disposal. More succinctly, translational competence involves even more than the competence of a native speaker who has mastered one or more foreign languages, thus achieving two or several linguistic competences. Native (as well as acquired foreign language) competence enables speakers to make use of the repertoire of variable linguistic means in either their first or second tongue. In each case they dispose of their variable linguistic knowledge or expertise in a **monolingual setting**, be it in their mother or their foreign languages. Thus, the variants they use are either those of language one (L1) or language two (L2). More specifically, their range extends from phonetic or accent peculiarities across lexical and grammatical specifics to stylistic and register markers in their mother tongue and, if they are proficient enough, though often to a lesser extent, in their acquired L2 usage.

In other words, language variants of this kind exist in relation to other variants of that very same language (L1 or L2). They are normally chosen because they correspond to the background and upbringing of the speakers (such as accent or dialect) or they are conditioned by the stylistic, functional, and social norms of the speech community. Those variant features of a language lend themselves to detailed description as components of the phonetic/phonological, grammatical or lexical subsystems. Furthermore, they may be identified as register variants or, sometimes, sociolectal variations. In short, their status as variables is measured with regard to their place values in the language system and its (various) norms. It is in terms of these specifics as particular language variants that they become incorporated into texts, or that texts can be analysed as containing the individual variants or clusters of them.

By contrast, looking at translations as variants of the original implies a primarily global perspective. A TT being a variant of an ST makes only sense if the former is taken to be a replica of the latter. Translations must be viewed as **total variants** and not as individual or habitual selections from various usages or norms within a language. (Of course, there is also an element of choice if we take the number of languages into consideration which can variably serve as target languages.)

The target text then is a variation on an original. Its shape and substance is again the result of a subtle putting together of target language items exhibiting choices from the ways in which this new medium is variably structured. But – and this is our main point – the final version decided upon by the translator is **not** determined by the individual variabilities of the ST. Though at the beginning and time and again in the course of solving their often frustrating task, translators seem to focus, at least temporarily, on individual item for item correspondences, they eventually cannot but resort to the overall context of the text and the demands of their translational commission. And the final choices they settle upon are much more of a top-down than a bottom-up process. This is the result of the global textual needs that the translation is meant to fulfil in the target community, and may also be a response to the demands of the translation native of either L1 or of L2.

To put it very generally, translations figuring as L2 variations on or of L1 originals enjoy this status as specimens of text productions in the context of different linguistic communities. Translators serve as communicators across language boundaries. In a way, then, translations are variable expressions of the world communities, i.e. the users of different languages. They are variable modes of discourse. No doubt they do not exhibit their variability on one time level as do linguistic varieties, which are characteristic of individual languages being deployed by groups and in regions in particular periods in time. Functional and social varieties, though open to change, govern usage contemporaneously. Translations, however, show **directedness** (Neubert 1986). TT follows ST. Uni-directionality prevails. Backtranslations hardly deserve mention outside perhaps a teaching context but not even there since using a TT as a source for retranslation makes the concept of ST altogether spurious.

Interestingly, one original may, and, in fact often does, have several translations in its wake. This remarkable fact is the cause of what are aptly-called *comet-tail studies*, which compare the various translations of one original that have appeared either over several generations or even centuries or within one lifetime (cf. the most informative, annual volumes of the Göttingen research group on literary translation beginning with Schultze 1987). The sequence or cluster of target versions represent reflections of the source text under the constantly changing conditions of the TT community. It is a well-known fact that new generations and often new social situations and cultural contexts encourage new attempts at translating what is often seen in a new light. Existing translations may not only be outdated but may clash with new ways of looking at the original. Thus translations take on the character of varied texts not only, as is normally expected, in relation to the ST, they also vary with regard to themselves, i.e. different translations of the same original. Translated discourse varies itself over time and place, sometimes among persons achieving the 'same' task often within a few years in response to repeated commissioning by various or the same publishing houses. In essence, this is also what happens when an ST is translated by a number of competitors for a jury or by a class of excellent students in a translation workshop as part of an advanced translation study programme. The TTs produced are particularly good examples of varied texts in the double sense just noted above.

It goes without saying that the concept of translations as varied texts takes on an additional dimension when we, as I think we have to, take into account that new translations do not only relate to the original but also to previously produced TTs. Consequently, it is almost impossible to tell how much of the total achievement of a new TT or rather the particular 'last' version of a translation owes its detailed shape to the translator's attempt to recreate the passages of the ST and how often he or she borrowed from other translators. Yet however tricky or practically impossible the precise disentanglement of 'home-grown' and 'imported' elements in a concrete translation under analysis may be, the very fact that the 'final' translator wrote up his or her work can be safely taken as a kind of 'signing off'. The TT as a whole should be judged as the one translator's version of the ST. In our context, this final product functions as **the** TT variant of the original, in whatever stages it was achieved. After all, previous translations, if available to the translator, are but part of the vast corpus of reference materials which are not only accessible for consultation but should necessarily enter the translator's decision process as part and parcel of his or her responsibility. It goes without saying that translators should not be denied the right to take into account and, in fact, exploit what their predecessors, though at different times and often under different conditions, have come up with as their particular solution. Making use of previous TTs as positive or negative feedback in the course of the new task leading to incorporation or rejection of old choices has been a continual practice in translation. It should not be seen as plagiarization.

The after-life of an original under the guise of its subsequent translation is a perfectly legitimate topic. It takes into account how translators, especially literary translators but not only they, have viewed their efforts at dealing not only with the original, however primary this may be, but also with the various historical appearances this ST has had in the target language. These appearances, just think of the broad range of Shakespeare translations into German or of the countless translations of classical Greek and Roman writers into many modern languages, have become deeply ingrained in the cultural life of the target speech communities. Translations have significantly expanded and enriched the cultural experience of the receptor societies. The thought worlds and the emotional reverberations of literate twentieth-century men and women cannot be imagined without the integrated contributions of the most diverse translations of texts from the past as well as from the present. In addition to the trivial fact that we are what we are as a result of our everyday experiences, there are many cultural overlaps weighing deep in our consciousness. Translations are the agents through which currents and fragments of otherness keep percolating into our seemingly indigenous storehouse of knowledge. Each individual new translation recaptures a **varied experience of reality**, real and invented, from another life source. It enhances as well as universalises particular ways of conceptionalising our experience of life. As translations concern practically all walks of life, from belles lettres to the media, from science and technology to business, from sports to all kinds of entertainment, from religion to everyday affairs, etc., we can say that our reading, viewing, and listening is actually flooded with alternative ways humans have imagined and expressed various modes of reality and irreality. This is what is meant by looking at translations as offering variable pictures of the world, variable in that these pictures, however fragmentary, contribute slightly or totally different perspectives on how people more or less different from us think and feel. Taken together, or at least gradually accumulating, these varied texts offer a kind of multiperspectivity. In other words, they can pave the way for a potential world culture.

Unfortunately, this truly humanistic view of the role of translations is not borne out by reality. It is rather a **virtual** world culture which translations are in a position to offer their potential recipients. Apart from the fact that the sorry state of literacy in many countries makes the use of translations by many, particularly, but not only, in the third world unfeasible there are other reasons restricting the opportunity to access translations whenever this is desired. It must be admitted, instead, that there has never existed a worldwide policy directed at making all kinds of translations universally available to everyone everywhere. In stark contrast to the well-intentioned idea of a generally available abundance of translations in all corners of the globe there have always been restricted policies, restricted by financial or ideological considerations, to channel and, indeed, to limit the flow of translations. Especially the choice of texts has never been fully free, with often underpaid translators' jobs depending on commissioners who again have to remain in business or, worse, are willing partners in politically, religiously or other ideologically affected systems of power relationships.

Theoretically, the concept of translations as varied texts highlights a **potentiality**. A translation can break up what were idiosyncratic, habitual, normative, or sometimes monolithic views. It can cross boundaries, though in actual fact policy makers in the interest of the status quo have time and again blocked or channelled the unimpeded flow of information through translations. Often enough translations were even used to strengthen conservative views by carefully choosing just those STs that lent themselves to their favourite views of the world. The history of totalitarian states, in recent years, is a particular case in point. But o..e could quote just as well many examples of restrictive translation policies in the past, in fact, in all ages.

On a smaller plane, however, and without reference to matters of content, which figure prominently in translation policies, TTs represent ST variations in more subtle ways. They are text-linguistic new-creations of STs. It is indeed the challenge of a translation to match its original by singling out just those linguistic means of the target language (TL) that are not the sum of individual 'equivalents' but a global *gestalt* functioning as an adequate TL variant of the ST. Translators, in order to achieve this task, must have developed a unique **competence** that transcends the competence of SL speakers, native and acquired, as well as that of native and acquired TL speakers. **Translational competence** may in fact be defined as the capacity of a text producer to create a TT that recovers an ST under the conditions of the TL text world taking into regard the syntactic, semantic, stylistic and pragmatic requirements which an ST would demand if it were to be formulated for a TL audience. One can clearly see that this definition is closely related to our starting hypothesis about translations being variant texts, that is, TTs varying STs, or, in short, STs changing their textworld. It is actually derived from this hypothesis.

Translations as communicative variants

This leads me to the **second** part of my argument. How can the variant concept enlighten us with respect to our view of translation in general? In other words, how does variability come in when we look at translation as a communicative process in contrast to all other modes of communicating, more concretely, as against monolingual communication.

When I pointed out above that the incidence of linguistic variants also accounts for language use by fluent speakers of foreign languages, this fact by no means implies that near-perfect knowledge of a second (or third) language is a sufficient qualification for translators. This knowledge is, of course, extremely important, though there have been cases in translation history which have demonstrated that mastership of the TL, mostly the translator's mother tongue, may be and, in fact, was often more crucial than knowledge of the SL. This fact may run counter to the prevalent opinion that translators are people who know two languages.

By contrast, the idea of a translator recreating a TT as a variant of the ST points the way to a better understanding of this seeming paradox. Integrating a translation into a new universe of discourse no doubt presupposes highest proficiency. It is after all only the TT that reaches an audience. Even the best understanding of an ST, analysing the ins and outs of its linguistic structure, its semantic potential, and its stylistic ramifications, is no guarantee that all these insights come across. Of course, translators have to be skilled experts in ST comprehension. But more importantly, because the fledgling TT cannot make any excuses referring to its SL origin, it is exposed to the demanding world of TL discourse. It cannot hide behind SL 'difficulties', difficulties with regard to their SL recodability. It is like 'walking in open TL daylight clothed in a garb with ST rags showing through'. The new version is relentlessly accessible and open to criticism by the publisher's editors and, of course, by the TL audience. From beginning to end, translators are faced with the challenge of giving the ST a new lease on life in the shape of a translation. And particularly during the final stage of their work, they have, sometimes painfully, settled upon or often resigned themselves to a bottom line solution. In the process they often half-heartedly, but always conclusively, had to abandon all the various preliminary attempts at tackling a tough passage or an intricate decision problem affecting the whole text.

I can hardly think of a more accurate description of this frustrating plight of the translator than Martin Luther's comments in his famous *Sendbrief vom Dolmetschen*, written in 1530. Having sometimes laboured almost "vierzehn Tage, drei, vier Wochen" to translate a minor passage of the Bible, he is convinced that his German readers cannot possibly have the slightest idea of the enormous amount of hard work he as translator has been involved in. Instead the reader "stößt nicht einmal an, wird aber nicht gewahr, welche Wacken und Klötze da gelegen sind, wo er jetzt drüber hingeht wie über ein gehobelt Brett, wo wir haben müssen schwitzen und uns ängstigen, ehe denn wir solche Wacken und Klötze aus dem Weg räumten, auf dass man könnte so fein daher gehen". Of course this cleaning away of rocks and stumps cluttering the original ground exists only in the translator's view. An adequate TT presents quite another picture. In Luther's words: "es ist gut pflügen, wenn der Acker gereinigt ist. Aber den Wald und die Stubben ausroden und den Acker ausrichten, da will niemand heran" (Luther 1530, quoted after Störig 1993: 20).

The TT does not, in fact should not reveal anything about the intract-
ability of the translator's SL original and his or her first and several other
drafts. The ST variety, in order to be transformed into the final TT variety, as
a rule, undergoes a series of rewriting stages until the final version eventually
appears and, sanctioned by the translator, is handed over to the commissioner
or publisher of the translation. They would normally like to take the quality
of the TT for granted though they may try to make sure by having it looked
though by a revisor. Whether revisors actually compare it with the original is
a moot point. Their time scheme rarely permits them to perform a contrastive
analysis sentence by sentence. Mostly they focus on those words and passages that strike them as awkward, strange or just wrong in terms of a TL
context. More precisely they step in where the translation 'has not made it'
into the TL discourse, its usages and conventions, for instance, collocations
or stylistic features which sound out of the way. With the translator not
around the publishers may enter or even usurp the TT and try to inculcate
their different, perhaps more TL-oriented way of thinking, sometimes running the risk of corrupting the text in spite of the best of intentions. Anyhow,
what the readers of the translation read is then often a joint product. From my
own experience I remember cases where a publisher's editor changed passages inserting phrases that I had originally in mind, too. Actually, I was
convinced that they might have been a better choice, at least on a local level.
Yet I had rejected them because, on second or third thought, they clashed
with other parts of the TT or they left out something that I thought should be
kept the way it corresponded to the original text, that is on a global level.

In the final analysis it all boils down to the frustrating fact that good translators know only too well how much is getting lost on the way across the text
boundary, from the ST author to the TT translator. They are, indeed, their
best critics. But their final version, however perfect or imperfect it may be, is
the result of an individual decision process (overlapping, in the case of a revisor's intervention, with other individual choices). Translations are products
of an intricate interplay between mental bottom-up and top-down processes
where local decisions are continually matched by global considerations.
Translators, as a rule, are acutely, if not painfully aware of the **inherent
variability** distinguishing everything they select and leave out in the course
of managing the vacillating formulation job. Each step is dependent upon
several others. In line with the procedures discovered by game theorists a
translator's individual moves to recast the original in its sequential and intertextual build-up are provisional at any particular moment in time but take on
at least tentative permanence when viewed along with new moves envisioned
or previous ones already made earlier in the text. Translations are thus networks of moves, which hopefully support each other. Yet these networks
cannot possibly be identical with the textual network of the originals. In-

variance on this level is impossible. TTs represent, in exchange, **variant texts** where the individual moves of the translators, though seemingly different from the details of the ST, add up to compete with the moves of the original text producer 'on a higher plane', that of the world of the communicative needs of the target audience. This is what I meant by *equivalence* of the TT to the ST in a new communicative space. In short, TL communicative norms, which cause variability, at the same time safeguard, in fact, recreate the conditions for **communicative equivalence**, or **sameness in difference.**

Applications of the variability hypothesis

1. Translation practice

Within the context of translation studies a number of fundamental questions remain. Can this 'sameness', which in fact is an often strikingly different 'variation', be practically justified and theoretically founded? Is the translational variant of the source an acceptable, genuine, valid, adequate, legitimate variant of the original? This question remains the translator's burden when the final touch has been given to the job. And it is not only the critical response of the audience – if this is vented at all – it is the conscience of responsible mediators who know best what the translation is lacking or what stands in the way when they compare the target with the source. Often this text matching is done in their minds. TT recipients being (by definition) denied access to the ST cannot possibly comprehend the translator's frustrations, as Luther and many other before and after him knew well. Where should we look for criteria to test or even measure the extent of the variability hypothesis? Is it verifiable at all or is it, which would be by itself, just a good analytical tool, a pertinent explication of the translation process?

First, how far does the variability thesis reflect translation practice? Do translators apply it themselves? I think one of the clearest indications that this is so is the irreality of backtranslations. TTs are variants of STs in such a way that they incorporate so many individual and TL-conditioned specifics that any attempt to recreate the ST back from them would be doomed to failure. The very practical steps, their indistinguishable sequence and their unique complexity, of the translation process extend in one direction only. Describing translators' moves shows them as irreversible. Translators may and do, of course, retract individual steps when they, in the course of the translation process, think of more suitable solutions. So there is an element of reversibility as part of the decision-making at the local level of a text. But once the finished product is decided upon as **the** final version there is no return. The TT has turned into a global discourse unit, which compares with its original as a new *gestalt* of which the sum total of its grammatical and lexical elements, even its individual sentences can no longer be rigorously traced back to their original stimuli. If translation critics try to do it they can only succeed in those parts which point to ST features they think should have been rendered differently. But what they often forget in this locally perfectly sensible venture is to take into account all the other consequences that a minor correction would necessarily entail and which the original translator for various reasons may have also considered but had given up in favour of the choice he or she had actually made.

Beyond the everyday realm of translation criticism the history of translation abounds in cases where TTs for a great number of reasons make a particular point of varying from their STs. There is a whole gamut of reasons, social, political, legal, commercial, cultural, philosophical, religious and others (Delisle/Woodsworth 1995, Neubert 1997), which can be cited as being responsible for the special kinds of variety that translations were supposed to represent in relation to their respective originals. Hypothesising TTs as varied texts, well-intentioned though sometimes wilful variants of STs enables us to describe this abundant stream of translations over the ages. Translations of highly divergent kinds, often bordering on the realm of paraphrases and adaptations, yield descriptions which cover the reality of bilingually mediated communication much better than any narrow approach to translation, which singles out only those TTs that are more or less close replicas of their STs.

Describing how translations take on their variable shapes and contribute to our understanding of the vagaries of translational history is only one application of our proposed hypothesis. If it qualifies as an adequate mode of describing how translations have come about in the past, the hypothesis of tranlations as varied texts should equally help us to supply insights into the translation practice of the present. By this I mean not just the work of practising translators. Their job is in fact already covered by the above mentioned historical perspective. Presently, as well as in the past, professionals, as well as part-timers, conduct their work according to the needs of their clients. The TT variants they produce stand in a line with the work of their thousands of predecessors. They adapt the originals to suit the TT communities and their textual conventions. And if these conventions and the TTs newly embedded within them are a far cry from the norms of ST world, then the translation varies more from the original than if there is little contrast. This shows that the variable hypothesis is not an absolute. True to its very nature it applies to different text types or genres in different ways. As a rule, it is less applicable in highly 'ritualised' or formulaic texts, such as patents, legal statements, etc. By contrast, it is characteristic of all those cases where the ST world is already rich in variable shapes. In order to assess the range of variability open to the translator, it is, therefore, expedient to combine the necessary analysis of the ST with an assessment of its variability within its SL genre before translators can take variability as their guideline for producing the TT. In addition, translators or their commissioners may want to control the degree to which TTs should resemble their STs. There has always been a lively debate, not to say quarrel, about whether translations should be perfectly accommodated to the TT conventions or whether they should still look like translations. The latter case, propagated by people like Venuti (1995), may be said to be almost an attack on the hypothesis proposed in this paper. It purports to keep a translation as close as possible to its ST since not doing so is regarded as doing a disservice to or even 'violating' the original.

2. Translation teaching

There is, secondly, another important area of application. The variability hypothesis relates to what may be termed *potential* translation practice, namely the field of training prospective translators. Looking at how individual variables determine the translation process from beginning to end in subtle ways yields a rich mine of pedagogical clues that can sensitise both teachers and students in their attempts to emulate the best practitioners. Approaching translations as variant texts does away with single-minded prescriptivism. Instead, a new realism gains ground facilitating students and teachers to cooperate more closely. Translating is no longer looked upon as imitating what can actually not be imitated at all (viz. the ST). Creating a new TT becomes a pragmatic adventure. This is bound to affect students in their classroom performance and teachers in their evaluation procedures. Learning to translate and solving translation problems successfully become closely linked to the student translators' decision processes. Adequate translations will no longer be modelled on an objective translation ideal but may be derived **by variable means** from individual perspectivisations when approaching the ST in view of the communicative needs of the TL addressee. Integrating top-down and bottom-up strategies leading to highly effective TL variants of SL originals gives individual learners sufficient leeway to come up with translation solutions which doubtlessly enliven classroom discussion. They yield an often amazing potential of 'variable equivalents' on the lower text levels allowing truly variable global solutions on the higher and global text levels.

A most conspicuous side-effect of this variegated treatment of simple and complex translation problems is the growing awareness on the side of the students of the **relativity of translation** (Neubert 1986). In a nutshell, this means there are always various ways to arrive at an adequate TT. It goes without saying that the grading of translation performance and of the translation product, which is the task of the teachers (and, luckily, sometimes volunteered by gifted and versatile co-students), can also profit immensely by not sticking to an immutable TL model. There is actually no limit to the un-tapped resources of the TL waiting to be exploited for the benefit of hitting upon a particularly suitable match. And since several translators may have structured their TTs differently (e.g. compared to the moves of their fellow-students in class) there is usually a diversity of fitting equivalents that match different individual TT proposals according to variable TT slots. The state of the TT at any particular moment of its development, that is, viewed by the translator in this phase of his/her work corroborates a chosen (set of) local equivalent(s). Eventually, the final state of a TT, again viewed by the trans-lator in retrospect, gives the green light to the sum of local renderings as well as to the global *gestalts* of TL means. Translation teachers are well advised to judge the students' performance in response to the sequential variants and, after the TT has been handed in, in consideration of the students' global tex-tual efforts. In all cases, locally and globally, translations provide pervasive expressions of variability. There is nothing straightforward or even predict-able in the translation process. All steps are relativised by previous steps. The TT as a variant text of the ST and as variant of other TTs, previously or con-temporaneously produced, is a function of the translator's overall strategy as well of the tactical choices taken under way.

Theoretical implications: a new definition of translation

In the light of these procedural consequences, I think it is worthwhile to con-sider their theoretical implications. If translations are variant texts what, then, justifies us to speak of a TT as a category at all? If everything is in flux where do translations stop? Referring to the applications analysed above, we should be in a position to state when translators have gone too far (or not far enough, for that matter) and abused their job. Or, more specifically, when have students failed their task and/or when have teachers misjudged the work of the prospective translators entrusted to them?

These are serious questions, which lead well beyond translation practice. They touch a vital nerve of what we have been used to call translation. On which foundation does our ambitious discipline rest? The subject matter of translatology must not disappear in a sea of varieties. How can we yet locate some 'islands of invariance'? They should exhibit a unity in diversity such as some sort of recoverable, though variant relationship to original texts. It is this feature of ST derivation which distinguishes any TT from other TL texts. But it is not a mere recoding or imitation of an original that marks off a translation. In order to justify the multifaceted quality of translations past and present we have to come up with a new and more realistic definition, which can serve as a reliable guideline. Variability turns out to be not a result of irresponsible relativism. It is variability in the service of the translation's function. A translation functions by virtue of a new communicative need. It is precisely in terms of meeting these needs, often diverse and different from the ST that a translation can be identified as a new variant text. Thus all TTs are variably related to STs.

Taking this functional variability as our practical **and** theoretical premise we can redefine a translation as a **ST-induced TT**. For functionality to be integrated in the definition we have to specify the translation process as initiated or commissioned by either SL or TL people or their agents who are interested in or who express a need for the translation. A more comprehensive definition would then be: **translating is ST-induced TT production for a third party** (Neubert 1985, Neubert/Shreve 1992). Within this frame of reference we are now in a position to account for whichever direct or indirect renderings of the original are or were called for, and/or which changes or additions and cuts etc. were or are in order to meet the challenges to the ST under the auspices of the TT world. Indeed, there is room for an immense range of versions reaching from the almost literal recoding to the most liberal recreations. The re-textualization of the ST for a new audience not only entitles but forces translators to invest their expertise and their creativity. It is here that their translational competence is taxed to the utmost (Neubert 1994, Neubert 2000).

A *theory of translation*, though the term *translation studies* would perhaps be more opportune at the present stage of development of the discipline, would profit immensely from this variable approach. Above all, it would free translation from the narrow bounds of linguistic correspondences. In exchange, it places investigation in the light of pragmatic and social dimensions. There is no doubt that contrastive linguistics and even linguistic typology have much to offer by way of pinpointing detailed recoding procedures. Yet the reality of translating is not describable and certainly not explainable by recourse to contrastive linguistics but requires a communicative framework which can account for the immense varying strategies translators have to deploy in order to meet the third party's requirements at any moment in time. Actually, translating involves a profound analysis of a particular situation, any translational situation for that matter. As a result of their experience translators have identified **types** of such situations. Generalising their methods, even customising the most frequent tasks of their daily routines, they are well aware of when to rise to a unique occasion or perform a run-of-the-mill job. Translation students as well as translation teachers have learned immensely from such case studies. It is true, empirical research has still a long way to go towards producing a scenario of the multifarious translation scene, where a great variety of strategies are in order. Instead of claiming hard and fast rules for 'translating from one language into another',

translation studies have come across highly divergent tactical steps functioning as components of overall textual procedures. Actually, any individual
translation is a unique variable of a more general translation type. Both types
and variables of them may be identified as located on a historical plane
between the SL and the TL communities. Types such as the translation of
advertising or the translation of annual company reports, of business letters
or of mail-order catalogues, of tenders or commercial agreements, to name
just a few sub-types of the macro-type of business communication, all call for
specific textual reorientations from the ST to the TT. Realising the sentence-
by-sentence or phrase-by-phrase reconstruction of the originals presupposes
the translator's keen awareness of the specific **differential** obtaining between
a particular (sub-)type in the respective communicative spheres of the ST and
the TL. Concentration on just the words and structures would mean not
seeing the wood for the trees.

Any realistic theory of translation has to reflect this differential. And it is
precisely the variability hypothesis which can take the globally conditioned
requirements as well as the locally identifiable consequences into account. A
detailed classification of empirical data based on detailed contrastive comparisons between (groups or types of) STs and TTs should yield a corroboration
of translational variability governing the concrete shape from the text level
down to the structural and word levels. The multi-levelled differential characterising each individual translation, as it results from the translator's
tactical steps, no longer bewilders the theorist. Translational individuality
and one-offness falls into place as soon as it is viewed as the most natural
outgrowth of text-type specificity. For example, there is no doubt a clearly
discernible relation between the degree of variability and text types or genres
across the translation spectrum. Some texts exhibit greater normativity and
thus more rigid, even ritualised grammatical and lexical reshaping in the TT
in relation to the ST formulation than others. On closer analysis these texts
turn out to be members of different text types respectively. Translational
variability is thus a matter of degree, depending on the textual gradient
between the ST groups and TT groups.

Theorising on how and why TTs are variant texts, varying STs under
translational conditions, allows predictions about the translator's repertoire
of top-down requisites and about how to go about implementing the necessary bottom-up steps leading to the equivalent TL variant. Thus translation
studies allow us to draw an adequate map of the complex territory of translation. Reading this map and knowing one's way about is the translator's
competence. In the midst of an extremely rich and multi-faceted diversity
translators take their orientation, at the same time, through a highly systematic network of roads and paths which lead the way from the original to its
TT variant.

References

Delisle, Jean/Judith Woodsworth, eds. (1995): *Translators through history*. Amsterdam/Philadelphia: Benjamins/Unesco Publishing.

Luther, Martin (1530, 1993): "Sendbrief vom Dolmetschen". Quoted after Hans Joachim Störig, ed. *Das Problem des Übersetzens*. Stuttgart: Goverts, 14-32.

Neubert, Albrecht (1968): "Pragmatische Aspekte der Übersetzung". Albrecht Neubert, ed. *Grundfragen der Übersetzungswissenschaft* (= Beihefte der Zeitschrift Fremdsprachen II). Leipzig: Enzyklopädie, 20-33.

Neubert, Albrecht (1985): *Text and translation* (= Übersetzungswissenschaftliche Beiträge 8). Leipzig: Enzyklopädie.

Neubert, Albrecht (1986): "Translatorische Relativität". Mary Snell-Hornby, ed. *Übersetzungswissenschaft. Eine Neuorientierung*. Tübingen: Francke, 85–105.

Neubert, Albrecht (1994): "Competence in translation: a complex skill, how to study and how to teach it". Mary Snell-Hornby/Franz Pöchhacker/Klaus Kaindl, eds. *Translation Studies. An Interdiscipline*. Wien/Philadelphia: Benjamins, 411-420.

Neubert, Albrecht (1997): Review of "Jean Delisle/Judith Woodsworth, eds. Translators through history". *Zeitschrift für Anglistik und Amerikanistik* 4, 367–369.

Neubert, Albrecht (2000): "Competence in language, in languages, and in translation". Beverly Ahab/Christina Schäffner, eds. *Developing translation competence*. Amsterdam: Benjamins (in print).

Neubert, Albrecht/Gregory M. Shreve (1992): *Translation as text*. Kent/London: Kent State UP.

Schultze, Brigitte, ed. (1987): *Die literarische Übersetzung, Fallstudien zu ihrer Kulturgeschichte* (= Göttinger Beiträge zur Internationalen Übersetzungsforschung). Berlin: Schmidt.

Snell-Hornby, Mary (1986): "Einleitung. Übersetzen, Sprache, Kultur". Mary Snell-Hornby, ed. *Übersetzungswissenschaft. Eine Neuorientierung*. Tübingen: Francke, 9-29.

Venuti, Lawrence (1995): "Introduction". Lawrence Venuti, ed. *Rethinking translation. Discourse, subjectivity, ideology*. London/New York: Routledge, 1-17.

Christoph Gutknecht/Lutz J. Rölle *(Hamburg)*

Translation factors

Translation is an "intriguing yet highly complex subject" (Shuttleworth 1997: v). Experience shows that for numerous SL texts there are many potential TL alternatives. The reason is that there are many different contexts of utterance and purposes of translation. This gives an idea of the many and multifarious factors influencing translation. Ross (1981: 11) comments: "The complexity of translation, the number of factors involved, is enormous." Given an SL text and given a specific set of such translation factors, the translator will come up with a specific TL rendition. This is translating by factors – this is translating.

An example will make this point clear.[1] Usually the English pronoun *I* will be translated into German as its literal equivalent *ich* – cf. (1) and (2). But if *I* in (1) occurs in a scientific text and is used as an authorial statement, then German prefers impersonal constructions such as (3).

(1) I will show that ...
(2) Ich werde zeigen, dass ... [literal translation]
(3) Diese Untersuchung will zeigen, dass ... ['This study will show that ...'[2]]

Of course, no one would claim that *I* can 'mean' *diese Untersuchung (this study)*, but *I*, together with the translation factor *conventions of German academic texts* does allow for this rendition. This shows the substantial influence that translation factors can have.

We devoted an entire book to the topic of translating by factors (Gutknecht/Rölle 1996, henceforth TF). The idea itself is nothing new. In fact, translators cannot help but 'translate by factors'. As the existence of both (2) and (3) as possible renditions of (1) shows, one unique rendition of an SL text does not exist. So presetting factors to indicate the direction that the translation is to take is simply inevitable. Either the translators' clients will by themselves give general instructions about how they want their SL texts to be translated, or the translators will have to ask the clients or have to decide themselves which translation factors to adopt. This has been true ever since the very first translation was made thousands of years ago. Sometimes clients are not satisfied with the translators' rendition because they expected some-

---

[1] This example was inspired by Kussmaul (1978: 54).

[2] Cf. Gutknecht/Rölle (1996: 238).

thing different. Holz-Mänttäri (1987) even reports of a lawsuit in such a case. She concludes that a 'product specification' prior to commissioning a translation is inevitable. This shows the importance of translating by factors. There is no alternative to it.

This leads us to the question of whether *translating by product specification* and *translating by factors* are one and the same thing. The answer is simple. The clients cannot be expected to think of **all** the factors the translators are to take into account when they perform their professional work. All the clients can do is give some general guidelines for the translators to go by, such as free or literal translation, pro or contra explanations for the sake of facilitating the TL hearer's understanding, a rendition that reveals or conceals the fact that the TL text is a translation, etc.[3]

Such product or task specification agreed with the clients or SL authors is seen by Wilss (1994: 148) as just one out of "four main factors involved in the process" of decision-making, tne other three being the translators' cognitive system, their knowledge bases, and problems specific to the particular text-type.[4]

In practice, these factors cannot be seen in complete isolation from each other. The task specification may, for instance, include TL invariance of SL text type (such as *scientific text*). The competent translators' knowledge base will then include differences of this text type in the two languages involved (such as SL *personal* vs. TL *impersonal constructions* – *I* vs. *diese Untersuchung*).

This means that one *macrofactor* (such as *text type*) will entail lots of *microfactors* (such as the specifics of this text type). Generally, only macrofactors will be discussed with the clients. Microfactors are the translators' domain governing the hundreds of decisions they make when they create a TL text. Both macrofactors and microfactors are translation factors guiding the translators' actions. Holz-Mänttäri (1984: 162) aims at "elucidating the factors guiding [their] actions". Likewise many other translatologists refer to factors of the translation process.[5] But is it really necessary to use the term *factor* at all?

Classen (1997: 157) suggests one might just as well speak of *elements*, *aspects*, or *categories*. His suggestion was obviously inspired by our very definition of *factor*, which includes the notion of *element*: "any of the circumstances, conditions, etc. that bring about a result; element or constituent

---

[3]   Cf. Savory's (1968: 54) list of contradictory translation principles.

[4]   See also Shuttleworth/Cowie (1997: 37).

[5]   Cf. our list of publications on translation featuring the term *factor* (TF: 1f.). Kashkin (1998: 96) holds that translations of grammatical forms develop as a process of making choices governed by various factors.

that makes a thing what it is".[6] Accordingly, note that the essential feature of translation factors is their *"bringing about* renditions or *making* them what they are" (TF: 5; italics added).

This crucial characteristic of factors – their causative or creative power – is not expressly conveyed by use of words like *elements* alone. *Element* typically merely denotes "a constituent part" of something (Webster 1993a: 323, s.v. *element* 2), which is not necessarily, as is a factor, "something that *actively contributes* to the production of a result".[7]

In our initial example, for instance, the translation factor *conventions of German academic texts* actively contributes to producing the rendition *diese Untersuchung*. If we were to speak about this vital active aspect of translation factors in terms of elements, we would necessarily have to add a relative clause along the lines of our above definition, and say, "translation element that makes a rendition what it is". But why use such a long expression when we can simply say *translation factor?*

As does *elements*, so *aspects* and *categories* typically refer to static descriptions of things. Certainly description is involved in translating, but it is only the first step. To take up our first example again, a statement about the membership of the SL text in question to the class of academic texts is merely a description of the nature of this text. What is far more important is that, as a consequence, this text class acts as a factor to bring about a TL rendition that vastly departs from the ordinary equivalent of part of the text.[8] This shows that the factor *text class* performs a function – it revises the standard correlation of *I* and *ich*. Hence it may be referred to as a *revision factor*.

Other translation factors perform different functions, as the following example shows. Usually the German word *Amphibienfahrzeug* will be rendered in English as *amphibian*. Now suppose that for some reason some native German students interpreting a spoken text for some of their friends do not know this TL word. Being native German speakers, however, they of course know what the German word refers to and would be able to explain what it means when they hear it in the spoken SL text. Because it refers to a simple concept, this explanation could certainly also be given in English.

---

[6] TF: 5, as quoted from Webster (1983b: 656, s.v. *factor* 2).

[7] Webster (1993a: 359, s.v. factor 2), where the example *Hard work was a factor in their success* is given. As a first step, we would accept using terms such as *translation elements/aspects/categories/features/variables*, etc. But when these become functional, contributing to the creation of TL renditions, the term *factors* will be more appropriate because it semantically includes this causative aspect.

[8] The (non-literal) textual equivalence of *I* and *diese Untersuchung* is an extreme case of what Gallagher (1998b) refers to as *possibilities and limits of equivalence*.

And this is exactly their 'rescue strategy'. They could paraphrase the unknown TL word *amphibian* by saying, *vehicle that can travel on either land
or water*.

We may say that the interpreting students' ignorance of the TL noun
corresponding to the SL one acted as a *blocking factor* to verbalizing this TL
noun. And the availability of a paraphrase comes to their rescue as a *compensation factor* for their ignorance.

Now Malmkjær (1998: 156) wonders "what 'value added' is involved in
formulations such as the following: 'insufficient competence of TL modal
nouns acts as a blocking factor to their rendition (TF: 259)'". She wonders if
this means "more than, say, ... 'If you don't understand modal nouns, you
can't translate them'".

First, the correct paraphrase of our statement would be, "If you don't
know the form of certain TL modal nouns, you can't use them for a rendition".

Second, her question is like asking, "What 'value added' is involved in
formulations such as the following: 'This is the subject or theme of the
sentence'? Does this mean more than, say, 'This is what is being talked
about'?" The obvious answer is that scientists use languages for specific
purposes (LSP) terminology to denote abstractions based on observations
they make. In our case, the point about unknown modal nouns is just one
observation. Other observations include:

- You can't translate an English syntagma of the form *adjective plus noun*
  by a congruent German syntagma if the adjective does not semantically
  denote a characteristic of the referent of that noun (*blue sky* – *blauer
  Himmel*; but: *medical student* – **medizinischer Student*).[9]
- You can't translate the English personal pronoun *I* into German if you do
  not know as a reference point the class of text it occurs in (usually: *ich*; in
  scientific texts renditions such as *diese Untersuchung*).
- You can't translate the English personal pronoun *you* into German when it
  is used as a form of address if you have not checked the text it occurs in
  for the kind of relationship that holds between speaker and hearer (if informal: use *du*; if formal: use *Sie*).

All these statements are abstractions because they contain linguistic terminology (*syntagma, adjective, noun, semantical, referent, personal pronoun*,
etc.). They are formulated along the lines of Malmkjær ("If ... you can't ...").

Now the translatologist may take one further step in the direction of abstraction and say that in each case the translation is 'blocked by a certain

---

9   The asterisk (*) denotes ungrammaticality.

actor'. From here it is only another small step to referring to this factor in terms of its function and call it a *blocking factor*.

The 'value added' that is involved in formulations containing this term may be stated on the basis of the well-known scientific principle that more general statements will be more powerful in terms of description and explanation. In our case this means that **all** the observations listed above are cases of translation blockage due to blocking factors. And such blockage may be 'circumvented' by making use of compensation factors[10] – the possibility of paraphrase (*a vehicle that can ...*), of forming compounds (*Medizinstudent*), of co(n)textual disambiguation (*du* or *Sie*), and so on.

It must be emphasized that terminological abstractions in terms of translation factors and their functions are no luxury. Renditions being blocked and having to be compensated for, standard renditions having to be revised – these are typical working-situations commonly experienced by all professional translators hundreds of times each day.[11]

It is quite obvious that translators will be better prepared to cope with these situations if they are trained to recognize them better by being supplied with terms expressly characterizing them for what they are. It is exactly here that terms such as *blockage, compensation,* and *revision,* as well as their sources, i.e., *blocking factors, compensation factors,* and *revision factors* come as handy tools for developing translation strategies or techniques. The most basic form of one such strategy is, "Whenever you are faced with a blocking factor, try to find a compensation factor (to still arrive at the goal of an adequate rendition)."

According to Thiele (1998: 75, col. 2), TF "can be considered ... as an (exemplified) guideline for acquiring translation strategies". This makes it a practical resource for translation trainers. Jones (1998: 149) attests TF that "by covering a full range of techniques required in translation, the text provides a rich assortment of tools for research on factors, and so is an excellent resource to develop a 'factor approach' for translation projects or training courses". Gallagher (1998a: 94, col. 2) suspects that the factor analyses "could open up fresh possibilities in the field of translation teaching".

---

[10] It would be possible to draw 'cognitive translation maps' depicting 'paths and circumventions' on the basis of these factors. Such maps would, of course, be highly relevant to machine translation.

[11] All blockages to renditions are translation problems. Wilss is aware of their existence and the possibility of solving them by 'circumventing' them: "Von interlingual hochstandardisierten Texten abgesehen, gibt es kein problemloses Übersetzen ... Übersetzungsprobleme sind wie Stromschnellen, um die man vorsichtig herumlavieren muß, wenn man aus einer Textvorlage eine sprachlich und außersprachlich akzeptable Übersetzung machen will" (Letter to the editor, "Übersetzungswissenschaft", *Frankfurter Allgemeine Zeitung* 63, 3/16/1987, 11).

More specifically, Niven (1997: 4) argues that TF "might also be used in a German-English/English-German translation course, as it points out and systematically analyses many differences between the languages". Luelsdorff (personal communication) actually used TF as required reading for his 1997 university-level German-English contrastive analysis course which he called "Translating by factors"; and Pym (personal communication) used TF diagrams in class – cf. his 1998 review. Meidl (1997: 4) thinks that TF "will be a valuable aid to instructors of interpreters and translators". And for Prokop (1997: 4) there is no doubt that intermediate and advanced learners of German or English "would benefit enormously from ... 'thinking in factors'".

What exactly has the trainee translator to know about translation factors? Böhm (1997: 357) aptly summarizes the factor approach to translation:

> The approach argued for in TF ... provides a two-fold matrix of translation factors: a classification into *kinds* along the familiar semiotic dimensions, giving rise to syntactic, semantic, pragmatic, etc. translation factors, and a (cross-)classification of these factor kinds into functional sets on the basis of the *functions* they may serve in the translation process. (italics as in the original)[12]

The matrix of translation factors for the examples covered above is presented in Table 1.

---

[12] The desirability of a translation matrix is also pointed out by Prokop (1997: 1): "Clearly, texts are characterized by many different grammatical, semantic, and pragmatic features ... that need to be taken into account to produce a 'satisfactory' translation. The process of identifying, assessing, and weighing of the source language (SL) text features should ideally result in a reduplicable matrix for which grammatical, semantic, and pragmatic equivalencies can be found in the target language (TL)."

Table 1: Kinds of factors and their functions

Example		Kinds of factors	Factor functions
medical student		TL syntax and semantics	act as blocking factors
		TL morphology	acts as compensation factor
I	situation 1	knowledge of SL text	
		class *academic texts*	acts as revision factor
	situation 2	ignorance of SL text class	acts as blocking factor
		finding out SL text class	acts as compensation factor
you		SL pragmatics	
		(ignorance of speaker-	
		hearer relationship)	acts as blocking factor
		relevant SL co(n)text	acts as compensation factor
amphibian		TL lexicology	
		(ignorance of TL noun)	acts as blocking factor
		semantics (paraphrase)	acts as compensation factor

Most of the above examples show the same sequence of factor functions – *blocking factor(s) circumvented by compensation factor*. The kinds of factors fulfilling these functions are more diverse: morphology, lexicology, syntax, semantics, pragmatics, and text class – in short: the entire range of linguistics. So we could make the general statement that "linguistic factors act as blocking/compensation factors".

At a less general level, we may say that "morphological factors, lexical factors, syntactic factors, etc. act as blocking/compensation factors". Such more or less general statements are suitable for describing the principles of the translators' path along the translation process.

At a still more concrete level, we have to speak of individual factors such as ignorance of TL noun, possibility of paraphrase, knowledge or ignorance of SL text class, of speaker-hearer relationship, etc.

At an even more concrete level, factors include the paraphrase of a special noun (hyponym) by means of a more general noun (its hyperonym) plus a relative clause that denotes the special content of the special noun.

Finally, we arrive at the most concrete level of the example at hand, for instance, *amphibian* being paraphrasable by *vehicle that can travel on either land or water*.

So when asked which kind of factor acts as the compensation factor in the last example, we could give different answers, depending on different levels of abstraction:

- a linguistic factor;
- a semantic factor;
- the possibility of paraphrase;
- the possibility of paraphrasing a hyponym by means of its hyperonym postmodified by a relative clause denoting the special contents of the hyponym;
- the possibility of paraphrasing *amphibian* by *vehicle that can travel on either land or water*.

Accordingly, translation rules or techniques may be formulated at different levels of abstraction (The first, most general one, was already given above. It merely refers to factor functions.):

- If you can't translate an expression due to some blocking factor, try to find a compensation factor.
- If you can't translate an expression due to some linguistic blocking factor, try to find a linguistic compensation factor.
- If you can't translate an expression due to some lexical blocking factor, try to find a lexical compensation factor.
- If you can't translate an expression due to the blocking factor of ignorance of some TL lexeme, try to find a lexical compensation factor.
- If you can't translate an expression due to the blocking factor of ignorance of a TL noun, try to use the compensation factor of paraphrasing this noun by means of its TL hyperonym postmodified by a relative clause denoting the special contents of the hyponym.
- If you can't translate *Amphibienfahrzeug* due to the blocking factor of ignorance of the corresponding English noun, use the compensation factor of paraphrasing it by saying, *vehicle that can travel on either land or water*.

As they stand, all of these 'rules' may be useful for the (trainee) translator. General rules such as the first one mentioned are useful because they cover virtually all cases of renditions being blocked and suggest one universal solution strategy. Specific rules such as the last one mentioned are also needed because general rules are of no practical use unless the translator gets to know how to implement them on the 'bottom' level of individual translation problems.

It is the specific rules that ultimately permit the translator to come up with concrete renditions. How many such rules are needed? What should be their point of reference? In our last example it is the word *Amphibienfahrzeug* that is the object of the rule. This seems to be appropriate because it is, after all, individual words such as this one that translators are faced with. This does not, of course, mean that it is invariably word for word that gets translated. Word-for-word translation is rather an exception compared to the more common commission of 'freely' translating whole sentences or even whole texts. So it is necessary to evolve translation rules for the sentence and text levels. But in many cases the levels of word, sentence, and text are interwoven, and reference to one level somehow involves consideration of the others, too. This means that for each SL lexical item there should be a list of all possible translation factors influencing its rendition in various cotexts – i.e., (types of) sentences and entire texts – and contexts – i.e., situations – in which it occurs, and its respective renditions in these co(n)texts.

Actually, as can be imagined, there are many intricate cases where some discussion of the factors involved will be necessary. Therefore, ultimately a mere list of the factors involved will not do. What is called for is in fact an encyclopedia of the translation factors potentially affecting rendition of every single SL word or group of words.

We have tried to take one step towards such a project by writing TF. Here one group of lexemes, the English and German modals, was chosen for a case study of the factors relevant to their translation from one of these two languages into the other. The idea was firstly to focus on one field of language in order to show that even for a small group of words there can be myriads of translation factors. Secondly, our aspiration was to make the translation situation transparent by systematizing translation factors.[13]

Much of this factor system offered in TF is not restricted to the field of modality but relates to many issues that are of general interest in translation studies. This is why Hall (1998: 80) feels that "the topics covered in the book's eight chapters are relevant to a wider audience than one would expect of a book on German and English modals". Hall in fact found that we "bring in almost every issue of any importance in translation ..." (1998: 84).

Chapters were organized according to the major kinds of factors, referred to by us as *factor dimensions* (TF: 3). They were treated in the following sequence: formal factors – syntax and morphology – semantic factors,

---

[13] A three-page review of TF summarizing its main points is provided by Camón (1998). Further reviews appeared in *Anglia. Zeitschrift für englische Philologie* 4, 1998, 517-519 (by A. Neubert); *Applied Semiotics/Sémiotique appliquée* [Electronic Journal, Univ. of Waterloo, Canada] issue n° 5, 1998, 330-335 (by P.G. Michelucci); *Babel* 1, 1998, 93-94 (by S. El-Shiyab); *The Canadian Modern Language Review* 3, 1999, 426-428 (by J. O. Askedal); *Modern Language Quarterly* [Duke UP] 1, 1999, 240-241 (by D. Lewis); *Multilingua* (in print; by I. Werlen); *Selecta* 18, 1997, 46 (by C.W. Nickisch); *Studies in Second Language Acquisition* 21, 1998, 158 (by S. Colina); *Word* 3, 1998, 412-421 (by G. Crocco Galèas).

pragmatic factors, factors relating to spoken and written language, factors relating to translation units and types of equivalents, and essential factors of the translation situation.[14] Each factor dimension was broken down into its major and minor kinds of factors (dealt with in individual sections, subsections and subsubsections, respectively). Altogether more than 1,100 examples were presented to illustrate hundreds of factors in more than 20 functions. As such, TF is much more comprehensive than its predecessor written in German (Gutknecht/Rölle 1988), which explored the multifactorial translation situation of the modals of the German-English language pair.

In view of the complexity of the matter, however, even the goal of TF had to be modest: far from compiling an encyclopedia, all we could do was hint at several hundred factors and illustrate each by way of one or two examples involving one or two modals. But the actual number of translation factors affecting the modals is much greater. An all-inclusive presentation would require application of all factors to all of the modals. So an actual translation grammar or encyclopedia for the modals remains to be written.

Proposing to extend application of the factor approach, Mueller (1997: 682) suggests that the practical knowledge gained by applying this approach to the modals "may serve as a stepping-stone to factoring other grammatical phenomena as well".

Further expanding on this idea, Nicholas (1997: 41) states that the account given in TF "lays down a precedent for similar studies to be undertaken for different languages ....". By way of such studies, many kinds of factors may be found to be identical to those relevant in English and German. In areas where languages differ vastly, however, factors hitherto not considered may be expected to be relevant. This was demonstrated by Jones (1998: 149f.), who used the factor approach to illustrate the translation of sentence

(4) He can hear her.

into Japanese. Jones takes this sentence to be "quite clear grammatically", but as for translating it he feels that "it is hard to stop at grammar since many factors can only be fully exploited if the actual intent of the SL creator is seriously approached ....". He has in mind a special context of (4) as a spoken sentence: "Previously the speaker, a female, did not believe the man could hear her comatose daughter, and thus stressed the word *can*." In addition, factors relevant in Japanese include the factuality of hearing, the knowledge (or inference) of whether the sentence is spoken or written, the sex of the speaker, and the relationship of the speaker to the hearer. Jones emphasizes

---

[14] The chapter on the latter factor dimension, together with the final chapter on factors in translation theory, deals with what Hall (1998: 83f.) calls "the large scale problems of translation". He finds that "most of the statements and arguments in these last two chapters ... will be of major use to the novice translator" (1998: 83).

that "all these factors must be identified and compensated for" – in Japanese, they "would not be adequately conveyed if some compensation factors were not included".[15]

In other words: Factors not contained in the SL sentence itself but evident from the utterance situation are to be made explicit in the TL rendition. The blocking factor to an adequate rendition in this case is the insufficiency of consideration of linguistic factors in view of the additional importance of cultural factors.[16] And the compensation factor is the extraction of these factors from the utterance situation and their explication in the TL rendition.

In dealing with the language pair of English and Japanese, we come to find that one kind of factors – the cultural ones – plays an essential role; and these factors fulfill two of the three functions already dealt with: those of blocking factors and compensation factors.[17]

There is an interesting aspect to the third function mentioned, that of revision factors. Revising renditions is one of the most typical features of the translators' work. Pondering over the SL text in terms of the factors relevant for the current commission, they come up with a possible rendition. But soon further factors come into their mind which induce them to revise the rendition. Their revision is intended to be more than a mere change of rendition – it serves the purpose of improving it. Therefore the revision factors taken into account for the sake of improving the rendition may be referred to as *optimizing factors*.

In many cases attempts are made to optimize texts repeatedly. Stolze (1992: 82f., esp. n. 76) illustrates the "gradual process of optimizing"[18] a TL

---

[15] Jones discusses the following inadequate renditions:
(i) Kare wa kanojo ga kikoeru.
(ii) Kare wa kanojo no yutteiru-koto ga kikoetteiru.
A rendition that is based on the factors mentioned and "conveys all the information necessary for the Japanese" would be
(iii) Hontoni kikoerunda wa.

[16] On cultural translation factors cf. TF: 165ff., and Robyns (1994). Jones (1998: 151) takes up our suggestion (TF: 10) that use of the modals (such as *can* in (3)) involves a specific world view. He considers the study of culturally determined world views, a particular promising field of translation studies. He holds that views of life can and should be fully explored in the translation process and brought over in the rendition.

[17] For an overview of twenty-one functions see our *Glossary of factor functions* in TF, 5f., which "illustrates the complexity of the set of factors that the user has to take into account in the act of translating" (Thiele 1998: 75, col. 1). Our definitions of the twenty-one factor functions reveal that each of these functions is part and parcel of the "typical working-situations commonly experienced by all professional translators hundreds of times each day" (see above). This shows that translating by factors is no mere theoretical construct but mirrors the essential procedures of actual translation practice.

[18] Our translation.

text by quoting Paepcke's three-step revision of the printed rendition of the following sentence (taken from one of Albert Camus' texts):

(5) La vraie générosité envers l'avenir consiste à tout donner au présent.
(6) Die wahre Großzügigkeit der Zukunft gegenüber besteht darin, in der Gegenwart alles zu geben. (rendition in published text)
(7) Die [!] Zukunft zugewandt leben heißt, sich ganz der Gegenwart hinzugeben.
(8) Der Zukunft leben heißt ganze Hingabe an die Gegenwart.
(9) Der Zukunft lebt, wer alles der Gegenwart schenkt.

Trainee translators will maximally profit from such a stepwise improvement if they are not merely presented sequential renditions but also the optimizing factors leading to them. Only in this way will they learn to creatively optimize renditions themselves.

Stolze (1992: 72) refers to translating as a process in which the translator keeps on 'testing' until he or she finds an adequate expression. Creative ideas during translating deepen the translator's understanding of the SL text. Thus in a dialectic process gradually increasing understanding goes hand in hand with increasingly fitting renditions found. According to Stolze, the goal of translating guiding the translator in this process of optimizing renditions is the fidelity of the TL text to the SL text.[19] For Stolze, a rendition will be faithful if it is a felicitous, precise rendition of the SL text as a whole, if what is meant is effortlessly comprehended by the reader.

Can renditions (8) and (9) be expected to be effortlessly comprehended by the reader? Due to their archaic dative construction *der Zukunft leben* – an expression of highly elaborate poetic style – chances are that hardly any German of the younger generation will understand these sentences.[20] *Der Zukunft leben* is in sharp stylistic contrast with the everyday expression *envers l'avenir*.

Can renditions (8) and (9) be referred to as precise renditions? Certainly not – the *vraie générosité* extended to the future, still present in rendition (6), has in the final two renditions declined to a mere *leben*. This means that the German renditions (8) and (9) do not precisely match the French original in terms of denotative meaning. Moreover, in the final step from (8) to (9), addition of the relative pronoun *wer* in (9) personalizes in German what is

---

[19] "Sinneinheit zwischen Text und Übersetzung", i.e., "Stimmigkeit" (Stolze 1992: 72).

[20] What strikes us is that the definite article in (7) is utterly wrong – it must run *der Zukunft zugewandt*, because *zuwenden* (participle *zugewandt*) must be followed by the dative. In contrast, *leben* in (8) and (9) usually requires the accusative: *die Zukunft leben*. The dative *der Zukunft leben* is archaic style, but the article *der* might also be another misprint in terms of contemporary German.

expressed in French in an impersonal way. This sentence even markedly deviates from the original syntactically.

So in terms of Stolze's optimizing factors, it must be said that Paepcke's revisions are increasing departures from the SL sentence rather than increasing matches.

Most probably, however, the translator did consider his stepwise TL revision to be an improvement – otherwise he would not have undertaken it. And there is also an explanation of his way of revising the TL renditions: he must have had in mind other factors that guided his decisions as a translator – factors such as elevated style, terseness, and aphoristic trenchancy. This perspective is in line with Stolze's (1992: 82f.) point of presenting Paepcke's revisions: that the translator gradually immerses himself into the whole of the SL text, gets completely involved in it, and then relates the text message as if it were his own. Accordingly, Paepcke may have wanted to capture the very essence of (5) taken as a whole, irrespective of its internal structure.[21]

Stolze (1992: 83) also says that the translator designs his or her TL text to suit the client's purpose, in this way becoming the client's advocate. Justifying rendition (9) would presuppose a client that explicitly commissions a rendition reflecting 'esoteric' style suitable for an elite TL readership. On the basis of this translation factor preset by the client, the steps from rendition (6) to (9) must definitely be considered a process of optimization.[22]

The translator of the printed rendition (6), on the other hand, may also have progressed through a series of optimizing steps. He chose this sentence because for him it represented the optimum rendition. The factors guiding his decisions will have been those mentioned by Stolze: precision and expected effortless reception by the TL reader.

All this suggests that there is not just one optimal rendition to sentence (5) but several completely different ones.[23] Each of them is optimal in its own right because each is optimal **relative to** the background of different factor sets according to which the SL text in question is to be translated. In light of the factor set *lenience towards SL denotative meaning, TL elite readership,* and *TL esoteric style,* rendition (9) may be considered optimal. In light of the

---

[21] This would be in line with her concept of *hermeneutic translation.*

[22] If augmented by mention of the translation factors *lenience towards SL denotative meaning, TL elite readership,* and *TL esoteric style,* these steps are therefore a good example of our "stepwise approach to understanding ... texts and translating them by means of factors" (Thiele 1998: 75, col. 1). This approach qualifies TF as a "study toward a methodology for optimizing translations in general" (Mueller 1997: 682).

[23] This supercedes the "somewhat mythical belief, shared not only by naïve language users, but also by some professional translators and foreign language users, that there should be one 'ultimate' correct translation of each particular sentence" (Kashkin 1998: 109).

factor set *adherence to SL style* and *preservation of SL denotative meaning*, rendition (6) may be called optimal.

These reflections show that optimizing renditions is a multifaceted issue. The possibility of presenting **both** (6) **and** (9) as optimal renditions of (5) corroborates Stolze's (1992: 72) thesis that different priorities set within the translator's decisions may yield more than one optimal rendition of one and the same SL text.

In this connection she speaks of optimal fidelity **to the SL text**. We prefer her other remark about the translator designing his or her TL text to suit **the client's purpose** because our discussion has shown that it is fidelity to the latter that is criterial. Speaking of optimal fidelity to the SL text does not seem to make much sense when there are indefinitely many optimal ways of rendering it on the basis of indefinitely many different factor sets that a client may commission the translator to go by.

The possibility of optimizing renditions in different ways on the basis of different translation factors preset by the client illustrates the reality of translating by factors. It further illustrates the supreme role of the clients in determining which direction the renditions that they have commissioned are to take. As said near the beginning of this paper, the client may give general guide-lines for the translator to go by, such as free or literal translation, pro or contra explanations for the sake of facilitating the TL hearer's understanding, a rendition that reveals or conceals the fact that the TL text is a translation, etc.

Hence it is not the translatologists but the clients whose role it is to prescribe to the translators how they should translate, which factors they should follow. All the translatologists can do – but this is still quite a task – is "do research into the ways and means of creating optimum TL renditions of (different kinds of) SL texts in light of different factor sets" (TF: 304).

In terms of translation criticism, translatologists may check if renditions are successful or felicitous, i.e., whether translators have properly taken into account the factor set preset by their clients.

This factor-oriented approach to translation criticism makes obsolete the comparison of two renditions as such. There is, for instance, no point in saying that, *per se*, rendition (6) is better than rendition (9), or vice versa. Each may only be judged in light of its respective factor set applied to sentence (5). These differing factor sets make a comparison without reference to them meaningless.

At the same time reference to these factor sets is a means to justify and explain both renditions (6) and (9). This proves the factor approach to be "an approach and a system which has high explanatory power and provides an effective conceptual tool for the analysis of the 'fidelity' of translations" (Prokop 1997: 4). For Siepmann (1997: 16) TF achieves to "provide a set of criteria and a metalanguage which will promote consistency and precision in translation criticism".

Summarizing the advantages of the factor approach, Gallagher (1998a) expresses his conviction that TF "marks a distinct advance in dealing with translation problems in general" (95), and that "clearly there are considerable advantages in the kind of approach" (94, col. 2). Dressler (1999: 367) considers TF to be an important contribution to the theory and methodology of translation studies.

Böhm (1997: 359) regards TF as a "systematic study of the interplay of linguistic properties as factors determining the choice[24] of particular TL renditions". It explains "how and why certain renderings are appropriate or not, emphasizing the decision-making aspect of translating" (Leppihalme 1997: 94). Thus these factors "form an ideal basis for accumulating conditions and circumstances of decisions for translating" (Thiele 1998: 75, col. 2).

One of the advantages of the factor approach is that decisions are given an objective basis: The pertinent factors, even those that are only implicit in the SL text, are explicitated for evaluation in the decision process.[25] This intersubjective amenability makes it "a tested and testable framework for further research on the factors which may be required for 'high-fidelity' translations" (Prokop 1997: 1).

No wonder, therefore, that Golden (1997: 2) proposed that the factor approach "could be usefully applied ... to the development of natural language processing (NLP) rules for computational linguistics parsers ...". Gallagher (1998a: 94, col. 2) reckons that factor analysis "could facilitate the work of linguists responsible for designing MT systems". Nicholas (1997: 40) is even convinced that "one sphere where translation methodology immediately benefits from such an explicit analysis is that of machine translation".[26] In TF itself, we already hinted at the applicability of the factor approach to machine translation. Moreover, we construed a number of flowcharts for the sequential understanding of an SL sentence and its translation

---

[24] Cf. the "choice factor model" by Kashkin (1998: 105), who chooses to "dwell on the factors that influence the ... translator's choice of grammatical forms" (96). There are striking parallels between Kashkin's approach and ours, for instance his idea of "various factors ... having different degrees of influence and priority" (96), giving rise to a "choice hierarchy (the factors of choice)" (100), and our notions of *strength of factors (obligatory* vs. *optional factors)* (TF: 6) and *factor hierarchy* (TF: 282ff.).

[25] This extends also to evaluation of finished translations in the sense that "the factor approach gives translation criticism an objective yardstick for assessing the quality of translations by drawing upon the factor typology offered by the authors" (Köster 1997: 77).

[26] As an example, Siepmann (1997: 16) suggests that our findings about cotextual translation factors "could be fruitfully incorporated into MT software".

and suggested that this "step-by-step progression lends itself to machine translation also" (TF: 292).[27]

As for this special field of application, and also in general, TF must, however, be seen as an exploratory study only. Echoing our feeling that we have just taken a first step into research on translation factors, Nicholas (1997: 41) finds that TF "represents the beginning rather than the endpoint of a promising line of research"; Meidl (1997: 4) considers TF to be "an inspiration to other researchers"; and Gallagher (1998a: 95) states that, thanks to the factor approach, "future scholarship will now have a far more secure foundation on which to conduct research".

Which directions could such research take? Since the approach of translating by factors is not tied to any specific model or 'school' of translation, it is open in all imaginable ways. Its compatibility with the perspectives of others is evident from the fact that our "application of previous studies successfully integrates a variety of approaches" – Golden (1997: 1), who also found that "one of the most refreshing aspects [of TF] is its avoidance of any dogmatic considerations that would have to govern translation practice" (2). Similarly, Aijmer (1998: 124) points out that we "do not appear to be dogmatic" with regard to a specific approach.[28]

As far as we can see, all translatologists deal with factors anyway, so the concept of translating by factors could indeed be seen as some common ground of research. Even now Zgusta (1995 [1997]: 163) considers what is offered in TF "a unified theory of translation".[29]

---

[27] In this connection, we coined the acronym FAST (factor analysis in sequential translation).

[28] This is corroborated by Gallagher's (1998a: 94, col. 2) statement: "The authors crystallise translation theory into a neat and coherent form and endeavour to reconcile the divergent views put forward by translation theorists who have become embroiled in long-standing quarrels."

[29] Outside the realm of translation proper, the factor approach is also considered to be promising. Koktová (1998: 807f.) writes that TF "is not only significant for translation, but also addresses, in an insightful and inspiring manner, a number of issues relevant for theoretical, general, and comparative linguistics, pragmatics, and the philosophy of language".

References

Aijmer, Karin (1998): Review of TF. *The Translator* 1, 120-124.

Böhm, Roger (1997): Review of TF. *English Language and Linguistics* 2, 357-359.

Camón, Juan Bosco (1998): Review of TF. *TESL-EJ. Teaching English as a Second or Foreign Language* [Electronic journal] 2 (R 11), 1-3.

Classen, Albrecht (1997): Review of TF. *Schatzkammer der deutschen Sprache, Dichtung und Geschichte* 1&2, 157-159.

Dressler, Wolfgang U. (1999): Review of TF. *Linguistische Berichte* 179, 366–367.

Gallagher, John Desmond (1998a): Review of TF. *Lebende Sprachen* 2, 94-95.

Gallagher, John Desmond (1998b): "Möglichkeiten und Grenzen der Übersetzungs-äquivalenz". Wolfgang Börner/Klaus Vogel, eds. *Kontrast und Äquivalenz. Beiträge zu Sprachvergleich und Übersetzung* (= Tübinger Beiträge zur Linguistik 442). Tübingen: Narr, 1-30.

Golden, Sean (1997): Review of TF. *The Linguist List* 757, 1-4.

Gutknecht, Christoph/Lutz J. Rölle (1988): "Die multifaktorielle Translations-situation bei den Modalverben des Sprachenpaares Deutsch-Englisch". Gisela Quast, ed. *Einheit in der Vielfalt. Festschrift für Peter Lang zum 60. Geburtstag.* Frankfurt am Main etc.: Lang, 154–215.

Gutknecht, Christoph/Lutz J. Rölle (1996): *Translating by factors* (= SUNY Series in Linguistics). Albany, N.Y.: State University of New York Press.

Hall, Charles (1998): Review of TF. *The SECOL Review* 1, 80-84.

Holz-Mänttäri, Justa (1984): *Translatorisches Handeln. Theorie und Methode.* (= Suomalaisen Tiedeakatemian Toimituksia. Annales Academiæ Scientiarum Fennicæ B 226). Helsinki: Suomalainen Tiedeakatemia.

Holz-Mänttäri, Justa (1987): "Ausgangstext oder Produktspezifikation als Beurteilungsgrundlage? Ein Gerichtsurteil setzt Massstäbe". *Textcontext* 2, 177-178.

Jones, Andrew (1998): Review of TF. *Japan Association for Language Teaching Journal* 1, 148-151.

Kashkin, Vyacheslav B. (1998): "Choice factors in translation". *Target* 1, 95-111.

Koktová, Eva (1998): Review of TF. *Journal of Pragmatics* 6, 807-813.

Köster, Jens-Peter (1997): Review of TF. *IRAL* 1, 77-78.

Kussmaul, Paul (1978): "Kommunikationskonventionen in Textsorten am Beispiel deutscher und englischer geisteswissenschaftlicher Abhandlungen. Ein Beitrag zur deutsch-englischen Übersetzungstechnik". *Lebende Sprachen* 23, 54–58.

Leppihalme, Ritva (1997): Review of TF. *Neuphilologische Mitteilungen* 1, 94-95.

Malmkjær, Kirsten (1998): Review of TF. *International Journal of Applied Linguistics* 1, 152-159.

Meidl, Eva (1997): Review of TF. *Language, Society and Culture.* [Electronic Journal, University of Tasmania at Launceston, Australia]. Issue 1. Review article, 1-4.

Mueller, Magda (1997): Review of TF. *Language* 3, 681-682.

Nicholas, Nick (1997): Review of TF. *Dhumbadji! Journal for the History of Language* [Melbourne, Australia] 1, 37-41.

Niven, Bill (1997): Review of TF. *The Web Journal of Modern Language Linguistics* [School of Modern Languages, Newcastle-upon-Tyne]. Issue 2. Review 10, 1-4.

Prokop, Manfred (1997): Review of TF. *Zeitschrift für Interkulturellen Fremdsprachenunterricht* [Electronic Journal, Edmonton, Alberta, Canada] 3, 1-4.

Pym, Anthony (1998): Review of TF. *Target* 2, 397-399.

Robyns, Clem, ed. (1994): *Translation and the (re)production of culture. Selected papers of the CERA research seminars in translation studies 1989-1991*. Leuven: The CERA Chair for Translation, Communication and Cultures.

Ross, Stephen David (1981): "Translation and similarity". Marilyn Gaddis Rose, ed. *Translation Spectrum*. Albany, N.Y.: State University of New York Press, 8-22.

Savory, Theodore H. (1968): *The art of translation*. London: Cape.

Shuttleworth, Mark (1997): "Introduction". Mark Shuttleworth/Moira Cowie. *Dictionary of Translation Studies*. Manchester: St. Jerome Publishing.

Siepmann, Dirk (1997): Review of TF. *Mitteilungsblatt für Dolmetscher und Übersetzer* 3, 15-16.

Stolze, Radegundis (1992): *Hermeneutisches Übersetzen. Linguistische Kategorien des Verstehens und Formulierens beim Übersetzen* (= Tübinger Beiträge zur Linguistik 368). Tübingen: Narr.

TF = see Gutknecht/Rölle (1996).

Thiele, Wolfgang (1998): Review of TF. *Zeitschrift für Anglistik und Amerikanistik* 1, 75.

Webster's new encyclopedic dictionary (1993a): Springfield: Merriam Webster Inc.

Webster's new twentieth century dictionary of the English language (1993b): Springfield: Merriam Webster Inc.

Wilss, Wolfram (1994): "A framework for decision-making in translation". *Target* 2, 131-150.

Zgusta, Ladislav (1997): Review of TF. *Studies in the Linguistic Sciences* 1, 163-166.

Gottfried Graustein/Wolfgang Thiele *(Leipzig)*

Elements and relations again

0. Introduction

> As all simple ideas may be separated by imagination, and may be unified again
> in what form it pleases, nothing could be more unaccountable than the
> operations of that faculty, were it not guided by some universal principles,
> which render it, in some measure, uniform with itself in all times and places.
>
> David Hume, A Treatise of Human Nature 1739

After the upsurge of text linguistics in the 1970s and '80s ('a new cross-discipline'), the '90s have seen an opposite trend. The sheer complexity of the object text, the separate development of discourse analysis for spoken communication, the need to cope with a host of less accessible communicative features, and the waning prospect of achieving striking results in a limited period – possibly also the failure or minimal progress of electronic data processing to develop tools for automatic text analysis – have led to a deterioration of text-oriented work in linguistics. And the outlook for the next decade is not too promising either. Almost every field of linguistics, from language history to variety studies, is being investigated instead. In view of the persistent need to describe genuine communication, any attempt to partly reverse the trend or at least to prevent a further decline looks off-beat but is neither unnecessary nor unrealistic.

We want to attempt this in the field of elements and relations, an area where some of our earlier efforts lay (Graustein/Thiele 1987a; 1987b). For this we shall briefly survey previous work, then suggest a variation on this theme, and outline some ensuing details. The sample text "Allocating light" (ALG) to be used for illustration is a comment published in *The Guardian* (see Appendix 1; the numbers mark graphic sentences). If not indicated otherwise, examples are taken from ALG. It can be classified as an argumentative text: "Argumentation is the text type related to the cognitive process of *judging* in answer to a problem" (Werlich 1983: 40). Apart from their necessary brevity, comment texts have a complex and diversified text structure (cf. Thiele 1995; 1996) which sets specific standards to be met by the approach or model used for analysis.

1. Elements and relations in texts so far

Elements and relations figure prominently among the essential or basic aspects of combinatorial linguistics and thus text linguistics. The concept originated from different backgrounds. Most remote for our purpose is certainly a chemical definition like 'Element: A substance that cannot be decomposed into smaller substances (by chemical means)'. For elements in discourse this restriction does not hold, i.e. *element* here is synonymous to *unit, part, item, component*, etc.; we shall be using mainly *element* and *unit*. Elements in texts are neither limited to any particular form, either lexeme, phrase, clause, sentence, paragraph or the like, nor to any linguistic point of view, either semantic, syntactic, morphological, pragmatic or the like. *Relation* is "an aspect or quality ... that connects two or more things as being or belonging or working together" (Webster 1983: 994), with a similarly wider range of application in texts.

This definition of *relation* points to the organic combination of element and relation in all textual situations and contexts. Linguistic research can of course separate one or the other in order to pinpoint particular features, but this should not lead to eventual detachment or isolation. Previous work on element and relation (cf. Graustein/Thiele 1987b) exhibits some variation in this respect. The main trend appears to be an element-oriented approach with a kind of built-in relation. Besides Fillmore (1968) and Berndt (1970), Lehmann (1985: 71) argues that "the relation is *inherent* in one (or both) of the elements". Relation-only approaches have concentrated on the sequencing of language items rather than the elements that are being sequenced. Among the proponents of this are Quirk et al. (1985), Leech/Svartvik (1975), Halliday/Hasan (1976). A mixture of element (e.g. instrument – purpose; denial – correction) and relation (e.g., matching: coupling) approach is found in Hoey (1983) and Crombie (1985). Little attention is given to the interplay of horizontal and vertical (as well as intratextual) relations.

Our own concept (Graustein/Thiele 1987a) tried to give due attention to both aspects. Elements and relations were treated as sequential and vertical configurations:

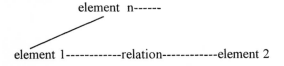

```
                element n------
                          /
                        /
                     /
                   /
 element 1------------relation------------element 2
```

For example, on level 8 of the ALG analysis (Appendix 2), there is the configuration

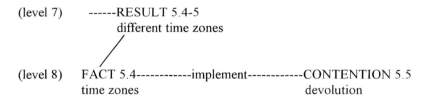

(level 7)   ------RESULT 5.4-5
             different time zones

(level 8)   FACT 5.4------------implement------------CONTENTION 5.5
             time zones   devolution

which is 'integrated' (level 7 of the diagram) into the unit RESULT 5.4-5
(different time zones). 5.5 (= element 2) thus states the way in which the
solution expressed in 5.4 (= element 1, i.e. the time zones) could be implemented.

The limitations or drawbacks of most of these notions are obvious: They
are too simple or unwieldy or they are too static. In our own version too much
was crammed into either individual labels or cumulative arrays of too many
diverse details. 5.4 would, for instance, be described as an assertion in front
position in the configuration and set off by a sentence final stop, a sentence
with a scope of 14 words, a complexity marked by one finite subordinate
(conditional) clause and three verbless clauses (= embeddings), elements of
the word systems 'time', 'problem', 'Great Britain', etc. The relation has a
semi-explicit relator ('perhaps'), more explicit would be an expression like 'a
possible way is'. The relation is marked by a sentence gap between 5.4 and
5.5, the connection between 'the problem' in 5.4 and 'this matter' in 5.5, and
'be solved' in 5.4 and 'vote' in 5.5.

2. From here

The disadvantages of previous element and relation approaches should be
remedied from the point of view of the specific textual angle. For this, we
suggest a concentration on those items or aspects that are most relevant for
the course and progression of communicative events qua texts.

One way of implementing this is to consider elements and relations as
linked to or part of rhetorical devices. Rhetoric shares with text linguistics the
assumption that "texts are vehicles of purposeful interaction" (de Beaugrande/
Dressler 1981: 15). This view may overcome an artificial subdivision of linguistics into its traditional disciplines and also subsume monological as well as
polylogical communication, i.e. utilise the common factor in speaking and
writing.

Rhetoric has undergone major revisions in its long history. In the ancient
world it was used as a kind of checklist on mental acts which a rhetorician
could use when investigating and collecting arguments on a subject (e.g.,

definition by genus and differentia, comparison and contrast, cause and effect). It dates back to the work by Aristotle.

Nowadays rhetoric is reflected in the social sciences differently:

> In the late 20c, rhetoric has an explicit and an implicit aspect. Explicitly, many 20c professionals refer to rhetoric as archaic and irrelevant, while for some philosophers of communication and for many teachers of writing it is a significant and lively issue. In the latter circles, there is a discussion of a 'new rhetoric' that blends the best of the old with current insights into the nature of communication. (McArthur 1992: 864)

It is indeed philosophers of communication, literary scholars (e.g. Müller in Nünning 1998: 463-465) and teachers of writing (cf. Jordan 1984) who positively assess rhetoric and its application in various fields of communication. In linguistics it often had a negative meaning, although it is regaining esteem, particularly because it always has been concerned with units beyond the sentence, i.e. the communicatively basic units of language (which are especially relevant in text linguistic work), and has treated the text as a vehicle of a message. In this view rhetoric can be interpreted as a genuine 'generative' approach to the analysis and description of texts.

Our attempt to make use of principles of rhetoric for text analysis and description coincides partly with and is encouraged by ideas born within the framework of rhetoric. The *rhetorical structure theory* (= RST) as developed by Mann, Thompson and co-workers and based on *rhetorical predicates* (Grimes 1975), makes statements about how meaning and intentions are structured and combined. It "identifies hierarchic structure in text. It describes the relations between text parts in functional terms, identifying both the transition point of a relation and the extent of the items related. It provides comprehensive analyses rather than selective commentary" (Mann/Thompson 1988: 281). Scholars of this school make "the parallel claim that 'clause combining is a grammaticalization of the rhetorical organisation of discourse' but they support this claim not by reference to spoken language or earlier stages of the same language, but they appeal to the parallelism between clause relations within prosodic sentences and sentence relationships within larger texts" (Haimann/Thompson, 1988: xi). Their concept works with relational propositions, like 'justification, solutionhood, evidence, motivation, enablement', and 'circumstance' (Mann/Thompson 1986), which – although it puts the relations on an equal level with the elements – at the same time separates them from the elements and conflates them with parts of the (second) elements.

Mann/Thompson (1986: 63) would describe the configuration 5.4-----5.5 as "'enablement', in which one part of the text provides information that *enables* the addressee to comply with the directive". Matthiessen/Thompson

(1988: 292) are more specific – but also less linguistic – and define the proposition as "a portion providing the means which enable the reader to comply with the directive or take advantage of the offer".

The advantage of this approach is that the analysis disregards the various other details which sometimes make complex analysis almost impossible, such as the interactional aspects which are implied in the meaning of language utterances or the manifold realization forms which express the element and relation meaning. FACT 5.4, e.g., could be interactionally characterized as 'stating', since the writer wants to make a fact known to the reader (wants to state something) – a description which partly overlaps with FACT because facts are often 'stated'. Another advantage may be seen in the situational variation which the usage of the devices is connected with. 'Solutionhood, evidence', or 'enablement' are labels determined propositionally, but also depend on the function of these 'relations' in the progression of the text.

The limitations of this approach are partly connected with their advantages. This is – with regard to text-linguistic work – not surprising if one has in mind the complexity of the object of analysis and description. Besides the overlap of element 2 and relation characterizations mentioned above, relationally dominated meaning analyses do not adequately cover the linguistically relevant factors of the meaning expressed. 'Enablement' for 5.4-----5.5 in ALG disregards that element 1 (5.4) is – as the subject matter in its textual relevance – a FACT stating time zones, and element 2 (5.5) expresses a CONTENTION (devolution) to be implemented. Moreover, the inventory of categories, labels and their definitions is not conventionalized and thus does not allow generalizations applicable to different texts, text types, or text forms. Another problem is that the rhetorical devices proposed by Mann, Thompson and co-workers may be confused with stylistics, since the most effectual shaping of the communication may be at variance with the subject matter.

3. Meaning

What does this rhetorical orientation mean for our own configurational description of elements and relations in texts? As far as we can see, relations require more new thinking than do elements.

Elements are units or components characterized or characterizable by *topicalization*, and this holds also for a rhetorical interpretation. Integrating topicalizations into a rhetoric framework means, however, that the concept is dynamic rather than static. The "topicalization is the ... conventionalized, socially standardized or established part" of the unit meaning (Graustein/ Thiele 1987a: 54). Topicalizations summarize the subject matter in their textual relevance, they are therefore 'more' than macropropositions (van Dijk 1980). For this we use our established labelling. The list of labels is not finite, but reflects what has resulted from several years of analytic work on texts of different provenance, although we would not neglect culture-specific variation in details. The unit size is not fixed, but in the present essay we do not want to descend very much below clause level in order to avoid mixing details of phrase or sentence grammar with text-analytic moments.

The following examples illustrate the use of topicalizations:

> TOPIC 1.1-2 (level 2) = the title and subtitle of the text (comment), here: announcing both the problems of light and devolution
> BODY 2.1-5.5 (level 2) = the main body of the text, developing the subject(s) announced in the TOPIC
> PRO 2.2-3.6 (level 4) = arguments in favour of sth., here: the British keeping summer time throughout the year for various reasons
> CON 4.1-5.5 (level 4) = arguments against sth., here: the attitude of Scotland which wants to keep winter time

The topicalization labels can be supplemented by propositions, which state the specific content or meaning referred to in the structure of the text. They are usually expressed in a reduced way and not restricted to a specific kind of syntactic wording. They are complementary to the topicalizations in the element description of the textual units. Within the dialectics of general and unique features they characterize a text and distinguish one text of the same or another type from another text. Propositions support and (by referring to subject matter) give reasons for the application of specific topicalization labels and thus substantiate the labelling. This inclusion of propositions in the unit characterization is one of the essential differences from RST, where 'conceptual entities', derived from the literal text portions (Mann/Thompson 1986: 59), are taken to be the arguments of the relational propositions.

Thus the propositions at level 4 for

> PRO 2.2-3.6: abolish winter time and save lives and avoid casualties

and

> CON 4.1-5.5: Scotland against this

are semantic explications of the PRO and CON configuration, including its contrasting meaning relation.

For units which in their literal formulation have sentence- or phrase-like status, the proposition characterization may be redundant and thus not necessary. This holds, for example, for

> (level 3)
> STATEMENT 1.1 (= Allocating light)

and
SUBSTANTIATION 1.2 (= It's a ripe subject for devolution).

In such cases a propositional generalization is not useful or appropriate from the point of view of the text structure, particularly if the units are considered also in their hierarchical relatedness: The TOPIC 1.1-1.2 is labelled 'announcement'. In other cases, propositions may overlap with topicalizations (i.e. they are more or less tautological), since the subject matter expressed by the unit and its textual relevance are very close to each other, e.g. level 2, unit 1.1-2. (TOPIC and 'announcement'). These problems deserve further investigations in connection with text analytic work.

On the highest level in the element and relation structure the text as a whole is characterized. The topicalization label QUALITY CONTENTION for ALG is typical of comment texts (Thiele 1995; 1996). Other text types have different labels, e.g. we found HYPOTHESIS TESTING for the presentation of findings pertinent to a hypothesis, ENVIRONMENTAL IMPACT for a fable, TECHNIQUE DESCRIPTION in operational reports (e.g. on an artificial heart valve) and others (cf. Graustein/Thiele 1987a).

Relations are more than just the content of the relation expressed by element 2 with regard to element 1 as suggested earlier (cf. Graustein/Thiele 1987a: 59-65). They should be considered more prominently than before in their role in communication, i.e. as rhetorical acts and not as static but as dynamic features. We do no longer ask: What **is** element 2 in relation to element 1, but what does element 2 **do** with regard to element 1? For the types of relations this requires a reconsideration or re-interpretation of the list we have used so far (cf. a, below). A switch to another variant (cf. b, below) does not seem more convincing at present.

Just as the unit size is not fixed, relations do obtain between any two or more elements, but for the time being we do not go below sentence level.

(a) Reconsideration of the previous list

Because element 2 is now seen in a different connection to element 1, our previous list has to be reconsidered and modified. The example quoted in 1. illustrates the problem:

(level 8)
FACT 5.4---implement---CONTENTION 5.5

The old-type analysis, which would have indicated that element 2 (CONTENTION: devolution) is 'processual' in relation to element 1 (FACT: time zones), has been replaced by the rhetorical relation 'implement', i.e. the suggested devolution for Scotland could and would implement the different time zones.

Another point to be considered, though secondary, is that element-relation combinations in previous analyses were partly tautological, e.g. TOPIC---explicative---DEVELOPMENT, which would be our characterization of level 2 in the ALG analysis on the basis of our former approach.

The following list includes the relation types we used so far and the rhetorical relations as reconsidered or re-interpreted. For a definition of the old relation types, see Graustein/Thiele (1987a: 59-65).

Relation types (old) element 2 [is ... to] element 1	Rhetorical relations element 2 [does this to] element 1
additive	adds
adversative	contrasts
alternative	alternates
---	answers
descriptive	describes
evaluative	comments [on]
explicative	details
	develops
causal	reasons [that]
concessive	concedes [that...despite...]
consecutive	follows [from]
	concludes [from]
final	purports
conditional	conditions
comparative	compares [with]
instrumental/processual	implements
local/temporal	circumstances

Note that not all rhetorical relations find an equivalent in the relation types. The inventory is certainly not definitive and exhaustive, but in our analyses it was sufficient to cover most of the configurations encountered in real texts.

Our rhetorical relations can be compared with categories of the *rhetorical structure theory* (RST) as they also "do not rely on morphological or syntactic signals", but rest "on functional and semantic judgements" (Mann/Thompson 1988: 249f.). Their list of relations shows some degree of similarity with our inventory (e.g., 'circumstance, cause, condition, evaluation, contrast'), but the two are not identical. This is above all due to the fact that Mann/Thompson do not clearly distinguish between element and relation characterization, as signalled by labels like 'solutionhood, background, enablement' (cf. our argumentation above). Another essential difference is our introduction of 'answer' as a relation, which is a dynamic concept evolved from interactional text linguistics. Also different is RST in its insistence on relational propositions as combinatorial phenomena, which do more than simply relate parts of texts, convey "essential subject matter" and join "subject-matter-specific concep- tions to each other" (Mann/Thompson 1986: 58 and 76).

The elements and relations of text ALG outlined in appendix 2 describe the relations in configuration. Here are a few examples:

    (level 2)
        TOPIC 1.1-2---develop---BODY 2.1-5.5
    (level 3)
        STATEMENT 1.1---comment---SUBSTANTIATION 1.2
        CONTENTION 2.1---answer---SUBSTANTIATION 2.2-5.5
    (level 4)
        PRO 2.2-3.6---contrast---CON 4.1-5.5
    (level 6)
        GENERAL 2.2-4---add---SPECIFIC 2.5-7

Note that there is generally no fixed combination between element and relation. Other configurations could be e.g.

        GENERAL---contrast---SPECIFIC
        GENERAL---detail---SPECIFIC
        GENERAL---condition---SPECIFIC.

Some relations allow serial combinations: add, alternate, compare, circum- stance, e.g.

        VARIETY I---compare---VARIETY II---compare---VARIETY III.

This serial combinability suggests another parallel between RST and our ap- proach: There (Matthiessen/Thompson 1988: 289) the relations are conceived as *nucleus – satellite*, where one member of the related pair is 'ancillary' to the other (e.g. 'motivation, elaboration') and as *list* (neither member is ancillary), reminiscent of traditional paratactic predicates. These concepts do, however, remain hierarchical only, and do not cover equal and horizontal relations.

(b) Adopting a variant
Certainly basic are the relations suggested by Gray (1977: 192) though a detailed explanation is missing there. They are called *inter-assertional relations* which also transgress the boundaries of grammar and rhetoric:

        DESCRIPTIVE: continue, contrast
        EXPLANATORY: conclude, support
        RHETORICAL: question, answer

The latter pair would tie in well with the extension of our list ('answer').

Although it looks similar to the nucleus and list approach of RST, this variant is not consistent, and not specific enough for our purposes. It also favours a preconceived quantitative grading: Most commonly an assertion is related to the previous assertion as a continuation. Less common is the relationship of contrast. Relatively uncommon are: concluding, supporting; least common are: questioning and answering. This is contrary to the textual function, since an 'uncommon' relationship can be crucial in the text progression.

One important aspect is not covered by these variants: the relation at the uppermost level of the textural structure. The answer to the question 'What is the text related to?' is too difficult to answer here, but we think it should be part of a realistic and adequate element-relation approach. The text constitutes an element. What is the other element of the configuration? It is clearly external to the text, and as such can be content and/or form, e.g.

(a) the comment section of the Guardian, the Guardian newspaper, the news coverage in Britain,
(b) the discussion about GMT, Scottish time, the European discussion of the semi-annual time switch,
(c) the reader and/or writer of ALG in interaction with each other and with the text.

This must remain one of the problems for future work. Efforts are also required for elucidating the vertical relations in the hierarchical structure of the text, which so far have been treated summarily as 'detailing' the level below and 'integrating' the level above (cf. 1.).

4. Realization

"By realization we understand the discoursal, grammatical, lexical, and phonological/graphic forms that serve to express ... the external and internal features of the content/meaning" (Graustein/Thiele 1987a: 65). The problem here concerns quantity as well as quality. The wealth of linguistic details that have been detected in words and phrases multiplies in any description of a text which is longer than two sentences and leads to a huge amassment of details that cannot be assessed or used. The other extreme – leaving out or neglecting realization features altogether – is one of the drawbacks of rhetorical studies: "all of RST is pre-realizational since it makes statements about how meanings and intentions are structured and combined, but not about how they are realized" (Mann/Mattiessen/Thompson 1992: 45).

Therefore we favour – different from the rhetoric approach – an organic combination of meaning and form, though not as a 1:1 relationship. Form in this sense also includes naming meanings which are not signalled explicitly by a linker and can only be gleaned from other parts of the text, e.g.

Henry likes pasta. John prefers baguettes. (= contrast, typical linkers would be *but, whereas*)

The principle here is to refer to linguistic devices of any kind in their rhetoric function, their importance in signalling progression. In the example quoted the contrast is signalled by the different persons and the different (regional) food.

Realization is not central to the present argumentation and only included as part of the complex view of texts. This means that a number of grammatical and other details, as listed for example by Biber in his factorial studies (1988; 1995), are disregarded here in favour of a few outstanding aspects. A few of these minor forms were quoted above in the element-relation sample (FACT 5.4---implement---CONTENTION 5.5).

Some realization forms in ALG:

(level 2)

TOPIC 1.1-2: headline, bold face, brevity (nonfinite clause in *-ing*), unusual meaning (*allocate*), *light* without a determiner and modifier (cf. *daylight* in 2.2)

BODY 2.1-5.5: positive question as a starter, running text with chunks, lexical cohesion or linkage, return to headline (*devolution*) at the end

develop: [in developing the TOPIC, this is] marked by indentation, capitals, wh-question

(level 4)

PRO 2.2-3.6: list of facts and/or statements, nondefinite NPs (5.2 *everyone*, 5.3 *anyone*), that-clauses, *lifestyle* as a kind of frame (2.2 *suffer* – 3.5 *lifestyle reasons*)

CON 4.1-5.5: brief statement as a starter, argumentative items (4.2 *opposition – 5.2 pros and cons – 5.4 problem ... solved*)

contrast: [in contrasting PRO before CON, ALG uses] a negated question as a linker at the end of the opening (i.e. PRO) paragraph (3.6), verbless clause with a proper noun as an answer

(level 6)

STATEMENT 5.1: assertion, simple sentence, nondefinite NPs and proforms, resumption of main subject: 2.1 *save ... lives* – 2.8 *reduction in road deaths* – 3.3 *deaths ... reduced* – 3.5 *casualty figures ... overwhelming* – 4.2 *reduction in road casualties*

OUTLOOK 5.2-5: argumentative chunk with contrasting clauses (5.2 *if* – 5.3 *But* – 5.4 *if* – 5.5 *perhaps/whether*), Scotland contrasted to England, subjunctive verb forms, return to subtitle 1.2 (*ripe, devolution*)
concede: onset of complex sentences, *therefore* could not be inserted

(level 8)
FACT 5.4---implement---CONTENTION 5.5: as described in 1 above

(at sentence level (here for illustration only))
FACT 2.2a: assertion, non-personal, negative connotation
CONSEQUENCE 2.2b: subordinate clause [as object], prospection, nondefinite pronoun (extensive)
conclude: subordinator, direct object of metacommunicative verb

5. Conclusion

Though it looks very promising and has brought about first encouraging results, the present attempt is far from being definitive. The variations our own work has undergone so far are indicative of continuous development, but even if the results were less transitory, the complexity of the object language itself would necessitate and enable laborious progress in a combination of theoretical work and practical analyses. Confirmations and modifications in the sense of improvements depend on

(a) the principled affirmation – highly probable – or disapproval of element and relation as essential aspects of text linguistics,
(b) the confirmation of the validity of the rhetoric approach – highly aspired – to these phenomena,
(c) progress in text linguistics for other criteria – clearly indicated – ,
(d) the compatible description – urgently needed – of elements and relations below sentence level: What is the equivalent of rhetoric aspects at sentence level?

Despite these desiderata and necessities, the description of our sample text ALG with topicalizations, propositions and rhetorical relations has provided a reasonably clear picture of a mainly symmetrical comment text (PRO, CON) and a differently structured subdivision (PRO – more STATEMENT, FACT; CON – more diversified elements). The relations are characterized by fewer neutral listings (add, explicate) and more argumentative concepts (answer, contrast, concede, follow). Among the advantages over RST is the fact that elements and relations are not conflated and that our rhetorical relations unlike the relational propositions of RST are not treated as basic – which would mean – unrealistically – that the non-relational units (our topicalized units) were derived from the relational propositions.

The possible outcome of our attempt in its completion could be that the rhetorical structure constitutes the discourse structure, or – more realistic – that the rhetorical organisation exists as focused relations within the discourse structure (Hoey 1983: 179) – but then the question of the ensemble of the discourse organisation arises anew.

References

Berndt, Rolf (1970): "Transformational generative grammar and the teaching of English". *Zeitschrift für Anglistik und Amerikanistik* 3, 239-261.

Biber, Douglas (1988): *Variation across speech and writing*. Cambridge: CUP.

Biber, Douglas (1995): *Dimensions of register variation*. Cambridge: CUP.

Crombie, Winifred (1985): *Process and relation in discourse and language learning*. Oxford: OUP.

de Beaugrande, Robert/Wolfgang Dressler (1981): *Introduction to text linguistics*. London: Longman.

Fillmore, Charles J. (1968): "The case for case". Emmon Bach/ Robert T. Harms, eds. *Universals in linguistic theory*. New York: Holt etc., 1-88.

Graustein, Gottfried/Wolfgang Thiele (1987a): *Properties of English texts*. Leipzig: Enzyklopädie.

Graustein, Gottfried/Wolfgang Thiele (1987b): "Relations revisited". *Zeitschrift für Anglistik und Amerikanistik* 1, 58-67.

Graustein, Gottfried et al. (1987): *English grammar. A university handbook*. Leipzig: Enzyklopädie.

Gray, Bennison (1977): *The grammatical foundations of rhetoric. Discourse analysis*. The Hague etc.: Mouton.

Grimes, Joseph E. (1975): *The thread of discourse*. The Hague etc.: Mouton.

Haimann, John/Sandra A. Thompson, eds. (1988). *Clause combining in grammar and discourse* (= Typological Studies in Language 18). Amsterdam/Philadelphia: Benjamins.

Halliday, M.A.K./Ruquaiya Hasan (1976): *Cohesion in English*. London: Longman.

Hoey, Michael (1983): *On the surface of discourse*. London: George Allen & Unwin.

Jordan, Michael P. (1984): *Rhetoric of everyday English texts*. London: George Allen & Unwin.

Leech, Geoffrey/Jan Svartvik (1975): *A communicative grammar of English*. London: Longman.

Lehmann, Christian (1985): "On grammatical relationality". *Folia Linguistica* XIX, 1-2, 67-109.

Mann, William C./Christian Matthiessen/Sandra A. Thompson, eds. (1992). *Discourse descriptions: diverse linguistic analyses of a fund-raising text*. Amsterdam: Benjamins.

Mann, William C./Sandra A. Thompson (1986): "Relational propositions in discourse". *Discourse Processes* 9, 57-90.

Mann, William C./Sandra A. Thompson (1988): "Rhetorical structure theory: towards a functional theory of text organization". *Text* 3, 243-281.

Matthiessen, Christian/Sandra A. Thompson (1988): "The structure of discourse and 'subordination'". John Haimann/Sandra A. Thompson, eds. *Clause combining in grammar and discourse* (= Typological Studies in Language 18). Amsterdam/ Philadelphia: Benjamins, 275-330.

McArthur, Tom, ed. (1992): *The Oxford companion to the English language.* Oxford: OUP.

Nünning, Ansgar, ed. (1998): *Metzler Lexikon Literatur- und Kulturtheorie.* Stuttgart/ Weimar: Metzler.

Quirk, Randolph et al. (1985): *A comprehensive grammar of the English language.* London: Longman.

Thiele, Wolfgang (1995): "An approach to the integrated analysis of argumentative English discourses". Wolfgang Riehle/Hugo Keiper, eds. *Anglistentag 1994 Graz. Proceedings.* Tübingen: Niemeyer, 513-529.

Thiele, Wolfgang (1996): "Diskurseigenschaften geschriebener englischer Kommentare". Rudolph Beier, ed. *Festschrift für Günter Weise.* Frankfurt a. M.: Lang, 217-225.

van Dijk, Teun A. (1980): *Macrostructures.* Hillsdale: Erlbaum.

Webster's ninth collegiate dictionary (1983): Springfield: Merriam Webster Inc.

Werlich, Egon (1983): *A text grammar of English.* Heidelberg: Quelle & Meyer.

Appendix

1) Sample text: ALG

1.1 **Allocating light**
.2 It's a ripe subject for devolution

2.1 WHAT would it take to persuade politicians to save well over 100 lives a year and avoid hundreds of unnecessary casualties at no cost to the puplic
.2 purse? Yesterday's annual ritual of putting the clocks back means that everyone will suffer an extra hour of darkness at night in exchange for an
.3/.4 hour of daylight in the morning. Hardly anyone benefits from it. Opinion
.5 polls indicate that 80 per cent of the population are against it. The vast majority of lobbies from the Royal Society for the Prevention of Accidents to
.6 Age Concern and the Police Federation want change. Research has shown that it would cut crime, boost tourism, reduce energy wastage and add to our
.7 enjoyment of life. Those benefits alone ought to make it a political priority.
.8 But the main reason for change is that there would be a big reduction in

road deaths, particularly of children, including in Scotland where most
opposition has been focused.

3.1   Statistics proving all this have been available for years and never seriously
  .2   contested. Recently, the Department of Transport asked the (privatised)
       Transport Research Laboratory (TRL) and the Department of Statistical
       Science at University College, London (UCL) to do the most exhaustive
       analysis yet on the likely effects of an extra hour of daylight in the
  .3   evenings throughout the year. They found that deaths would be reduced by
  .4   between 104 a year (according to UCL) and 139 (TRL). The number
       seriously injured would be reduced by 339 (of whom 200 would be
  .5   pedestrians). Even if these statistics didn't exist there would be a very
       strong case for extending daylight time in the evenings for lifestyle reasons –
  .6   but the casualty figures make it overwhelming. So why hasn't it happened?
4.1/.2 In one word, Scotland. There is, understandably, more opposition there
       even though the statistics show that the reduction in road casualties would be
  .3   only slightly smaller proportionately than in Great Britain as a whole. For
       this reason Labour, which is facing opposition from resurgent Scottish
  .4   nationalism, isn't interested. The only vehicle for change now is Lord
       Archer's proposal (as stated in Saturday's Guardian) which would be
       counterproductive since it centres on the benefit to London of an extra hour
       as part of his mayoral campaign.
5.1/.2 In fact everyone would gain from fewer road casualties. If Scotland,
       having weighed to pros and cons, decides it would prefer to have lighter
       mornings and darker evenings despite the cost in road deaths and casualties
  .3   then that is the country's democratic right. But it shouldn't entail the rest of
  .4   England and Wales having to do as well. The problem could easily be solved
  .5   if Scotland and England had different time zones. Perhaps, the newly
       devolved administrations in Scotland and Wales should vote on this matter
       for themselves to test whether time is ripe for devolution.

Source: The Guardian 26-10-98, 17

2) Structuring in ALG: Elements and rhetorical relations

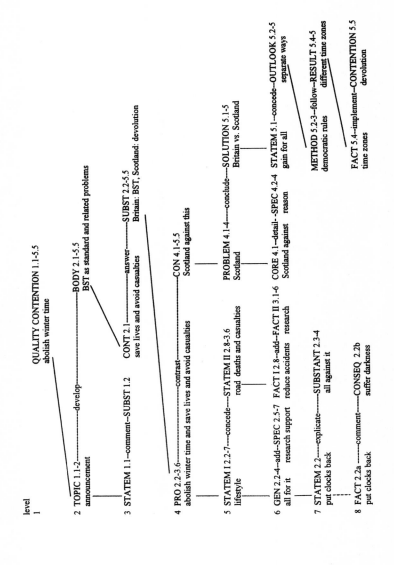

level
1

         QUALITY CONTENTION 1.1-5.5
         abolish winter time

2 TOPIC 1.1-2————develop————BODY 2.1-5.5
   announcement   BST as standard and related problems

3 STATEM 1.1—comment—SUBST 1.2   CONT 2.1————answer————SUBST 2.2-5.5
         save lives and avoid casualties   Britain: BST, Scotland: devolution

4 PRO 2.2-3.6————————contrast————CON 4.1-5.5
   abolish winter time and save lives and avoid casualties   Scotland against this

5 STATEM I 2.2-7————concede————STATEM II 2.8-3.6   PROBLEM 4.1-4————conclude————SOLUTION 5.1-5
   lifestyle   road deaths and casualties   Scotland   Britain vs. Scotland

6 GEN 2.2-4—add—SPEC 2.5-7   FACT I 2.8—add—FACT II 3.1-6   CORE 4.1—detail—SPEC 4.2-4   STATEM 5.1—concede—OUTLOOK 5.2-5
   all for it   research support   reduce accidents   research   Scotland against   reason   gain for all   separate ways

7 STATEM 2.2————explicate————SUBSTANT 2.3-4   METHOD 5.2-3—follow—RESULT 5.4-5
   put clocks back   all against it   democratic rules   different time zones

8 FACT 2.2a ————comment————CONSEQ 2.2b   FACT 5.4—implement—CONTENTION 5.5
   put clocks back   suffer darkness   time zones   devolution

Christian Todenhagen *(Chico)*

Point de capiton as textual metaphor

Research in the cognitive aspects of language analysis has reached a high level of maturity in the area of text production, comprehension, and recall. A distinct sign of its sophistication is the ready availability of a large number of models in these domains whose primary functions are visual representations of the complex interplay of cognitive linguistic processes.

For text comprehenders who depend on their linguistic intuitions the cognitive tasks involved are usually simple and straight forward, but may, of course, also be knotty and ambiguous. It is here that models of text representation find themselves in a particularly challenging position because their explanatory power is put to the test in a novel situation. Such a novel situation is given by two radio commercials differing virtually only in a concluding sentence but creating two radically different symbolic realities. The challenge to competing text models is to explain the cognitive skills demanded from text comprehenders to discern these two realities.

The two texts in question are radio commercials broadcast in 1998 in the Toronto area of Canada. Both were designed to create good will and commercial interest in a product of Canon, Canada, a unit of Canon Inc. of Japan. The first advertising spot ran (very much) like this:[1]

1	MOM:	Here's my presentation - what do you think?
2	KID:	Mom, honestly, it's like stone age.
3	MOM:	Well, I wouldn't go that far.
4	KID:	Mom, you need a Canon big time.
5	MOM:	A big gun?
6	KID:	A Canon BJC 4300 Color Bubble Jet Printer.
7	MOM:	Oh well, I'm sure they're all about the same.
8	KID:	Hello? The Canon BJC 4300 has Canon's patented PhotoRealism which gives you amazing photographic-quality images, plus Canon has something new and very cool: it's called DMT.
9	MOM:	DM what?

---

[1]   The text was reconstructed on the basis of the *Wall Street Journal* article "Kid says darndest things in ad, and Canadians say, 'Spare us'" (De Santis 1998), and the (second, revised) original of the "Smart kid radio copy revised". The author is very much indebted to Marshall Thompson, Chico, for his generous gifts of time and enthusiasm.

10	KID:	DMT -- you know, Drop Modulation Technology. It is the newest generation of photo quality color printing.
11	MOM:	Really?
12	KID:	Yea, and it gives you images with even less graininess and richer tones.
13	MOM:	Oh.
14	KID:	But best of all, with the optional scanner cartridge the Canon BJC 4300 can scan images right into the computer.
15	MOM:	You seem to know a lot about this Canon BJC ...
16	KID:	BJC 4300 Color Bubble Jet Printer.
17	MOM:	Right: How'd you get so smart?
18	KID:	I'm a graduate of grade seven. Duh!

To the incredulous dismay of the advertising agency's script writers, however, the radio spot prompted dozens of complaints: "People were concerned about what they saw as a perennial problem – kids' lack of respect for adults – and called to complain" (De Santis: loc. cit.). A spokesman declared: "We did not intend it as being rude. We wanted to show a kid who was knowledgeable about technology" (quoted by De Santis: loc. cit.).

The advertising agency came up with a revised version which differed from the original in two places only. The script writers eliminated the kid's "Hello?" (8) and replaced it by "Not.", and they cut out 18 completely and substituted for it the words: "I don't know, I guess I just inherited it."

Of these two editorial changes it is clearly the last one which turned around the meaning of the commercial to receive the approval of the Canadian radio listeners. It provides, too, the clue to the theoretical linguistic explanation of the cognitive strategies involved. Trabasso (1989: 74) proposes the strategy of *goal intervention and substitution*: There is the original goal of a mom who wanted her kid evaluate her presentation. It is interrupted by the formation of a 'more valued goal'. The proud mom now wants to find out how her kid got so smart. "This goal becomes a first order goal. The original goal is over-ridden and abandoned ..." (Trabasso: loc. cit.). Indeed, the dialogue of the commercial ends without any explicit statement of whether the mother took her daughter's advice to buy a Canon printer. The positive note of the new first order goal pushes the negative feel generated in the context of the original goal completely into the background and substitutes for it.

The cognitive strategy of *goal intervention and substitution* can be formalized in Trabasso's (1989) *causal network model*. As Trabasso works with narratives, the radio dialog must be translated into a narrative format (Graesser 1981; Trabasso/Sperry 1985).

| 1 | There was a mom |
| 2 | who had prepared a presentation. |

3   After she had finished writing it,
4   she wanted to have it evaluated.
5   She asked her kid what she thought of it.
6   The kid said it was stone age.
7   She wanted to persuade her mother to buy a Canon printer
8   and therefore listed all its technical advantages.
9   The mom was very impressed by her daughter's smartness
10   and asked her how she got so smart.
11   The kid said: "I don't know, I guess I just inherited it."

Trabasso (1989: 69ff.) analyses a narrative into one or more planning episodes which consist of six components: settings (S) – the background social and personal context; events (E) – the changes that affect existing goals; reactions (R) – mental events such as cognitions, decisions, perceptions, emotions; goals (G); attempts (A) – actions that are carried out to achieve the goal; outcomes (O) – changes that indicate success or failure of attempts to achieve a goal. These categories of information occur diachronically. Their order and the arrows connecting them will express the enchainment of cause and effect. Comprehension is thus viewed as the reader's task of setting up a series of categories of information causally connected to link a text opening to its final conclusion.

In this causal network model the narrative about the 'Smart Kid', revised version can be graphically presented in Figure 1:

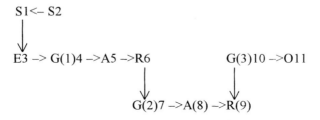

Figure 1

G(1)4 indicates the first order goal as expressed in sentence 4, G(2)7 indicates a subgoal expressed in sentence 7, and G(3)10 finally represents the 'more valued goal' replacing G(1). The mom's strategy of *goal intervention and substitution* is formally expressed by the gap between R6 and G(3)10. The first planning episode is not completed by a concluding 'outcome' O because the mom wanted to know how her kid could be so persuasive about reaching subgoal G(2).

The gap in Figure 1 clearly marks the distance between two planning episodes and projects graphically the impression that the narrative operates with two distinct types of intersubjective relationships, the first one characterized by the kid's smart-alecky attitude and the second one by the kid's deferential one. But does the narrative contain a dramatic tension based on these two perspectives? Is it not rather the case that the last statement "I guess I just inherited it." defines the mother-daughter relationship throughout the story as loving and respectful?

Jacques Lacan (1977) gives an unambiguous affirmative answer to this question and – indeed – would challenge the legitimacy of the dilemma which Trabasso's (1989:74) *intervention and substitution* strategy creates. The theoretical construct with which he works is the *point de capiton* which is based on his conviction of the primacy of the signifier and his idea of the endless movement of signification. His first position is an inversion of de Saussure's order of the signifier and signified and his second one calls into question de Saussure's 'cut' which stops the flux of signifier and signified and unites them in the sign.

Lacan's emphasis on the predominant role of the signifier – fundamental to the *point de capiton*[2] – rests in his own practical experience as a psychotherapist (for example Lacan 1977: 197f.) and his reading of S. Freud. Freud, for example, likened the dream – one of the windows to the unconscious – to a rebus. In a rebus it is the acoustic images of the pictures presented which through various manipulations – elision, addition, fusion, etc. – lead to the discovery of a hidden signifier, a word, a phrase, sentence or text. The signified of the pictures is not a matter of importance nor is their signification related on a manifest level to that of the solution. Neither is the orthography of the signifiers of any relevance but rather their spoken form. This observation deserves special mention here because Lacan (1977:149) frequently stresses Freud's anticipation of de Saussurean linguistics. Lacan thus inverts Saussure's formula of a sign which is

$$\frac{\text{signified}}{\text{signifier}}$$

to

$$\frac{S}{s}$$

where the capital S iconically represents the dominant signifier and the lower case s below the line the subordinate signified.

---

[2] This term is frequently translated as *anchoring point* but since the terms *quilting point, nodal point, key signifier, master signifier* and *Knotenpunkt* are also very common in English, Lacan's original term has been preserved here.

To move to the second pillar on which the concept of *point de capiton* rests, one may point out that for de Saussure and Lacan the value of linguistic signs rests on their oppositional relations between them on the paradigmatic and syntagmatic axes of language. For de Saussure the linguistic sign corresponds to a connection between two amorphous masses which are in constant flux. It constitutes itself by a 'cut' which fixes an idea in sound as a signified at the same time as a sound sequence constitutes itself as a signifier. The famous opposition between *why choose* and *white choose* which differ only in the placement of the 'cut' – the plus juncture – can serve as a brief illustration here of this conceptualization.

Like de Saussure Lacan talks about the endless movement of signification. In contradistinction to de Saussure, however, Lacan stresses the diachronic (or temporal) aspect of the utterance. As each utterance progresses the value of a sign is determined by those which went before and – most importantly – by those which are yet to come. Thus – by way of illustration – if a hotel clerk offers a guest a room in the 'luxury' category, the guest better not interrupt the clerk and listen which other categories are available since in some hotels 'luxury' means the very cheapest.

Lacan replaces the 'cut' with the *point de capiton* which stops the flux of signification and only then delimits and determines the value of the sign and unites the signifier with the signified. It is typically the last term of a sentence or text which completes their signification, each term in the utterance itself anticipating the following term and inversely determining the signification of the preceding ones retroactively.

The elements of the *point de capiton* discussed so far are expressed in this graph, Figure 2 (comp. Lacan 1977: 303ff.):

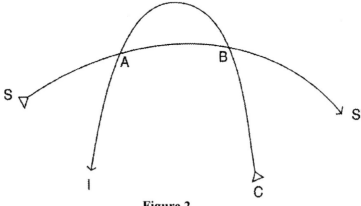

Figure 2

The lines with their arrows indicate that an utterance and its meaning develop diachronically. The vector SS' represents the signifying chain. This chain has to be segmented to become meaningful, thus the stretch AB signifies the process of segmentation. The meaning of the various segments standing in opposition can only be determined retroactively; therefore, the vector BA effects retrograde divisions of the signifying chain SS'. Finally, the creation of a specific signifying effect depends on the intention of the speaking subject. This intentionality enters the signifying chain at B from C and results in two intersections A and B capturing the speaker's influence on the structure of the message. Thus CI accounts for the two versions of the 'Smart Kid' commercial.

Lacan's *point de capiton* exposes the illusion that in a narrative an effect logically and naturally follows a ˜ause as expressed in the causal network model. There is no immanent necessity leading to an unavoidable conclusion. Rather signifier and signified are in Lacan's words separated by a bar which establishes their independence. No signifier will attain its specific meaning until the signifying chain has reached a final period which "stops the otherwise endless movement (glissement) of the signification" (Lacan 1977: 303). This final period retroactively fixes the meaning for a chain of signifiers, provisionally only to the extent that another nodal signifier may follow or that it may be replaced by another one, as was the case in the two radio commercials.

The peculiar semantic effect of the different *points de capiton* of the two versions of the 'Smart Kid' commercial are the result of the signifying function of metonymy and metaphor as understood by Lacan. In his formula

$$f(S \ldots S')$$

(Lacan 1977: 164) the signifier as defined by the metonymic function is the relation of contiguity between two signifiers. It is anticipated but receives its complete signification only after the fact. This Janus-faced function of metonymy is illustrated by the "Hello?" of the first version which is anticipated and confirmed by the final "I'm a graduate of grade seven. Duh." When this line was changed to "I guess I just inherited it.", the marker "Hello?" seemed out of place and was replaced by the script writers with "Not." If the last sentence of the first version is seen as expected, this signifying effect is metonymic, too, and therefore dependent for its effect on the entire context of the dialog.

The *point de capiton* of the second version of the radio commercial "I guess I just inherited it." cannot be referred to by metonymic ellipsis. Its function points to the function of the signifier S' in the expression

$$\frac{S'}{s}$$

in which S' is over the bar. It appears in Lacan's algorithm (1977: 165) for a metaphor

$$f(\tfrac{S'}{S})S \cong S(+)s$$

The S' – the sentence "I guess I just inherited it." – gains authority over the S of the text as produced so far and – as the right hand side of the equation indicates – determines its meaning by crossing the bar as ex-pressed by the vertical line of the plus sign.

The formula for the metaphor immediately calls up Lacan's algorithm for the sign

$$\tfrac{S}{s}:$$

the lower case s implying the constrained nature of the primary subject of the metaphor. The totally new reading of the 'Smart Kid' brought about by the introduction of "I guess I just inherited it." illustrates very well Lacan's state-ment (1977: 664) that "the metaphoric structure indicat[es] that it is the substitution of signifier for signifier that an effect of signification is produced that is creative or poetic ...".

There have been a number of studies which support the view that the use of a particular metaphor motivates the construction of a particular conceptual basis for interpreting a text (see Gibbs 1996: 215ff.). Kemper (1989), for example, familiarized her subjects with the superordinate metaphor "Love is war" and found clear evidence that they comprehended the derived sub-ordinate metaphor "The eager suitor assaulted her defenses" faster than the literal expression "The eager suitor wanted her affection". She thus proved that metaphors establish an interpretative domain which facilitates and en-courages a specific construal of a text. In the case of the *point de capiton* "I guess, I just inherited it.", its effect of signification shows that a metaphor can act retroactively as the organizing principle of a text. It provides the listener/reader with the schematic knowledge necessary to make sense of the presented event. However, it does not just create a unified verbal experience but also places it securely into a particular social reality with its specific rules of social conduct.

This last observation about the relationship of language to (social) reality reflects Lacan's thoughts about the synchronic function of the *point de capiton*. He sees in it the source of language in the child in which "the child raises the sign to the function of the signifier, and reality to the sophistics of signification ..." (Lacan 1977: 303f.).

How far do students in a linguistics class raise "reality to the sophistics of signification"?

Sixty-four students – varying in age between 18 and 48 years – familiarized themselves with the first version of the radio commercial of the 'Smart Kid'. Two students did not find the commercial objectionable: "This particular add (sic) does not bother me at all." – "I like it just the way it is." Forty students were somewhat bothered by the commercial. When they were asked to revise it, six of them eliminated the two discourse markers "Hello?" (18 above) and "Duh." (18) and in the majority of cases replaced "Hello?" by "Not exactly." or "Not really."

Twenty-five students made additional changes. They edited out and partly replaced other discourse markers and also targeted "it's like stone age" (2) and "big time" (4). Of these 25 students twelve rewrote the last line. Their *points de capiton* fell into distinct groups. The choice of the first group closely followed the example of the original: "Please, Mom, I'm in the 7th grade!" (3 students), "I have used the printer at school." (2 students), "I'm a graduate of computer freaks of America.", etc. Five students, however, came up with these suggestions which look like paraphrases of "I guess I just inherited it.": "Guess I take after you." (2 students), "It must run in the family.", "I'm your son." and "Because you are my Mom."

If one now looks at the remaining group of 22 students who found the radio commercial quite disrespectful, three observations can be made:

1. Their strong objections are not reflected in a large number of editing steps. They average four.
2. There is a definite shift of attention to the last line of the commercial. 19 students changed it.
3. Of these 19 students a large majority – 14 students – reformulated the last line to read: "I (must) take after you, Mom." (3 students), "I got it from you, Mom." (2 students), "Like mother like daughter.", "The apple does not fall far from the tree.", etc.

The students thus raised reality to the symbolic reality as Lacan envisioned it. They effected their control over their social environment by realizing those linguistic changes which they deemed necessary. A large group of students saw the problem in the mother-daughter relationship which could be straightened out by representing the mom as the ultimate and conclusive source of the kid's smartness. They did not bother with making a large number of changes because they 'knew' that linguistic entities are 'floating signifiers' whose meaning is specified retroactively in context. And finally they showed in practical terms that their intentions at signification could most efficiently be achieved by the *point de capiton* as textual metaphor to set the interpretative frame of the radio commercial unambiguously.

Within the narrow confines of this study, J. Lancan's *point de capiton* has offered at least a new, interesting way of dealing with a particular textual phenomenon. It has explained both in terms of comprehension and production cognitive linguistic strategies of native speakers/listeners, and has done so not in an ad hoc fashion but as an integral concept of Lacan's structural linguistic interpretation of Freud. While more studies are needed to secure Lacan's *point de capiton* its appropriate place in the cognitive linguistic enterprise, its promise for future research cannot be doubted. What makes this concept especially attractive is its significance both for the linguist and the psychoanalyst inviting collaboration and venture into unfamiliar intellectual territory.

References

Borch-Jacobson, Mikkel (1991): *Lacan: The absolute master.* Stanford, CA: Stanford UP.

De Santis, Solange (1998): "Kid says darndest things in ad, and Canadians say, 'Spare us!'". *The Wallstreet Journal*, March 22, 1998: B 1.

Dor, Joel (1997): *Introduction to the reading of Lacan: the unconscious structured like a language.* Judith Feher Gurewich/Susan Fairfield, eds. Northvale, N. J./ London: Jason Aronson.

Gallop, Jane (1985): *Reading Lacan.* Ithaca/London: Cornell P. U.

Gibbs, Raymond W., Jr. (1996) "Metaphor as a constraint on text understanding". Bruce K. Britton/Arthur C. Graesser, eds. *Models of understanding text.* Mahwah, N. J.: Erlbaum, 215-236.

Graesser, Arthur C. (1981): *Prose comprehension beyond the world.* New York: Springer.

Kemper, Susan (1989): "Priming the comprehension of metaphors". *Metaphor and Symbolic Activity* 4, 1-18.

Lacan, Jacques (1977): *Ecrits. A selection.* New York: Norton.

Lacan, Jacques (1978): *The four fundamental concepts of psycho-analysis.* Jacques-Alain Miller, ed. New York: Norton.

Lacan, Jacques (1988): *The seminar of Jacques Lacan. Book III. The psychoses 1955-1956.* Jacques-Alain Miller. ed. New York/London: Norton.

Lemaire, Anika (1979): *Jacques Lacan.* London/New York: Routledge.

Muller, John P./William J. Richardson (1982): *Lacan and language: a reader's guide to ecrits.* New York: International UP.

Ragland-Sullivan, Ellie/Mark Bracher (1991), eds. *Lacan and the subject of language.* New York/London: Routledge.

Trabasso, Tom (1989): "Causal representations of narratives". *Reading Psychology: An International Quarterly* 10, 67–83.

Trabasso, Tom/Linda L. Sperry (1985): "Causal relatedness and importance of story events". *Journal of Memory and Language* 24, 595–611.

Zizek, Slavoj (1997): *Looking awry: an introduction to Jacques Lacan through popular culture*. Cambridge, MA/London: MIT.

Wolfgang Lörscher *(Leipzig)*

Nonverbal aspects of foreign language classroom discourse

1. Introduction

"We speak with our vocal organs, but we converse with our entire bodies. Conversation consists of much more than a simple interchange of spoken words." This statement by David Abercrombie (1968: 55) denotes what is generally taken for granted; however, it has not been given its due attention by those disciplines which investigate social interaction. Medicine and psychology may be exceptions here. The other disciplines which are concerned with social interaction have, for a long time, only considered the verbal component of communication and have either neglected or ignored the manifold nonverbal phenomena. Only very recently has there been a growing interest in the nonverbal component of human communication. It has become a focus of investigation in anthropology, sociology, pedagogics, linguistics and the science of information.

The investigations which are carried out today under the heading of *nonverbal communication* are rather heterogeneous. First they approach their object of investigation by using rather different methodologies and with distinct epistemological interests. Second they very often concentrate on particular nonverbal phenomena which are transmitted through specific channels, such as the visual and the auditory media. This specialisation very often leads to the fact that the entirety of communicative behaviour becomes obscure and a systematic conception of a theory of nonverbal behaviour is hindered rather than helped.

Apart from the investigations of nonverbal behaviour communicated by different channels, research projects have been developed which try to capture verbal and nonverbal phenomena as comprehensive integral communication systems. Such multi-channel analyses (Mehrabian 1972; Scherer 1973), however, have not yet reached higher levels of elaboration.

2. Nonverbal and paralinguistic phenomena

Nonverbal communication has mainly been distinguished from verbal communication in a negative way, i.e. that verbal communication has been defined and everything else which is considered to have a communicative value is called nonverbal communication. A positive definition which distinguishes nonverbal phenomena such as gestures, mimicry, proxemic behaviour, speech pauses, pitch, etc. from spoken or written language has not been sufficiently elaborated so far. When looking at the relevant literature on nonverbal communication one soon realizes that the notion of nonverbal communication still requires scholarly consensing. Those authors who favour a broader notion of communication come to the conclusion that nonverbal signs are not always coded in an unambiguous way and are not always transmitted in an intentional way. They often use the notion of *nonverbal behaviour* in this way.

Other authors consider the distinction between verbal and nonverbal to be so complex that they choose terms which denote both phenomena in their interplay. For example Wescott (1965) and Kendon (1979) use the term *coenetics* which is defined as "the study of behavioural management of social encounters" (Ciolek et al. 1979: 5). Coenetics comprises the study of language and all interactional, nonverbal ways of behaviour. Another integrative approach is employed by Birdwhistell (1973). He uses the term *kinesics*, the study of body movements. According to Birdwhistell they represent a system analogous to language in human communication. Both these terms, *kinesics* and *coenetics*, have not been taken root in the disciplines concerned with communication.

The object of nonverbal communication is defined differently by different authors. According to Argyle (1972a; 1972b) the following ten phenomena constitute nonverbal communication:

1. bodily contact
2. proximity
3. posture
4. physical appearance
5. facial and gestural movements
6. direction of gaze
7. timing of speech
8. emotional tone of speech
9. speech errors
10. accent

Knapp (1972) considers the following seven nonverbal phenomena:

1. body motion or kinesic behaviour
2. physical characteristics
3. touching behaviour
4. paralanguage
5. proxemics
6. artefacts
7. environmental factors

Although this list could easily be supplemented the enumeration reveals a core area of nonverbal phenomena which includes body movements, proxemic behaviour and paralinguistic phenomena. The latter very often represent a special area because in contrast to the other nonverbal phenomena, they are of a vocal kind, i.e. they are produced by our vocal organs. Some scholars do not subsume them under the notion of *nonverbal* for this reason.

There is no agreement on what is considered to be paralinguistic. However, the following areas which are mentioned by Crystal (1974: 270–273) may be considered to be the proper subject matter of paralinguistics. They are:

1. the speed of speech or the speech tempo
2. rhythm
3. key
4. register
5. voice volume
6. intensity
7. articulatory characteristics
8. type of voice

Pitch, stress, juncture phenomena and intonation are often not considered to be paralinguistic but verbal phenomena.

According to the German psychologist Scherer (1973), misunderstandings often arise when the term *nonverbal* is used because both visible phenomena such as gesture and mimicry as well as audible phenomena such as speech style and speech quality are subsumed under this notion.

Therefore, Scherer suggests not only distinguishing between verbal and nonverbal phenomena but additionally making a distiction between vocal and nonvocal phenomena. Accordingly, a gesture would be a nonverbal-nonvocal form of behaviour, whereas speech quality would be considered nonverbal-vocal.

3. Classification of nonverbal phenomena

In order to investigate the complexities of nonverbal communication in a systematic way it seems to be necessary to split the entire domain of nonverbal behaviour into parts. Two different models can be found in the relevant literature.

3.1 Scherer's observational categories scheme

The first model comprises observational categories. It classifies nonverbal behaviour by means of the channels through which they are communicated from a sender to a receiver, and by means of the sensory organs by which the receiver

perceives them. This mainly receiver-oriented approach is used by Scherer (1973).
His categories are as follows:

Channel	Non-verbal phenomena perceived
visual/ eye	- mimicry (facial expression) - direction and movements of gaze - gestures and body movements - proxemics (interpersonal distance and spatial orientation)
auditory/ ear	- voice quality (pitch, stress, key) - way of speaking (voice-dependent variation: intonation, pronunciation, change of loudness; time-dependent variation: speed, duration, utterance length, pauses, turn-taking organization, variation of speech continuity, dialect, accent)
factory/ nose	- smells
gustatory/ tongue, nose	- tastes
tactile/ skin	- touches
thermal/ skin	- temperature and changes of temperature

3.2 Argyle's behavioural categories scheme

In the second model, *behavioural categories* are used for the classification of nonverbal phenomena. This approach which is propagated by Argyle focusses on the different observable ways of behaviour of a sender which are or can be expressed in a social interaction. The following list of categories goes back to Argyle (1972b: 90ff.):

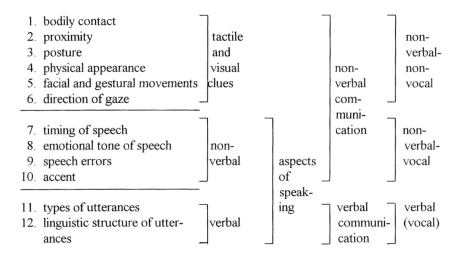

The behavioural categories as used by Argyle can easily be related to the observational categories by Scherer. The two classification systems are thus complementary by nature.

4. Aspects of the importance of nonverbal behaviour in foreign language classroom discourse

The considerations made so far about nonverbal behaviour have hopefully revealed the importance of nonverbal behaviour for human communication in general and by implication for communication in the foreign language classroom. Nonetheless, nonverbal phenomena in the classroom have hardly been investigated so far. One reason for this deficit must be seen in connection with what was said earlier, namely that only recently has the importance of nonverbal communication been realized and become an object of investigation in the disciplines involved in the study of communication. As far as communication in the foreign language classroom is concerned it is obvious that nonverbal behaviour plays an especially important role. At least four aspects are worth mentioning (cf. Hüllen/Lörscher 1989; Lörscher 1983):

1. Communication in the classroom is highly organized. The teacher and the pupils communicate mainly to reach specific aims which are largely given in advance. The teacher as an expert in her or his field knows the aims and has to achieve them in the most economical way possible. The teacher's function is to organize the

communicative resources available by the pupils so that the aims can be reached in an optimal way. This very often requires the use of nonverbal signals.

2. In the foreign language classroom there is a specific constellation of the participants in the discourse. There is one teacher and a group of pupils. Due to this specific constellation and the largely asymmetrical role relationship between the teacher and the pupils in class, the ﹍ommunication which takes place is between one teacher and a group of pupils. This, however, does not mean that there is no interaction at all between a single pupil and a teacher. The therapeutic measures which the teacher often uses after a learner commits an error, for example corrections or repairs, are first and foremost directed to the individual learner. But at the same time, these therapeutic measures have an important function in preventing errors among the other members of the group. With very few exceptions the teacher's utterances are also directed to the entire group of the learners. Thus supra-individual repertoires of knowledge are built up and the reality of the classroom as such is constituted. Part of the classroom management thus consists in signalling to the learners that the relevance of utterances concerns the whole group, even though in specific situations utterances are directly addressed to single members of the group. This signalling is mainly brought about nonverbally, above all by means of eye contact and gesture.

3. In the foreign language classroom the primary aim of teaching and learning is the acquisition of the foreign language code and its appropriate use. Therefore, the teacher's feedback is usually directed towards the correctness of the propositional content of the pupils' utterances as well as towards its correct realization in the foreign language. It can, therefore, be assumed that the reference of the teacher's feedback on either the formal realization or the content of the propositions uttered by the pupils is signalled nonverbally by the teacher and thus understood by the pupils.

4. As certain nonverbal signs can replace verbal ones it can be expected that both the teacher and the pupils make use of this substitution function of the nonverbal signs in the foreign language classroom. The teachers may use nonverbal signals in order to transmit information which they think that, if verbalized in the target language, will not be understood by the pupils; and learners may use them to transmit information which they are unable to express in the foreign language. The function of amplification in emphasizing, illustrating, and interpreting verbal signs by nonverbal forms of behaviour must be seen analogously.

In what follows nonverbal phenomena, especially those which are visually perceivable, will be described in their functions and modes of realization as they occur in thirty recorded foreign language classroom periods. The topics of the periods are grammatical phenomena of English, the analysis and interpretation of a work of literature, cultural aspects of Great Britain and the United States of America or the repetition of a textbook chapter which the pupils already knew from previous periods. The latter is a fixed type of foreign language lesson in Germany called *repetitive classroom discourse* in which the teacher asks questions about a textbook chapter and thus makes his or her pupils repeat it in small sections. The English lessons were videotaped between 1979 and 1994, with teachers and pupils from different types of schools in Germany, from form 6 to form 13. Due to the abundance of the data collected and our epistemological interest, only some aspects of the nonverbal behaviour detected in the data could be concentrated on:

i. Only the nonverbal signals of the teachers were observed. This delimitation was necessary because only two cameras were available for the recordings. One camera recorded the teacher, the second recorded the class as a whole. In this way it was not possible to systematically observe the nonverbal behaviour of one particular pupil.

ii. The investigation restricted itself to that segment of nonverbal behaviour which was visually observable, i.e. the nonverbal-nonvocal phenomena. Modes of behaviour communicated by the tactile, the thermal, or the olfactory channel could obviously not be observed but may play a secondary role in the classroom.

iii. With regard to the specifics of classroom communication in general and foreign language classroom communication in particular those types of nonverbal behaviour were concentrated on which occur:
a) in phases in which communication on fictitious reference systems took place, i.e. on topics about a fictitious rather than the real world of here and now. Examples are a chapter of a textbook like the story about Peter and Betty on Uncle Henry's farm or a literary work like *Macbeth*;
b) in phases of classroom management and those aside of the discourse topic in which the teacher gives information and/or directives or asks questions with nonfictitious that is real reference systems. Examples would involve a teacher directive such as "Please take out your excercise books.", or a teacher request such as "Who can go and get some chalk?"
c) in phases in which the didactic communication is about the foreign language code and its appropriate use;
d) in phases in which the teacher feeds back utterances of the pupils. These feedback utterances can be realized as the third element of an initiation-response-feedback structure and thus as evaluations of or comments on a preceding utterance by a pupil. But they can also be realized as confirmation or critical remarks during the utterance of a pupil. The latter case is called *back-channel behaviour* (Duncan/Niederehe 1974).

4.1 Nonverbal phenomena within phases in which communication with fictitious reference systems takes place

In those periods in which the teacher and the pupils talked about fictitious stories from a textbook, the number and intensity of the nonverbal signals were especially high. This holds true independent of the particular personality of the teacher. Didactic questions, i.e. those questions to which the teacher already knows the answers in advance, are often asked with reference to fictitious information and are often asked with a strongly artificial facial expression. This may be true for didactic questions in general. But it occurs often and emphatically in connection with fictitious information. It can be observed in the data that the nonverbal behaviour of the teacher and the pupils was most conspicuous when the teacher and the pupils acted as if they actually were in fictitious situations and really performed fictitious actions. It can be assumed that the intensity of this very artificial nonverbal behaviour serves to play down the triviality of many of the questions referring to fictitious reference systems. Thus the teacher's questions should create the impression that they were of high importance, which in fact they were not. To give an example: In one of the stories in the textbook the teacher and the pupils used during a period there were Peter and Betty who spent their holidays on Uncle Henry's farm. Both, the teacher and the twelve-year-old pupils, knew the story very well. One can readily imagine that the teacher's question "What did Peter and Betty do during their holidays?" was of a very trivial nature. By asking the question with concomitant nonverbal behaviour that suggested that the teacher did not know the answer to this question, its triviality and artificiality increased rather than decreased. Trivial questions on information with fictitious reference systems can only be justified if their function is to make the pupils practice the foreign language. The importance of these questions is therefore not, as the nonverbal phenomena may suggest, their informational content but their instrumental function with regard to the major aim of any foreign language teaching, i.e. making the pupils learn the foreign language code and its appropriate use.

4.2 Nonverbal phenomena in phases of classroom management and in connection with utterances with non-fictitious reference systems

In phases of classroom management and in those teaching phases in which communication about information with non-fictitious reference systems takes place there is a significantly smaller number and lower intensity of nonverbal signals. Those nonverbal signals which are used for classroom management can hardly be distinguished from those to be found outside the classroom. One reason for this may be the fact that the pieces of information dealt with in phases of classroom management are neither in direct connection with the specific learning goals and thus do not have to be learned nor have they an instrumental function in attaining specific learning goals. The teacher's allocation of the turns to speak represent by far the largest part of the utterances of classroom management. The allocation of turns can be performed in a primarily verbal way, i.e. verbal plus nonverbal-vocal. It can be performed exclusively nonverbally, i.e. nonverbally-nonvocally or by a combination of verbal and nonverbal signals. The most frequently occuring cases are nominations, verbal utterances like *yes*, *hm* with rising intonation or the more direct but often rather impolite address form *you* with falling intonation, in co-occurrence with eye-contact to the specific pupil, a deictic movement towards him or her and often in connection with a step towards him or her to make the distance between the participants smaller. The two first-mentioned nonverbal phenomena can allocate the speaking role even without verbal nominations and thus have a quasi-emblematic nature within specific communicative situations.

4.3 Nonverbal phenomena in phases in which communication on aspects of the foreign language code and its situationally adequate use takes place

Due to the partial competence of the learners in the foreign language many teachers often make use of the substitution and amplification function of nonverbal signals, especially in order to semantisize lexemes in the foreign language which are unknown to the pupils without using the learners' mother tongue. Mimicry and gesture are especially suitable for this purpose. By means of mimicry, emotional states can easily be expressed as denoted by adjectives such as *happy* and *sad*, or by adverbials and/or nouns such as *joy* and *anger*. Gestures are especially suited to express qualities, actions and/or objects which denote spatial relationships or movements such as adjectives like *tiny* or *fast*, adverbs or verbs like *climb* or *walk*, nouns like *clearing* or *fight* and prepositions like *up* or *towards*.

The nonverbal phenomena just mentioned generally occur in connection with verbal signs, and because of this co-occurrence they can also serve as aids for memorizing unknown lexemes to be learnt in a foreign language. The nonverbal signals used by the teachers for semantisizing lexemes in the foreign language are often idiosyncratic. Verbs of movement such as *pass by*, *walk* etc. can be expressed or clarified by movements of the head, of one or both hands or by the teacher changing her or his position in the classroom. It is important, however, that these different ways of behaviour can all be reduced to the abstract concept of movement. The concrete mode of movement which is denoted by the specific verb can, if at all, only be captured in a rather imprecise way by the nonverbal signals. Idiosyncratic nonverbal signs which cannot be interpreted in a pictographic way are thus less suitable as aids for semantisizing new lexemes in the foreign language. Rather they are used as signals for the retrieval of lexemes which have already been stored in the long-term memory of the pupils.

In this function they can be found in the lessons and especially in those phases in which communication takes place which is not primarily focussed on the foreign language. Nonverbal signs often fulfill the function of highlighting or emphasizing information which is considered to be important by the user of the signs. Since the major goal in the foreign language classroom is the teaching and learning of the foreign language, those stretches of discourse which have a metalinguistic orientation, in other words those which deal with the correct use of the foreign language are considered to be of special importance. This is why discourse phases in which aspects of the foreign language code are communicated reveal a large number of nonverbal signals of emphasizing and stressing information.

The amplification and the substitution function of nonverbal signs in connection with metalinguistic information occur less frequently in more advanced foreign language classrooms. Here the foreign language has already been mastered to a higher degree, such that metalinguistically oriented phases occur less frequently. Interpretations of texts and free conversations are performed in which the amplification function of the nonverbal signs concerns the thematic contents of the discourse such as the arguments put forward in an interpretation or the points made in a free conversation. Only in cases of gross violations of the target language norms does the discourse shift from the thematic to the metalinguistic level and the amplification function of the nonverbal signals changes accordingly.

4.4 Nonverbal phenomena and teacher feedback

Nonverbal feedback of the pupils by the teacher occurs with or without concomitant verbal utterances. The main function of the teacher's feedback is to comment on or to evaluate learners' utterances in a positive or in a negative way. In the foreign language classroom, positive feedback can refer to the contents of the pupils' utterances or to their formal linguistic realization or to both of these aspects, which is generally the case. Exceptions occur when pupils' utterances are linguistically or topically extraordinary good. In these cases positive evaluations either refer to the form or to the contents of the utterances. The nonverbal signals for emphasizing used by the teachers in these particular cases differ from those observable in other discourse phases. When aspects of the contents of an utterance are positively emphasized signals such as smiling, for example, are used. When the emphazing signals refer to the linguistic realisation of an utterance other signals are employed such as deictic gestures. The nonverbal signs used obviously fulfill an important indicator function. They tell the pupils unambiguously whether the linguistic or the thematic reference system of the feedback is meant.

The nonverbal signals either occur as the third element of an initiation-response-feedback structure or as back-channel signals which encourage the particular pupil who holds the floor to continue her or his utterance. The labeling of the nonverbal signals as *referring to the language* and *referring to the contents* also applies to utterances of negative feedback. Negative evaluations of pupils' utterances can refer to their contents or to their formal linguistic realization or to both of these aspects together with the latter being an exception. Due to the major goal of the foreign language classroom, violations of the foreign language norms very often lead to negative evaluations. The most frequently occurring nonverbal signal, which even without concomitant verbal signs negatively feeds back a linguistic error, is the rising of the teacher's hand often accompanied by a negative facial expression or shaking his or her head. The high importance which most of the teachers attach to the negative evaluations of pupils' erroneous utterances becomes obvious by the numerous therapeutic measures which they use after the evaluations. In periods which focus on the formal linguistic correctness of utterances, content errors often play a subordinate role. As my data reveals their negative feedback did not lead to any single therapeutic measure, only questions or comments on these erroneous utterances occurred although rather infrequently. The concomitant nonverbal signals differ considerably from those used after violations of foreign language norms. Either similar nonverbal signals are used with less extensity and intensity or the nonverbal signals are qualitatively different. Furthermore, the teachers' nonverbal behaviour seems to be dependent on the degree of fictitiousness and triviality of the contents to be communicated. In periods or phases in which this degree was especially high thematic errors were obviously considered to be rather unimportant and the nonverbal signals, if used at all, occurred in a less extensive and intensive way.

5. Concluding remark

The overwhelming majority of the nonverbal signals described so far were employed consistently by the teachers and were usually interpreted by the pupils correctly. This applies both to those nonverbal signs which where used by all or most of the teachers in my data corpus and to those nonverbal signs which were only used by one particular teacher. Consistency of form and function in the use of nonverbal signs is a necessary precondition for the fact that in the periods of my data corpus, and this may well be generalized, a specific system of nonverbal signals has developed which is mainly concomitant with the verbal system but can also replace it, at least in part. It is used and interpreted by the participants of the discourse with hardly any disturbances.

As a consequence of my considerations on the functions of nonverbal behaviour in the foreign language classroom two things should be kept in mind:

1. Nonverbal signals play a highly important role in the communication in the foreign language classroom.

2. Especially when nonverbal signs are used to interpret, comment on, or modify the concomitant verbal utterances in discourse or when they replace verbal signs they must be included in any discourse analysis.

References

Abercrombie, David (1968): "Paralanguage". *British Journal of Disorders of Communication* 3, 55-59.
Argyle, Michael (1972a): "Non-verbal communication in human social interaction". Robert A. Hinde, ed. *Non-verbal communication*. Cambridge: CUP, 243-269.
Agryle, Michael (1972b): *Soziale Interaktion*. Köln: Kiepenheuer & Witsch.
Argyle, Michael/Mark Cook (1976): *Gaze and mutual gaze*. Cambridge: CUP.
Birdwhistell, Ray L. (1973): *Kinesics and context. Essays on body motion communication*. Harmondsworth: Penguin.
Ciolek, Thomas M. et al. (1979): "Selected references to coenetics: the study of behavioral organization of face–to-face interactions". *Sign Language Studies* 22, 1-74.
Crystal, David (1974): "Paralinguistics". Thomas A. Sebeok, ed.. *Current trends in linguistics*. Volume 12. Den Haag: Mouton, 265-295.
Duncan, Starkey. jr./George Niederehe (1974): "On signalling that it's your turn to speak". *Journal of Experimental Social Psychology* 10, 234-247.
Ekman, Paul/Wallace Friesen (1969): "The repertoire of nonverbal behavior: Categories, origins, usage, and coding.". *Semiotica* 1, 49-98.
Hüllen, Werner/Wolfgang Lörscher (1989): "On describing and analyzing foreign language classroom discourse". Wieslaw Oleksy, ed. *Contrastive pragmatics*. Amsterdam: Benjamins, 169-188.
Kendon, Adam (1967): "Some functions of gaze-direction in social interaction". *Acta Psychologica* 26, 22-63.
Kendon, Adam (1979): "Some emerging features of face-to-face interaction". *Sign Language Studies* 22, 7-22.
Knapp, Mark L. (1972): *Nonverbal communication in human interaction*. New York: Holt, Rinehart and Winston.
Lörscher, Wolfgang (1983): *Linguistische Beschreibung und Analyse von Fremdsprachenunterricht als Diskurs*. Tübingen: Narr.
Mehrabian, Albert (1972): *Nonverbal communication.*.Chicago: Aldine, Atherton.
Scherer, Klaus R. (³1973): *Nonverbale Kommunikation*. Hamburg: Buske.
Scherer, Klaus R./Harald G. Wallbott, eds. (²1984): *Nonverbale Kommunikation: Forschungsberichte zum Interaktionsverhalten*. Weinheim/Basel: Beltz.
Wescott, Roger W. (1965): "Introducing coenetics: a biosocial analysis of communication". *American Scholar* 35, 342-356.

Hartmut Stöckl *(Chemnitz)*

Texts with a view – Windows onto the world. Notes on the textuality of pictures

1. Humans – visual animals?

The claim that ours is a visual age and that communication is drowned in a flood of images has become a commonplace both in impartial descriptions of modern forms of mediated communication as well as in current media critique. While it is certainly true that pictures[1] of diverse types are claiming ever more ground, particularly in journalism, but also in popular scientific and special language texts, where the invisible is made visible with powerful imaging technology, there are various ways of assessing the ubiquitous trend.[2] On the one hand the move towards the visual is seen as a symptom of our waning literacy, refined and cherished through many centuries and taken to be the distinguishing trait of our species. This attitude is reflected in the view that comics are an inferior type of literature for the uneducated. Likewise, television is often seen as a detrimental medium that erodes our reading abilities and fosters cursory perception and superficial thinking. On the other hand greater reliance on pictures and visual media in modern forms of communication is regarded as an achievement which facilitates the emergence of a new, visual literacy (Dondis 1973) and makes a contribution to visual culture (Mirzoeff 1998). The latter stance towards the visual image might well imply that, as psychologists do not tire of telling us, humans are not just articulate mammals (Aitchison 1998), but first and foremost visual animals, whose dependencies on sensory input via the eyes is crucial to their cognitive activity. Seen in this light the move towards pictorial information and image-based communication could be taken to be a return to a more immediate, less abstract and less mediated code.

---

[1] I will use the terms *picture* and *image* synonymously throughout this article despite a trend in semiotics to distinguish between the special case of depiction (*image*, German: *Abbildung*) and the general kind of picture.

[2] As Stafford (1996: 21ff.) shows very convincingly the trend towards a stronger reliance on the pictorial and a search for flexible and efficient means of visual expression as a counterbalance to the verbal is older than we are inclined to think. She traces it back to the enlightenment and particularly demonstrates the suitability of pictures for conveying spatial information, density of detail and objects/properties normally hidden to the eye.

Whilst this controversy is still in the making and has been fuelled by the recent advent of computer imaging technologies and the circulation of ever greater multitudes of pictures via computer networks,[3] academic and research interest in the visual is undoubtedly on the increase. Even though this growing devotion to studying pictures in communication is partly in response to a proliferation in ingenious research topics, it is not merely or not entirely hype. On the contrary, the resurgent interest in visual images can be taken as a pragmatic reflex of several academic disciplines which seem to adhere to the principle that everything that is prominent and crucial in a culture is worthy of investigation and systematic reflection. Originally a domain of philosophy, psychology and art history, questions of pictures, pictoriality or pictorial usage are increasingly being appropriated by other disciplines, notably semiotics (pictorial semiotics), linguistics and communication studies. Of course, sociological issues abound in picture use anyway, as we are invariably confronted with the question of why pictures seem to be gaining such a central importance in our (communicative) culture.[4] Addressing oneself to the subject of pictures, therefore, will necessarily have to be a transdisciplinary if not wholly interdisciplinary project. Within linguistics it is particularly on the level of text as the most complex unit in communication that we are confronted with pictures as integral parts of certain text types, particularly advertisements, journalistic texts, news, science writing, text books and so on. I would like, therefore, now to take up the question of whether pictures are texts and if so what exactly it is that is textual about visual images.

---

[3]   Such imaging technologies are for instance X-ray tomography (CT), which can expose bone structures, magnetic resonance imaging (MRI), which produces cross-sectional pictures of the brain in different 'cuts', and positron emission tomography (PET), which visualises brain activity in different phases (Stafford 1996: 24). At the centre of attention, however, are less specialised and more popular imaging techniques like computer programmes which can both retouch and manipulate images as well as literally generate them (e.g. Photoshop, Adobe).

[4]   A possible answer to this question highlights the importance of technological advances and constructs analogies between the advent of computers as popular media machines and the invention of printing. Kress (1998: 53f.), however, points out that "technology is socially applied knowledge, and it is social conditions which make the crucial difference in how it is applied". He conjectures that it may be the increasing amount of information produced and handled by modern societies and more effective processing of information facilitated by the visual that are responsible for the shift from the verbal to the visual.

2. In a maze of metaphors

It is an interesting phenomenon not altogether without relevance for the question I want to raise here that the visual is often conceptualised in terms of the verbal and vice versa. Lexemes and phrases like: *to see through something, to shed light on something, to put somebody in the picture, to get the picture, to paint something in vivid colours, to focus on something* and so on use categories derived from seeing, optics and the visual to metaphorically describe thought processes and intellectual activity. Thus, the black box phenomenon of the human brain and its cognitive mechanisms as little understood entities are made easier to understand by casting them into terms derived from real world sensory experience. Something common and familiar is mapped onto something mysterious and unfathomable. Conversely, when we talk about pictures we say things like: *visual language, the language of cinema, visual lexicon, pictorial utterance* and so on. So, here, more clearly on the plane of theoretical investigation into the nature of pictures, the visual is conceptualised as a language, an object with linguistic properties. Interestingly, this way of talking about pictures also reveals our uncertainty about and ambivalence towards them. Despite our manifold and varied interaction with pictures as viewers and image producers we understand little about them and can only make sense of them by way of metaphor. While metaphors as heuristic instruments are perfectly justified and almost inevitable they also create some problems as Hoey rightly points out:

> A side-effect is that we alter slightly our understanding of the familiar experience or object. ... It is a process ... essential to progress, but it is not without its dangers, particularly when metaphors are so often used that they are not seen for what they are (Lakoff and Johnson 1980). They seem so apt, or the authority of their inventor is so great, that they are taken as unadorned statements of fact. This is as true in linguistics as in other fields. (Hoey 1991: 27)

With respect to the linguistic metaphor applied to pictures two aspects need to be underlined. Firstly, conceptualising pictures as language will only take us some way towards understanding the ways pictures function in communication. There is in fact a certain danger here of losing sight of the specifically pictorial in images that distinguishes them from linguistic units. On the other hand, by mapping the linguistic system onto the picture we will go some way towards explaining how pictures contain signs and function as semiotic objects. Novitz points out the ambiguity of the picture-as-language metaphor:

> While we clearly must not overestimate the similarities between pictures and sentences, we must be as careful not to underestimate them. ... there are nonetheless important similarities between the two. ... The similarities that I have in mind are primarily a function of neither the surface nor the so-called

'deep' structure of sentences and pictures, but are a function of their use in communication. (Novitz 1977: 87f.)

Secondly, it must be borne in mind that unless the black box status of our intellectual and cognitive activity is diminished we will continue to feel compelled to apply metaphors and analogies to tricky sign phenomena and their functioning in communication. On a philosophical note, the meta-phorising may persist even after neurophysiological studies have convin-cingly shown in which format or modality pictures and language are processed, stored and accessed in the human mind. In other words, metaphors might be so much an ingrained cognitive reflex both in everyday explana-tions as well as in science that psychological certainties will not inhibit the tendency to draw analogies and map one system onto another for expressive clarity or theoretical insight.

To carry the metaphoric 'game' a bit further I should like to point out that even within text linguistics as one linguistic subdiscipline the object of study is often captured in metaphors. Whereas at first, the trans-sentential approach understood text organisation in terms of sentence grammar (van Dijk 1972), more recent theories conceive of texts as "interconnecting packages of information or opinion" (Hoey 1991: 34) which form networks of semant-ically related concepts. The former metaphor applies a lower-level unit to a more complex phenomenon, the latter seeks insights into text organisation by looking at how texts relate to one another. The metaphorising may well go on within text linguistics and outside. At any rate, the theoretical implications of heuristic metaphors have to be carefully examined and critically assessed. This is what I would now like to do for the picture-is-text metaphor.

3. What is textual about pictures?

Unless one defines texts to be exclusively verbal sign complexes (Rolf 1993: 19f.), there does not seem to be a problem about claiming that pictures are or behave like texts in many aspects. De Beaugrande/Dressler (1981: 218f.) write:

> In the broadest sense, any meaningful sign configuration is a text, and must possess textuality. Each individual sign occurs in an actual system that regulates and determines its function and sense. A science of linguistic texts might well be expanded and generalized to deal with semiotic texts of all sorts. Films, art works, billboards, concerts, political rallies, games – all these events (and many more) are composed of cohesive and coherent elements with relevance to the participants' attitudes and goals within the situation.

While many text linguists would not hesitate to agree with this, it would be interesting to have a cautious look at the presuppositions inherent in this claim when applied to pictures in particular. First of all, conceiving of pictures as text would seem to imply that they are composed of signs and function as semiotic objects. Although I would not regard this as problematic because image making seems to be inherently intertwined with meaning making, some doubt the semiotic status of pictures (Elkins 1998).[5] At least with respect to pictures in everyday texts, however, it seems safe to assume that their semiotic status as potentially meaningful signs is intended and relies on the capacity of pictures to convey meaning. The question of what kind of meaning they can convey and how they do this is clearly secondary here, although crucial for any theory of visual communication.

Another presupposition contained in the picture-is-text claim would seem to be that pictorial signs form a system that regulates their function and sense. At this point we encounter another metaphor perhaps most poignantly phrased by Kress/van Leeuwen (1996) as a "grammar of visual design". While I agree that pictures need to have some structural repertoire to differentiate meaning and accentuate utterances, I believe *pictorial grammar* to be far removed from verbal grammar. There are simply too many aspects of language grammars that translate into pictures badly or not at all. So even though visual images will have some kind of code it is by no means as explicit, well formed and structured as that of natural languages. Talking about a spatial grammar in contrast to a linear grammar may hint at a crucial difference in the functioning of visual and verbal syntax (yet another metaphor); in the final analysis, however, it does not reveal anything even vaguely resembling linguistic grammars. Though often attacked and rejected (Goodman 1968), the notion of iconicity[6] still seems the most suitable

---

5   Most of these antisemiotic accounts of pictures are rooted in phenomenological notions of perception, most notably that of Merleau-Ponty (1962). They deny that image making and visual communication are wholly based on pictorial representation and reject the idea that pictures are just symbolic constructs, be they cognitively or linguistically explained. Instead they argue that the pictorial surface "is constituted by nonrational forces – desires, drives, affectations, perceptions etc. – which are not necessarily reducible to intelligible models, to theorization" (Roberts 1998: 130). I believe the semiotic and the phenomenological approaches to be reconcilable and not mutually exclusive. In my view, it is important to stress that some types of pictures are rather strongly semiotic in nature, because they have come to be used with rather standardised meanings in certain media, whereas others, notably in art contexts, are clearly manifestations of the non-symbolic and non-cognitive factors highlighted in phenomenological picture theories.

6   After having rejected iconicity initially (Eco 1968), Eco has in the meantime come round to a general acceptance of the idea that iconic signs are based on similarities in the mental models we construct from real-world objects/scenes and pictorial signs (Blanke 1998: 286).

concept available to explain how we make sense of visual signs. Pictures mean something to us because we perceive similarities between the mental models of the signs and the objects they are supposed to depict. In other words the mental models we construct from visual sign complexes share important aspects with mental models from real world experience in our environment.[7] How we put the signs together to form complex utterances would also seem to have much to do with our real-world visual perception and the knowledge we accumulate in this process. In addition, however, there must be graphic conventions at best resembling a rudimentary code in order to accentuate visual propositions and constitute complex pictorial meanings.

Some of the examples of semiotic texts given in the de Beaugrande/ Dressler quotation seem to infringe on a workable notion of pictures as text, because in their understanding real-world events, like political rallies, concerts and games count as texts, too. If we were to take this idea to the extreme we would end up claiming that the world is a text and can be read, as has been put forward by a number of language philosophers (e.g. Derrida). With respect to events involving language this does not seem problematic, because here we judge the textuality of linguistic utterances as embedded into wider social action. Applied to pictures, however, it would seem necessary to differentiate real-world visual experience, i.e. seeing in our day-to-day experience, from looking at pictures as mediated visual experience. The medium of pictures and their technical characteristics as well as the factors that condition their making enter into any account of their meaning. Thus, for instance, paintings would, by virtue of their special circumstances of production, seem to have different semantic potential as compared with photographs or computer-generated images. As a consequence I would plead for a notion of picture-as-text that integrates the medium of signs as a vital component. Text in this view would necessarily mean a complex configuration of mediated signs.

Much of de Beaugrande/Dressler's (1981) notion of textuality is external to the text.[8] Textuality can therefore be seen more as a process, i.e. something text producers and recipients actively create, rather than a property inherent

---

[7] For different models of the iconic sign and in particular a current model that integrates a cognitive invariant (that is a mental representation of an object class) called type into the semiotic triangle see Blanke (1998).

[8] While still widely used as general points of reference in text linguistics, de Beaugrande/ Dressler's (1981) seven criteria of textuality have often been criticised for their vagueness. Apart from cohesion and coherence all criteria are subjective and over-generalised. It is in particular the claim that all seven criteria have to be fulfilled for a communicative occurrence to qualify as text which has been rejected.

in texts. While these functional-pragmatic views of textuality are justified and lend themselves particularly well to the study of pictures as text, they cannot completely deny the structural foundation of textuality. Just as no linguist would see much merit in exploring the function of single words as texts, visual grammarians would see little value in addressing themselves to the study of isolated pictograms. The point here is not so much that sign combinations of small complexity do not correspond to prototypical notions of text. What is more interesting is that cohesion and coherence of discourse as text-internal properties are better judged and explained on texts that have at least a minimal degree of complexity (i.e. two or more sentences). With respect to pictures structural complexity would seem to depend on the number of visible entities in a frame. The more visual objects the picture contains the more relations can be specified between them and consequently the more complex the text will be. On the other hand, even a minimal visual structure, say the picture of a house as one object, would seem to allow for a number of different utterances, as it displays the various properties of the object simultaneously. The viewer need just focus on them to create a text that would consist of more than one utterance/proposition.[9] The specificity of pictures, then, lies in their ability to make a number of interconnected utterances available as text on the basis of a minimal visual structure.[10]

When Kress (1998: 58) claims that "the landscape of communication of the 1990s ... is irrefutably a multi-semiotic one; and the visual mode in particular has already taken on a central position in this landscape", I would take this to mean that the prototypical text is now neither exclusively verbal nor visual. This has repercussions for a science of text as it particularly emphasises the need to come up with a comprehensive theory to explain the link between the two semiotic systems. The question that needs to be addressed is this: How does the verbal tap into the semantic resources of the visual and vice versa to form an overall textual message in reciprocal semiotic interaction?[11]

---

[9] The notion of propositionality with respect to pictures is contestable as pictures cannot explicitly (that is by means of a formal grammar) signal a proposition. In order for viewers to make sense of pictures, however, they need to attribute subject status to certain visual objects, identify their reference and construe a predication.

[10] It is a major function of co- and context to help the viewer construct an adequate message from the pictorial surface. The fact that the accompanying verbal text and knowledge about picture and text types focus the viewer on particular aspects of the visual image does not, however, preclude interpretations and observations of the picture less relevant to its communicative intention.

[11] This question and other related ones, especially methodological considerations of text analysis have been addressed in some of my own publications, notably Stöckl 1997; 1998a; 1998b.

On a higher level of abstraction, the claim about the multi-semiotic nature of communication also raises the question of the textuality of pictures. With a view to current communicative practice it would seem convincing to argue that pictures hardly ever occur without accompanying verbal text, however minimal it might be. Paintings in a picture gallery, for instance, still provide the viewer with an indication of a title and the artist, both functioning as verbal clues to a visual configuration of signs. This could be taken as justification for a stance all too common in text linguistics that regards writing as the primary medium and texts to be predominantly verbal entities. Such a view need not bother to define pictures as textual objects at all because it could claim that semantically deficient pictures and other visually mediated semiotic objects are merely integrated into a verbal text that ensures their meaningfulness. Contrary to this, I would like to argue that pictures as such already possess a certain amount of textuality and can function communicatively like texts. Pictorial textuality will certainly differ from verbal textuality in many important respects, but both will also share some central aspects. It is this common ground between visual and verbal textuality which makes the integration of pictures into verbal text so easy and communicatively efficient. My hypothesis then would be that pictures possess a residual amount of textuality and this, in principle, is what enables them to communicate of their own accord. Multi-semiotic texts consist of at least two textual elements, one verbal, the other visual, which come together as a cohesive and coherent whole in semiosis. In the following chapters I will try to outline the specificity of pictures as visual text using de Beaugrande and Dressler's (1981) seven criteria of textuality as a rough frame of reference.

3.1 Visual cohesion

Linguistic cohesion being the mutual connectedness of words within a sequence which is realised by grammatical dependencies (de Beaugrande/ Dressler 1981: 3; Hoey 1991: 3ff.), there would seem, at first glance, to be little resembling it in pictures. This cohesive deficiency has to do with the fact that the visual is no linear medium and that, although we metaphorically speak of a grammar of visual design (Kress/van Leeuwen 1996), pictures are not neatly composed of distinct units with morphosyntactic categories that bind them together according to strict rules. It is in this sense that pictures really are semiotic objects without a code (Barthes 1998; orig. 1964).

As, however, we believe pictures to have meaning – sometimes even a surplus of it – there needs to be a way of explaining how meaning enters into the picture. One way of doing this would be to say that in our quest for coherence we invest meaning into pictures. While that is certainly true, on closer inspection I think there are properties in pictures that contribute to their cohesiveness and serve as a basis for their coherence.

For one thing, pictures have a frame which restricts the number of sign complexes and delineates the visual text. Although this may sound like a platitude, I believe it is not. Frames act as indicators of pictures/texts and can be interpreted as an instruction to treat the elements in the frame as belonging together and being connected to each other in one way or another.

Secondly, despite often being regarded as functioning like a camera, seeing is a constructive process that adheres to principles, notably the principles of gestalt perception (Palmer 1992). Only if lines and shapes are arranged in accordance with gestalt principles will they build up into meaningful units and connect among one another. In many ways, then, the cohesiveness of pictures lies in their conformity to gestalt principles. Seeing is building cohesion into a graphic surface structure. On a more text-internal level, pictures as spatial patterns have proximity of signs as well as vectoriality (Kress/van Leeuwen 1996: 56ff.) as features that contribute to visual cohesion. Objects represented in the pictorial frame which are close to one another usually stand in some semantic relation; distance, on the other hand, signals disconnectedness. Vectors are lines – either complete or just indicated – that connect represented objects and convey the involvement of the objects in some kind of narrative structure. Colour and shape are further structural means of realising cohesion. Similar tones of colours link up different objects to form a larger unit of meaning. Complementing shapes suggest that objects belong together and interlock. Sifting through the different types of linguistic cohesion (Halliday/Hasan 1976; Lörscher 1995: 166f.; Hoey 1991: 3ff.), it can be seen that pictures may at best be capable of realising repetition (accumulating similar or identical visual objects), comparative reference (identity, similarity and difference of objects) and collocation (the co-occurrence of visual objects which belong to one frame/ script and open up semantic relations among one another).

On the whole it seems safe to argue that cohesion in pictures is less pronounced than in language and, due to the weakness of the pictorial code, more a matter of actively constructing it in the process of seeing rather than a structural property of the pictorial surface. Iconic in nature, pictorial signs immediately and more readily tap into our real-world experience and semantic concepts of them. Looking at a picture, therefore, immediately engages our sense of coherence, and it remains open to debate whether talking about pictorial cohesion can be done at all without recourse to meaning.

3.2 Visual coherence
Coherence as the mutual accessibility and relevance of concepts and the relations among them in the textual world (de Beaugrande/Dressler 1981: 4) would of necessity have to be very strong in pictures to enable them to have

meaning while their cohesive potentials are weak.[12] The way I envisage viewers to construct coherence in pictures is by linking up visually perceived objects with mental models and concepts stored in their minds as patterns of world knowledge. Seeing a picture therefore automatically activates mental frames, schemata and scripts, which allow a number of visible entities of the pictorial surface to be semantically integrated on a higher level of meaning. This way we allocate the visual entities we perceive to prototypical objects, situations, events or actions.

Two very general types of coherence generation would seem typical of the printed, that is static image. Firstly, printed images put viewers in a position to survey an array of visual objects and perceive their properties. Here, individual elements cohere because they correspond to stored patterns of objects. Crucial for this type of coherence, which operates within the confines of the pictorial frame, are spatial relations between visual entities and shape and colour of the objects depicted. Secondly, there is also a type of coherence which would seem to go beyond what we actually see. Here, we make educated guesses about the wider situational context of the visible elements of the frame. Conjecturing beyond the frame involves attributing situational circumstances, such as time and location and the 'before' or 'after', to the scene depicted on the visual surface. We thus transcend the textual world and by way of reference to real world elements we infer meaning not contained in the frame.

Inferencing procedures are generally very important for construing coherence in images as the pictorial surface, while making object recognition sufficiently easy, often leaves relations between depicted objects unclear and implicit. Whereas texts can express any kind of relation between concepts, pictures are clearly subject to restrictions. Analogy, contrast, causality and generalisation among others (like inclusion, specification, parts-of-a-whole etc.) are seen to be particularly suited to the visual medium (Messaris 1997: 182ff.), although, of course, the type of picture and its embedding as part of text into a text type would seem to enhance the potential of images to express relations. In sequences of pictures temporal relations can also be signalled easily.[13]

---

[12] In abstract paintings the relation between cohesion and coherence seems to be reversed. Here, coherence is weak, as reference to concrete objects and their integration into mental models (frames/scripts) is hardly possible. On the other hand, cohesion would seem to be strong, as colours, delineated areas, geometrical shapes, lines and interlocking patterns must all come together to create the pictorial surface of abstract images.

[13] Besides this, whole sets of pictures increase cohesion as more devices of repetition, substitution and even ellipsis become available.

At any rate, pictures are more ambiguous and polyfunctional with respect to the relations between concepts, simply because they are lacking in explicit cohesive devices, are weak in propositionality and do not have any meta-communicative elements to explain and comment on their own structure and meaning. As a consequence, while the sense of a verbal text "is not unduly unstable" (de Beaugrande/Dressler 1981: 7), the sense of a picture is clearly less stable. That is why coherence as a socially conditioned cognitive activity seems to be relatively more important in the production and reception of pictorial texts than it is in relation to verbal text. It is our quest for coherence that makes pictures meaningful and the subjective potential invested in this process must not be underestimated.

3.3 Intentionality of pictures
Intentionality as a producer-centred aspect of textuality would need to look at how pictures function in communication. An interesting observation concerns the fact that in principle one and the same picture can be used for many diverse purposes depending on how it is embedded into verbal text and anchored in a communicative situation. This is not to deny, however, that picture making as such is an intentional activity that follows some communicative goal specified in a plan. As a consequence there are structural properties of pictures and aspects of pictorial style which shape their usability in communication and predetermine them for specific functions. In my view, it is a pivotal part of a picture's intentionality that it be connected up with language in a wider textual context. Specific pictorial qualities have to be fine-tuned to serve this function.

The basic intentionality of pictures seems to be geared towards display (Kress 1998: 69), whereas that of verbal text aims at a sequence of events and actions which Kress calls narrative (Kress 1998: 72). Display should be understood as the general ability of the visual to show the salient properties of elements and their spatial relations. Technical drawings, fashion photographs and topographical maps would be good examples of this. While this distinction between the intentionality of the visual and verbal is generally true, more research is needed to fix various types of visual intentions and link them to aspects of pictorial style and design. Multi-semiotic text types would seem to be a useful category in this endeavour, as they are capable of drawing attention to the interface between visual and verbal text. Design and style of concrete pictures would then become understandable as geared towards the needs of the semantic and pragmatic link between the two semiotic modes (picture and language).

A large part of pictorial intentionality in my view rests on the iconicity and indexicality of visual images. The iconic nature of pictures entails that while perceiving visual images we construct mental models similar to those that result from our perception of real-world objects. In other words, both reality and pictures of it access the same cognitive invariants and make us perform similar mental operations and emotional responses. Pictorial intentions utilising the iconic nature of images are, for instance, the elicitation of attention, desire, warnings, demands, amazement, awe and other real-world emotional cues. Indexicality, on the other hand, is responsible for the trust we place in images, which is epitomised in the saying: "seeing is believing". This has to do with our perception of pictures (in particular photographs) as traces or effects of a reality which is out there to be recorded. Indexicality prompts the use of pictures as documentary evidence or proof of statements and claims.[14] This would seem to be another typical communicative function that pictures can perform more effectively than language.

3.4 Acceptability of pictures

Acceptability focuses on the receiver's attitude to a text and falls into two components: 1. A receiver finds a text acceptable because it has relevance for him or her and is useful in achieving some goal; 2. The text becomes acceptable because it conforms to minimal standards of cohesion and coherence. That pictures are relevant for us would seem to be beyond doubt. How else would we explain the growing reliance on them in media communication? Why would we bother to go to picture galleries? Some of the functions that pictures can perform, like display, elicitation of various types of emotion and documentary proof may have already hinted at a special relevance: Pictures do things for us that language cannot do at all or not as efficiently. On the other hand it is important to see the interdependencies of picture and language. In this light, pictures would seem relevant because they complement verbal texts. Equally, both picture production and reception involve conceptualisation which is strongly language-bound.[15]

Acceptability is, of course, relative and sensitive to the notion of text type. Consequently, receivers would assess the relevance of pictures within a social or cultural setting with recourse to the text type in which it occurs. To be relevant in a certain text type pictures need to comply with specific formal design and style features which have become customary in those text types and serve an efficient picture-text integration. Following on from my notion of picture as text, it would be useful to set up a category analogous to text type which I would propose to call image type. Such broad image types

---

[14] Our trust in pictures as evidence or proof is likely to crumble further as computer imaging technology spreads and raises awareness of the stage-managed, artificial and falsifying character of many pictures, particularly in popular media.

[15] For a concise treatment of some of the problems involved in the interrelation between picture and language see Stegu (1996).

would, for instance, be different kinds of photography (nature, product, fashion photography and so on), technical drawings, floor plans, diagrams, charts, maps and pictograms and so forth. Besides formal features of pictorial composition and design, image types would have to specify technical aspects of image making, typical functions of images resulting from their form and other facets of their socio-cultural use. Just like verbal text types, image types would not be hard-and-fast categories, but rough orientations overlapping and intermingling in many ways.

With respect to cohesion and coherence in pictures we have already noted that the former is generally weak and the latter largely actively constructed by the viewer in the process of reception. Pictures would, therefore, seem to be acceptable mainly on the basis of construed coherence, which is facilitated both by the recognisability of visual elements as specific or prototypical objects and by design features that increase 'readability' (another metaphor) of pictures. Just like in language where often the texts which work best are those which are lacking in coherence and cohesion and thus call on the reader to infer missing information, pictures as a rule rely on the viewer to make a contribution. This can take the form of the inquisitive gaze which explores the pictorial surface and probes every aspect of image design for structure and meaning. On the other hand, contributing to coherence may also involve inspecting the wider context of concrete pictorial usage. The integration of pictures into a verbal co-text and a synthesis of pictorial and linguistic meaning will be a natural consequence of this.

3.5 Informativity of pictures

The degree of informativity in texts is often judged with recourse to the categories *unexpected versus expected* and *unknown versus known*. Both with respect to verbal as well as to visual text informativity is thus clearly subjective as it depends on individual knowledge and experience. Taking into account that seeing has priority among our sensory modalities and that looking out for new images is an anthropological reflex, pictures would seem to be highly informative. This may be corroborated by the fact that pictures in multi-semiotic texts are experienced to be eye-catchers and a relief from the monotonous perception of print. In this sense, pictures are windows onto the world.

Tempting as it may be I would not want to hazard the guess that images are of necessity more informative than verbal text. In fact, some imagery has become so highly stereotyped that it carries a high degree of expectedness. This is particularly true for TV images, some press photographs and a great many magazine pictures which are more an embellishment than carriers of new information. The trend towards a decrease in informativity looks likely to grow stronger as pictures are centrally distributed by image banks and are used in more and more contexts and media.[16] On the other hand, many pictures, notably in advertising and popular journalism, are produced with the intention of providing a fresh and rather unusual look at things or to spark cognitive or emotional activity. Besides showing something thematically novel, this can be done by creatively applying the means of pictorial design, i.e. varying angle, distance, resolution, colours, lighting, perspective and so on, and by juxtaposing visual elements or unconventional montage. Similarly, some of the new imaging technologies create pictures that are highly informative in many ways. X-rays of our skeleton, computer scans of brain activity or infrared scans of temperature distributions in the atmosphere or solid objects are but a few examples of these powerful technologies. They pursue the aim of visualising objects or states that we can neither see with our own eyes nor, sometimes, even imagine. The technical or scientific image is thus in many ways the most ingenious and informative type.

3.6 Situationality of pictures

The notion of situationality is quite close to that of intentionality and, put in a nutshell, it claims that texts typically possess features which make them fit and relevant for a situation of usage. Conversely, text-external aspects of the situation (time, place, co-text, producer-recipient relation, intention, cultural background) exert an influence on the form of a text.

As already pointed out, a crucial part of most pictures' situationality in communication is their integration into and interdependence on a verbal co-text. It thus seems a fair claim that some aspects of the design, style and overall structure of pictures answer to the demands of the language-picture link. In a more extreme view we could argue that pictures are highly dependent on the situation of their usage and are only imbued with relevant meaning once they are used to communicate. This is precisely because they are lacking in propositionality, are devoid of modality, cannot perform speech acts, are not able to comment themselves and do not have deictic means to point to places, times, objects and persons. Claiming the paramount importance of situationality for pictorial texts means that their sense is greatly determined by their use in communication and only to a small extent by structural or formal features. On the other hand, depending on what sort of

---

[16] Pörksen (1997: 10f.) calls these rather standardised and recurring pictures *visiotypes*. The term obviously derives from stereotype. Just like our communication relies on key words we also seem to have key images (ibid. 28), he claims. Visiotypes are defined as special ways of accessing reality, certain styles of thought and standardised types of visualisation (ibid. 11).

message it is supposed to convey in a certain communicative setting, the picture is designed accordingly.

Let us look at two examples. A pictogram indicating a women's toilet can dispense with all graphic detail, the only thing that matters is that it can be distinguished from the corresponding male matchstick figure. Its function of pointing to the toilet would seem to greatly rely on a situational setting regulated by convention. Contrary, a fashion photograph in a mail order catalogue for women's clothes has to conform to a different kind of situationality. Here, efficient display is at the heart of its functionality and this is guaranteed by various formal means, for instance the pose of the model, lighting, focus, distance and angle, to bring out the texture and quality of the cloth as well as the colour and design of the garment. In both examples the situationality of pictorial usage would seem to influence the form of the visual image.

3.7 Intertextuality in pictures

Intertextuality, understood as "the way in which the use of a certain text depends on knowledge of other texts" (Malmkjær 1991: 469), allows for at least two basic interpretations. Firstly, a given text can depend on one or more previously encountered texts because it presupposes world knowledge about some state of affairs not contained in it but obtainable from other texts. Here, the text producer deliberately leaves gaps which he assumes the reader can fill upon reception as the text stands as a member in a whole chain of interconnected texts. The given text will contain clues which point to specific knowledge outside the original text that the recipient will have to invest into the text in order to make sense of it.

This kind of intertextuality based on world knowledge gained from dependent texts can be seen to be valid for pictures, too. When, for instance, a photograph in a newspaper intends to show the progress made on a specific building site, the concrete picture will only make sense with recourse to other pictures showing the beginning of construction work, various stages on the way to the present situation and perhaps the vacant plot of land in the context of the surrounding buildings. Likewise, many advertising images acquire relevant meaning only against the background of previous images in a campaign history. Silk cut provided an excellent example of this when they created a campaign in which every picture in the series was only fully understandable by reference to the first image. So only if one had seen the first picture, which transducted the literal meaning of the brand name "a cut in silk" into the visual medium by showing a piece of silk torn right through the middle, would one be able to understand the ensuing imagery.

The second type of intertextuality occurs in texts whose meaning would only be fully recoverable with recourse to knowledge about text genres and their characteristic features and patterns. Here a given text depends on others because, while belonging to a certain text type and fulfilling prototypical functions of that specific genre, it simultaneously activates knowledge about other text types whose features it selectively makes use of. Adverts in the style of a weather forecast, an encyclopaedic article or a news report would be good examples. This second type of intertextuality, where the use of one text depends on the knowledge of various genre conventions activated by it, also translates into pictures quite well. Here, pictures contain formal and style aspects that make them dependent on other pictures, or rather the knowledge of pictorial genres. It particularly concerns instances of 'art historical quotation', where typical genres and individual styles or techniques, like impressionism, surrealism, pop art or cubism and various photographic styles are alluded to in pictures. The allusion can be merely stylistic, but it may also work on a thematic level, where traditional and well-known subjects or scenes are depicted in new ways. While this kind of pictorial intertextuality might well be crucial to the understanding of a concrete visual image it need not necessarily be so. In many cases it will simply add a layer of meaning or nuances of expression to a pictorial composition that is fit to convey a basic message of its own accord.

4. Linking the pictorial and the verbal – Texts within texts

A number of important points should have become clear in my above exploration of the picture-is-text metaphor, popular but hardly pursued in detail within linguistics. First of all, while helpful and elucidating in many ways, the metaphorising stops short of the total specificity of pictoriality. This is hardly surprising, as we are mainly trying to transfer linguistic categories to pictures, which is what one would expect linguists to do. Although this limitation might be criticised one should also see the merits of this approach. By comparing picture and text (that is picture and language) it signposts crucial differences and similarities between the two.

The attempt to cope with pictures in linguistic terms and models is not just the reflex of a linguist who is bound to have a language-centred perspective on communicative processes. It also has its roots in the hermeneutic truth that in the final analysis the only way of making sense of pictures is to verbalise them. Recognising the strong link between pictures and language should not be regarded as a methodological weakness that seeks refuge in linguistics, but rather as a strength, because image making and (verbal) text making are intricately intertwined both in writing practice as well as in cognition. In fact, the precise nature and functioning of the link between pictures and language in two-code texts, and the influence of linguistic conceptualisation and phrasing on pictorial design and vice versa, represents a little explored field both in linguistics as well as in genuinely pictorial sciences. While not meaning to claim that pictoriality and textuality are identical, my short run through the textuality criteria highlights the fact that pictures in communication do share essential textual features with verbal texts.

Secondly, a point frequently made in my account was that while images can be likened to texts in many ways, their specific textuality rests on their dependence on co-texts and conte..ts which need to be investigated to get an adequate idea of the ways pictures function in communication. Even in those 'extreme' and rare cases where pictures are used in communication on their own, we must bring knowledge to pictures which we have acquired in the form of texts. The prototypical case of picture use is in two-code or multimodal texts, where the image constitutes but one, albeit important part of a text – a pictorial text – which is integrated into the text total by various verbal and visual means. Viewed in this light, cohesion and coherence would first of all seem to prevail between verbal and visual parts of text and their specificity will be sensitive to the text type. Exploring different strategies of building cohesion and securing coherence between pictorial and verbal text chunks and their dependence on overall text types or genres is clearly a desideratum in a modern type of text linguistics dedicated to two-code texts.

I believe that a great deal of the difficulty of getting to grips with pictures as semiotic objects and parts of texts has to do with the quest for standard criteria of pictoriality. The philosophy-inspired question of what a picture actually is has misguided our attention to seek a very general notion of picture and pictoriality.[17] This has obscured the obvious insight that the variability of pictures is in reality extremely large and that it is in fact misleading and inappropriate to talk and reason about **the** general or idealised picture. In communicative practice there is no such thing as the generalised, prototypical picture. What we are confronted with are images that automatically come as representatives of a specific image type whose core features they share and exemplify. The type of linkage between the picture and its verbal co-text as well as the image's embedding into the communicative situation at large is an essential part of its image type features, which in turn, of course, respond to the requirements of the overall text type or genre. When discussing pictures in communication we ought, therefore, to avoid talking

---

[17] Philosophical enquiry into pictures has concentrated mainly on the distinction between reality and depictions of it. In others words, how do we know that x' is a picture of x and under what circumstances is something a picture of something else? While some basic properties of pictures have been pointed out in those endeavours, I believe the philosophical way of asking questions to be too general and misguided in some aspects. In practice sign users know quite well how to distinguish between pictures and non-pictures. In fact, the communicative use of pictures is much more varied, complex and skilled as to be restricted to the general question of what a picture really is.

about pictures in general, but refer to concrete instances as individual realisations of image types.

Analysing two concrete examples of two-code texts I would now like to show how image types can differ, in what ways the two parts of text, i.e. picture and language, interlock and how they come to form a coherent and cohesive entity. In this I will try to illustrate some of the theoretical points made earlier. Particular emphasis will be put on formal and design features of the images and influences of the overall text genre on cohesion and coherence strategies.

5. Example 1: documentary image

My first sample text (Fig. 1) is a short report from the Geographica section of the National Geographic (September 1998). It tells the story of a trip across the Bering Strait and includes a total of four individual pictures put together in a specific way. One of the first general observations would highlight the fact that the visual and the verbal are roughly evenly distributed, perhaps with a slight predominance of the visual. The column of print on the left interspersed with two maps is balanced against a combination of two photographs on the right. Potential text recipients will perceive the two maps as belonging together and forming an independent unit of information which will then have to be integrated into the overall text. The same can be said for the two photographs in the right hand column whose montage clearly suggests they make up a coherent whole. Let us first take a look at design features of the individual pictures and then broaden our perspective to include relations between the pictures and between pictorial text and verbal text.[18]

---

[18] Three types of cohesion would need to be distinguished in this special case: Type 1 concerns cohesion within single pictures, type 2 would focus on cohesive elements that bind the individual pictures together (i.e. the two maps and the two photographs), and type 3 would address itself to phenomena of cohesion between pictorial and language sections of the text. The same could be stated about coherence types.

NATIONAL GEOGRAPHIC

Geographica

Crossing the Bering Strait—on Skis

About 55 miles separates Russia from Alaska at the narrowest point. But when veteran Russian Arctic adventurer Dmitry Shparo, 56, and his son Matvey, 22, made a historic first crossing of the Bering Strait on foot in March, they ended up traveling some 180 miles because the flow of the ice carried them northward.

They conquered choppy ice and snow, skirted open water, and avoided the occasional polar bear. "Never did I see a place with so bad an ice situation," says the elder Shparo. This was his fifth attempt to cross the strait.

Matvey hauled the sled carrying supplies (upper right). His father bore a backpack that initially weighed a hundred pounds; fierce winds often turned it into a sail. On their best days they skied ten miles; on their worst, less than two, spending nights in their tent (lower right). The trip took 21 days, far longer than expected, forcing them to halve their daily 5,000-calorie ration partway through. Dmitry lost 22 pounds. It was worth it, he believes. "This trip was my happiest because I was with my son, my good friend," he says.

Figure 1: Documentary image – *National Geographic***, 'Geographica' section** (September 1998)

The maps are in themselves a mixture of visual and verbal elements and due to their conventionalised reading allow for relatively stable and definite meanings. The small conically-shaped map is to give us a rough indication of where the story is set – it activates our geographical frame of knowledge and informs us about the dimensions of the area and some situational features, such as the extension of polar ice. The bigger rectangular map then by convention magnifies the area in question and gives us details about the route, the ice flow and the exact location. Although it can be argued that verbal elements play an important part in decoding the maps, there are also a number of cohesive devices which secure pictorial understanding even without reliance on the verbal. For one thing colours signal the two continents; for another their shapes can be recognised to be identical in the two maps. Furthermore, the red rectangle in the small map by convention marks the given area and acts as a signal for the ensuing enlargement. The claim then would be that the whole-part-relationship pertaining between the two maps can be signalled by cohesive pictorial elements and graphic conventions. It is merely made more explicit by the integration of verbal text into the maps. Textual elements, such as *Bering Strait, about 55 miles separates Russia from Alaska at the narrowest point, flow of the ice* act as cohesive devices, anchor the maps in the overall text and embed them in the communicative situation.

The cognitive work we have to perform in understanding the two photographs is different from that invested in the rather conventionalised reading of the maps. Here the recipient is called upon to identify objects against the white background of the snow, whose colour is again a cohesive element that links the photographs to the maps.[19] The main visual elements, skier(s), skis, sled, tent, backpack, hole in the ice, all cohere as they belong to one frame (polar expedition) and activate a common script which forms the theme of the text, namely travelling across ice. Cohesion between the two photographs is realised mainly by repetition (ice, sled, skier, skis present in both pictures) as is cohesion between verbal text and pictures (*skirted open water, hauled the sled carrying supplies, backpack, skied, spending nights in their tent*). In addition the text has metacommunicative signals (*upper right, lower right*) that expressly refer to the picture and indicate that the text describes what the picture shows. My claim again would be that the recipient could infer the general meaning of the pictures without recourse to the precise descriptions in the verbal text. He would be able to gauge from the

---

[19] The same could be said about the red colour which is used to mark the route on the map, including starting and end points, and connects with the red jackets and equipment on the sled in the photographs.

posture of the skier and his frame knowledge that somebody is trying to skirt the ice hole, that somebody is hauling a sled and that two adventurers have pitched their tent to spend the night in it. In order for the recipient to arrive at those interpretations he has to think beyond the frame of the pictures and to establish a relation between the conceptual worlds depicted in the two photoraphs. The conceptual relation between skiing and a pitched tent would in all probability have to be classified as temporal – the montage and reading of the pictures (above – below) indicating the sequence of actions in the mental script.

In conclusion, it can be seen that the pictorial text (photographs and maps) manages to present the setting of the story, identify the subjects and main objects of the story in general terms (the text then defines them, e.g. *Russian Arctic adventurer Dmitry Shparo, 56* and so on) and by way of inferencing predicate actions and attributes to the subjects and objects like skiing, crossing, camping. The images display dimensions, circumstances and properties of the objects involved, whereas the verbal text supplies circumstantial details, tells the story and thus verifies and enhances the interpretations of the pictures. The narrative potential inherent in language is perhaps best expressed in the direct speech passages of the text, such as *Never did I see a place with so bad an ice situation* or *This trip was my happiest because I was with my son, my good friend* – utterances the images could not make. Although indicated with graphic means in the maps, the argument about the ice flow increasing the distance to be covered during the crossing is only properly developed in the text. On the whole, pictorial and verbal text seem to largely run parallel to one another, building strong cohesive ties and supporting the same kind of coherence relations between concepts. In accordance with our knowledge of the text genre we take both the text (i.e. the story) as well as the images for real. The decoding orientation towards taking the depicted as reality is supported by the source of the information (*National Geographic*) and the indication of the producer of the pictures, who coincides with the main adventurer in the story (*Dmitry Shparo*).

Figure 2: Advertising image – AUDI advert
(*The Sunday Review*, 29 November 1998)

6. Example 2: Advertising image

Figure 2 (p. 102) shows my second sample text – an AUDI advert taken from *The Sunday Review* (29 November 1998) – which I will contrast with the analysis of the documentary text and thus show some typical properties of advertising images (texts). A first point one might notice is that the picture here occupies a large part of the format and seems thus dominant, at least in perception. This dominance is not founded on size alone, but is also supported by the frontal position of the picture which precedes the verbal part of the text. The recipient's gaze is thus arrested by the picture and engaged in its decoding before attention can be directed at the accompanying language.

The cohesive force in the image mainly derives from the silvery-brownish tint given to all visual elements in the frame.[20] Besides, it falls into two subsections: fore- and background which are signalled by differences in focus and resolution. The picture was taken in what is often called subjective angle (Messaris 1997: 29ff.) so as to put the viewer into the position of the driver and activate his real-world experience. In our case, this technique produces the odd side-effect that the recipient seems to be seeing two pictures, one of the car's interior, the other of a mountain scenery as framed by the windscreen. In a way, a third sub-picture is present in the frame of the rearview mirror. This effect is surely intended as a play on our activity of perceiving things visually and the possibility of an infinite regress of seeing (pictures within pictures).

More importantly, the visual elements are supposed to activate our mental script of driving and our knowledge frame of cars. While the winding road and the sharp bend straight ahead are meant to trigger the inference of danger and the importance of road-holding in driving, the dashboard is to simulate all the vital elements that make up the experience of sitting in a car. It is in this foreground part of the picture that visual coherence stops being frame/script-congruent, as the real wheel fitted in the car's interior clashes with our mental model of a dashboard which ordinarily comprises a steering wheel. This stage-managed replacement of a steering wheel by a normal car wheel, which also clearly hints at the doctored aspect of the photograph, can be described as a kind of rhetorical figure – a trope that substitutes one term for another.[21] Within the advertising context the intention of the visual metaphor

---

[20] Apart from the arty associations black and white photography usually has, the sepia tint also carries connotations of old age as it is familiar from photographs yellowed over time. This might be seen to tie in with the starting line of the body copy *Three thousand years later* and thus contributes to building cohesive links between picture and text.

[21] The substitutability of the visual objects is, of course, based on a formal analogy between both types of wheel.

or metonymy[22] might be to convey a message along the lines of: 'Gripping an Audi steering wheel is like gripping the actual wheel – it provides sensitive handling and sure road-holding'.

Genre knowledge is not only instrumental in making sense of the impaired pictorial coherence, it also makes a crucial contribution to understanding the very essence of the picture. For the advertising image to make sense the viewer needs to identify the car as an Audi. While the four chained rings on the wheel fitted to the dashboard can be read as a pictorial symbol for Audi (which is rather hard to make out for the uninitiated), it is rather genre knowledge about advertising that makes us infer that the depicted car must be an Audi, as a large majority of advertising shows the advertised object. Having established that the picture construes its textual utterance mainly by inferencing both on the basis of frame/script congruent elements as well as on the basis of frame/script incongruent visual metonymy, let us now take a look at how this pictorial message is linked up to the verbal text.

In contrast to the *National Geographic* example (Fig. 1) the advertising text does not contain any explicit or metacommunicative devices that would point to the picture. Cohesion is built in this case by repetition, that is by taking up visual concepts verbally: both steering wheel as well as the general wheel occur in the verbal text and are in fact core elements of its phrasing (e.g. "re-invent the wheel", "Audi gives you the steering wheel", "wheel to wheel"). Whereas picture and text in the *National Geographic* sample displayed a semantic parallelism and thus created informative redundancy, we notice that discrepancies and ambiguities arise from the interplay of image and language in the Audi advert. While the metonymic substitution in the picture which infringes upon visual coherence signals some kind of communicative relevance as illustrated above, it is only the verbal text which properly explains the visual trick by unfolding a technical argument: "The unique four-link front suspension reduces unwanted feedback from the road giving a more dynamic driving experience, wheel to wheel". None of this could possibly have been visualised directly. Pictorial and verbal elements thus come together and interlock to form quite a complex overall message which is more than the sum of its parts. So, while the picture provokes a cognitive clash, the text resolves it and determines its meaning.

A similar ambiguity is located in the headline "Audi re-invents the wheel", which with recourse to the picture could literally be read as fitting Audis with new types of steering wheels. This decoding is also suggested by the line

---

[22] For a detailed account of visual metaphor, its analysis and practice in advertising see Forceville (1996).

"Audi gives you the steering wheel". Alternatively, of course – and this is what the advertisement's claim spells out – re-inventing the wheel can refer to a new type of suspension which enables improved road-holding and steering. Viewed in this light, the picture makes a contribution to ambiguity, but also supplies a communicative incentive to resolve it via a cognitive engagement in the text.

7. Conclusion

The contrastive analysis of the sample texts should have shown structural and functional differences rooted in the different text genres and similarities grounded in the fact that both texts are confronted with the same task of linking picture and language. Noticeable differences are found in the pictorial functions and the kind of cognitive activity the pictures promote. Whereas the documentary image aims at mere display, the advertising image is geared towards facilitating a complex logical inference. Truth values in the images also differ: the documentary image is taken for real, the advertising image recognised for what it is, a doctored and stage-managed visual arrangement produced for aesthetic and cognitive effect. Cohesion between picture and language seems to work along the same lines in both two-code texts, although it is more explicit in the documentary text. Pictorial coherence is frame/script congruent in the documentary image, but deliberately incongruent in the advertising image. While it has to be conceded that a great deal of the recipient's text work to decode the images is guided by overall genre knowledge, my analysis has demonstrated that some structural and design features of the images and the picture-language interface play a crucial part in making sense of the images. The category of an image type seems therefore justified.

The two sample texts share one overriding similarity. In both examples pictures and prominent parts of the verbal text combine to form a minimal unit of information which summarily anticipates the content of the full text. In the documentary text maps and photographs are linked to the headline and the section title; in the advert the picture connects with the headline, the company logo and the slogan. The compact messages arising out of the combination of pictures and graphically prominent verbal cues provide cursory readers with a rough idea of the text's content at a quick glance, and thus serve as an efficient orientation in the information overload confronting recipients in our age.

While in perception images have priority and thus secure attention to texts, language seems to play a more important part in cognition and acts as the guiding medium in the detailed processing of two-code texts, particularly as it often helps to disambiguate images. In the final analysis, however, both codes, language and images are hardly separable in the practice of text production and reception. Just as in real life thinking and speaking cannot be cut loose from sensory experience, language and images in texts are but two ways of accessing the world that surrounds us.

References

Aitchison, Jean (1998): *The articulate mammal*. London: Routledge.
Barthes, Roland (1998). "Rhetoric of the image". Nicholas Mirzoeff, ed. *The visual culture reader*. London: Routledge, 70-73.
Blanke, Börries (1998): "Modelle des ikonischen Zeichens", *Zeitschrift für Semiotik* 3-4, 285-303.
de Beaugrande, Robert/Wolfgang Dressler (1981): *Introduction to text linguistics*. Harlow: Longman.
Dondis, D.A. (1973): *A primer of visual literacy*. Cambridge, MA: MIT.
Eco, Umberto (1968): *Einführung in die Semiotik*. München: Fink.
Elkins, James (1998): *On pictures and the words that fail them*. Cambridge: CUP.
Forceville, Charles (1996): *Pictorial metaphor in advertising*. London: Routledge.
Goodman, Nelson (1968): *Languages of art*. Indianapolis: Hackett.
Halliday, Michael A. K./Ruqaiya Hasan (1976): *Cohesion in English*. London: Longman.
Hoey, Michael (1991): *Patterns of lexis in text*. Oxford: OUP.
Kress, Gunther (1998): "Visual and verbal modes of representation in electronically mediated communication: the potentials of new forms of text". Ilana Snyder, ed. *Page to screen: taking literacy into the electronic era*. London: Routledge, 53-79.
Kress, Gunther/Theo van Leeuwen (1996): *Reading images: the grammar of visual design*. London: Routledge.
Lakoff, George/Mark Johnson, (1980): *Metaphors we live by*. Chicago: UP.
Lörscher, Wolfgang (1995): "Textstrukturen im Englischen". Rüdiger Ahrens et al., eds. *Handbuch Englisch als Fremdsprache*. Berlin: Schmidt, 165-168.
Malmkjær, Kirsten (1991): "Text linguistics". Kirsten Malmkjær, ed. *The linguistics encyclopedia*. London: Routledge, 461-471.
Merleau-Ponty, Maurice (1962): *Phenomenology of perception*. New York: Routledge.
Messaris, Paul (1997): *Visual persuasion: the role of images in advertising*. Thousand Oaks: Sage.
Mirzoeff, Nicholas (1998): *The visual culture reader*. London: Routledge.
Novitz, David (1977): *Pictures and their use in communication: a philosophical essay*. The Hague: Nijhoff.
Palmer, Stephen E. (1992): "Modern theories of gestalt perception". Glyn W. Humphreys, ed.*Understanding vision*. Oxford: Blackwell, 39-70.

Pörksen, Uwe (1997): *Weltmarkt der Bilder: Eine Philosophie der Visiotype*. Stuttgart: Klett-Cotta.

Roberts, Mark (1998): "The end(s) of pictorial representation: Merleau-Ponty and Lyotard". Hugh J. Silverman, ed. *Cultural semiosis: tracing the signifier.* New York: Routledge, 129-139.

Rolf, Eckard (1993): *Die Funktion der Gebrauchstextsorten*. Berlin/New York: de Gruyter.

Stafford, Barbara Maria (1996): *Good looking: essays on the virtue of images*. Cambridge, MA: MIT.

Stegu, Martin (1996): "Wie sprachlich ist die Bildsprache?". *Semiotische Berichte* 2, 3, 4: 305-320.

Stöckl, Hartmut (1997): *Werbung in Wort und Bild. Textstil und Semiotik englischsprachiger Anzeigenwerbung*. Frankfurt am Main etc.: Lang.

Stöckl, Hartmut (1998a): "Multimediale Diskurswelten zwischen Text und Bild." Bernhard Kettemann/Martin Stegu/Hartmut Stöckl, eds. *Mediendiskurse: verbalworkshop Graz 1996*. Frankfurt am Main etc.: Lang, 73-92.

Stöckl, Hartmut (1998b): "(Un)-chaining the floating image: Methodologische Überlegungen zu einem Beschreibungs- und Analysemodell für die Bild/Textverknüpfung aus linguistischer und semiotischer Perspektive". *Kodikas/Code*, Vol. 21/ 1-2, 75-98.

Stöckl, Hartmut (1999): "Ich weiß doch, was ich sehe! – Bilder lesen lernen? Visuelle Alphabetisierung in der Mediensozialisation". *Der Deutschunterricht* 3, Heft 2, 81-84.

van Dijk, T.A. (1972): *Some aspects of text grammars: a study in theoretical linguistics and poetics*. The Hague: Mouton.

Horst W. Drescher (*Mainz/Germersheim*)

Literati, literature, language; or, Patterns of identity

In *Humphry Clinker*, published in 1771, Tobias Smollett calls Edinburgh "a hot-bed of genius". The novel relates the adventures of Matthew Bramble's family party as they travel through England and Scotland. It is the Edinburgh of their day which Mr. Bramble has in mind, and indeed, a hot-bed of genius it was during the time of the Scottish Enlightenment between roughly 1740 and 1790. Most significant advances were made, and modern philosophy, historical studies, economics, sociology, politics, geology, chemistry, medicine, and agriculture are deeply indebted to the great Scottish thinkers of the eighteenth century and their practical concerns. "The central concept of the Scottish Enlightenment was that of human nature, and it was studied in all its aspects" (Broadie 1993: 69). Enquiry into the nature of society, man as social being, interest in literature and literary studies – these were prime objects of discussion and study among what generally has become known as the Edinburgh literati,

> professional men representing to a certain degree the legal *Èlite* of Edinburgh, a new class which had gradually taken over in social and political leadership when the influence of the nobility of Scotland was declining: literati in the true sense of the word; *men of business*, to introduce an eighteenth-century term. (Drescher 1989: 33)

Here Henry Mackenzie is to be mentioned, a still-recognized writer, 'primus inter pares' in that eighteenth-century generation representing Scottish thinking, cultural identity and literary tradition: a successful lawyer and public figure in Edinburgh and London, the trend-setting author of the *Man of feeling*. Mackenzie was also a prolific letter writer, essayist, biographer critic, and editor of two Scottish literary periodicals: *The Mirror* (1779-80) and *The Lounger* (1785-87). In the concluding number of the *Mirror* Mackenzie offers his definition of literati attitudes and interests:

> Cultivating letters in the midst of business, composition was to them an amusement only; that amusement was heightened by the audience which this society [Mirror Club] afforded; the idea of publication suggested itself as productive of still higher amusement. (*Mirror* 110)

A set of recent facsimiles, part of a series called *Scottish thought and culture 1750-1800*, edited by Richard B. Sher, is entitled *Lives of the literati* and includes Mackenzie's *Account of the life and writings of John Home*. Home,

a Presbyterian minister and one of the literati, was the author of *Douglas*
(1756), probably the most popular romantic tragedy of its time. The *Douglas*
controversy – Home was attacked by the presbytery of Edinburgh on account
of the play's alleged irreligious and immoral tendencies – produced a flow of
critical pamphlets, valuable sources of first-hand information about the
intellectual and socio-cultural climate at the height of the Scottish Enlightenment.

> At first glance the *Lives of the literati* looks like an opportunistic collection of
> old-fashioned books about a mixed bag of Enlightenment figures, but the
> opportunity it gives to contemplate the cultural synergy of the time and the
> ramifications of its legacy to its immediate successors, as well as to us
> two centuries later, makes this a very worthwhile publishing project ...
> (MacLachlan 1998: 12)

Mackenzie's *Account* was read to the Royal Society of Edinburgh on
Monday, 22 June 1812, and, in a later and revised version, published in 1822
as the first volume of his edition of the *Works of John Home*. The Royal
Society was very much a stronghold of the Edinburgh literati, Mackenzie
being one of its founder members (1783), then Vice President and President
of the 'Literary Class'. The intellectual stimulus provided by the existence of
numerous clubs and societies must not be underestimated. In addition to the
Royal Society there were the Philosophical Society, the Mirror Club, the
Select Society, the Poker Club, and the Speculative Society, to name but a
few: stock exchanges of thought and ideas, very much like the London
coffee-houses of earlier decades. Topics of discourse and debate were wide
and varied, learned, and commonplace, traditional and forward-looking,
highly pragmatic as well as nonsensical at times. Certainly, one area of
interest concerned matters of literature, including the status of language as
medium of communication.

In 1797, James Beattie, Professor of Moral Philosophy at Marischal College, published a kind of handbook entitled *Scotticisms. Designed to correct
improprieties in speech and writing*. Originally compiled by the professor for
the use of his students to help them avoid linguistic 'improprieties', the
publication shows that any analysis of the language issue in relation to
Scottish literature has to be placed in its socio-cultural context. There is a
continuous quest for identity, with sustained efforts to demonstrate cultural
and linguistic identity. Yet there also was the strong desire to escape paro-
chialism, and the literati of eighteenth-century Scotland may serve as an early
example of this ongoing dilemma.

> The language issue has always featured prominently in the debate about
> England's influence upon Scotland and, connected with it, the gradual erosion
> of the country's national and cultural identity. It reminds us of the inner con-
> flict Scottish life and letters experienced during the eighteenth century. There

were the outstanding philosophical, scientific and literary achievements of the Scottish Enlightenment as part of an all-European intellectual power game and, on the other hand, the embarrassing endeavours to avoid regionalism at all costs. (Drescher 1998: 65f.)

In the following, I propose to return to Henry Mackenzie's periodicals and hitherto unpublished literary fragments and notebooks. One of the regular contributors to the *Mirror* and *Lounger* was William Craig (1745-1813), his friend, Senator of the College of Justice and Lord of Session, a man very much representative of literati learning and attitudes. An essay from his pen appeared in *Mirror* 83, headed "Inquiry into the causes of the scarcity of humorous writers in Scotland". Craig opens by pointing out that

> in a paper published in Edinburgh, it would be improper to enter into a comparison of the writers of this country with those on the other side of the Tweed: but, whatever the comparative rank of Scottish and English authors, it must surely be allowed, that, of late, there have been writers in this country, upon different subjects, who are possessed of very considerable merit.

Craig admits that "the English excel in comedy ... in Scotland we have hardly any book which aims at humour ...", and he is "inclined to suspect that there is something in the situation and present government of Scotland, which may, in part, account for this difference in the genius of the two countries". A number of reasons and resulting consequences are conjectured upon: "Scotland ... before the union of the kingdoms, was a separate state"; for preferment or offices in public life Scots were "obliged to remove from home" to London, "a sort of foreign city". Obviously, "people in this situation are not apt to indulge themselves in humour" and it is "necessary for them to push their way in the world"; they are "obliged to do so among strangers". These and many other "circumstances may have had a considerable influence upon the genius and temper of the people of Scotland"; furthermore, there was no court or seat of the monarch in Scotland and "men living at a distance from the court become ... unacquainted with the rules of fashion which it establishes" while a

> great subject for wit and ludicrous representation arises from men's having a thorough knowledge of what is the fashionable standard of manners, and being able to seize upon, and hold out a departure from it, in a humorous point of view Scotland has become, in a certain degree, a provincial country, there being no fixed standards of manners within ...

Thus "one great source of ridicule is cut off, and an author is not led to attempt humorous composition".

But, as Craig goes on, there is still another particular reason which has "a very considerable effect upon the genius of the Scots writers, and that is, the

nature of the language in which they write". In support of his series of statements, the essayist concludes by drawing the attention of his readers to the
"nature of the language" in which the Scots writers write. English substitutes
the "old Scottish dialect". Although books may be written in English, "our
conversation is in Scotch", the "Scottish dialect is our ordinary suit". Allan
Ramsay's *Gentle shepherd* is quoted, as a work of literature "full of natural
and ludicrous representations of low life", written in "broad Scotch".
Equally, "many of our ancient Scottish ballads are full of humour". On the
other hand, "a Scotsman, who wishes to write English, cannot easily do this.
He neither speaks the English dialect, nor is it spoken by those around him:
any knowledge he has acquired of the language is got from books, not from
conversation". Craig sums up his argument and, himself a Scotsman,
confirms that he uses a language "in some respects foreign" to him. At a later
date he takes up the subject again in "Observations on comedy" (*Lounger*:
49), continued by Mackenzie in "Moral effects of Comedy" (*Lounger*: 50).

Even Mackenzie, in a way anglicized through his education and the study
of English law in London, had to admit that Scotticisms, i.e. "colloquial
improprieties and defects of language", may have found their way into *The
man of feeling*, his first novel. It was favourably received by the critics and
soon gained an international readership via translations into French, Italian,
German and even Swedish. However, *The Monthly Review* found fault with
the language which it claimed "abounds in provincial and Scottish idioms"
(*Monthly*, XLV, 1771: 418). In a letter of 24 June 1771 to James Elphinston,
educationalist and author of books on language such as *The contrast: A
specimen of the Scottish dialect, in prose and verse, according to the latest
improvements; with an English version* (1779), he asks his acquaintance to
suggest corrections:

> In case of another edition, I should take it as a singular favour, if you would
> point out any defects in language, or Scottish idioms, that struck you on a
> perusal of the book. In giving language to dialogue; one, whose ear is
> accustomed to hear such in this country, is very apt to slide into colloquial
> improprieties. (Drescher 1989: 56)

Indeed, the *Monthly* reviewer's criticism that the novel abounds in
"provincial and Scottish idiom" and that the "rare gift of true genius" was
missing in the anonymous author did more than just annoy Mackenzie. "They
will not allow me genius; but they have allotted me inspiration: for otherwise,
though I might easily have learnt *Scotticism*, I could hardly have acquired
provincial idioms" (Drescher 1989: 55f.). Mackenzie's reaction was typical
of his eighteenth-century background. The Scottish thinkers and literati
wanted to compete with their English fellow-writers on an equal footing.
Hence, they rejected Scotticisms in literature and, as a result, had to face up

to yet another paradox of Scottish literature and culture. And, socially speaking, this kind of paradox is still to be found in operation today:

> Obwohl das *Scottish Standard English* in Schottland heute zweifellos die dominierende Standardvariante ist, wird ... in bestimmten sozialen Gruppen, besonders in Kreisen des alteingesessenen Landadels, noch immer ein *English Standard English* mit RP bzw. einem 'near-RP accent' als Prestigenorm vorgezogen. (Hansen/Carls/Lucko 1996: 68)

The language issue is taken up again in the "Extraordinary account of Robert Burns, the Ayrshire ploughman", Mackenzie's influential review of the *Kilmarnock poems,* published in *Lounger* 97 on 9 December 1787. Mackenzie coined the name "heaven-taught ploughman" to stimulate the curiosity of an urban and fashionable readership. Burns was by no means an uneducated Ayrshire farmer; on the contrary, he was well-read in the classics and an excellent conversationalist. In any case, the review did serve its purpose.

> There can have been few contemporary authors more honest than Burns, and he was too alert not to realize that the concept of the 'Heaven-taught ploughman' ... fitted rather well into an aspect of the spirit of the age, that of Rousseau's noble savage ... (Strauss 1998: 81)

Written by Edinburgh's literary pundit it introduced Burns to the elegant society of the Athens of the North; it was, perhaps, the first step on the ladder to fame as a poet to becoming Scotland's popular national bard. In spite of all this, Mackenzie had no hesitation in criticizing the language of the poems, at least of those written in the 'dialect' of Scotland. At this point it should be remembered that the meaning of the word 'dialect' as applied by Craig, Mackenzie and other literary critics is synonymous with language.

> Even in Scotland, the provincial dialect which Ramsay and he [Burns] have used is now read with a difficulty which greatly damps the pleasure of the reader: in England it cannot be read at all, without such a constant reference to a glossary, as nearly to destroy that pleasure.

It becomes evident that Mackenzie's interest in the workings of language was linked with his self-critical assessment not only as the author of novels, plays and poetry but also as a writer of professional prose, treatises and essays on a variety of topics. Small wonder that his notebooks (NLS) contain numerous remarks and entries on the subject of language. A few examples may suffice.

Mackenzie knew French, some Italian and German, and had tried his hand at translating. In his opinion "learning a language by living in the country in which it is spoken ... would not give accuracy or elegance, but it would be less laborious and more pleasant than the regular acquirements of grammar and vocabulary". As far as grammar is concerned, he argues that

false grammar is so common in conversation and sometimes carelessly introduced into writings of a lighter kind that it does not strike us as incorrect
though greatly so in a grammarian's eye, as for example 'a Rose smells sweet'
or 'that dish tastes well'; both these phrases are in the active instead of the
passive, as a rose cannot smell, nor a dish taste, but is smelt and tasted.

Inaccuracies of the same kind may also be detected in the works of "eminent
writers" such as in William Robertson who, in his *History of Scotland during
the reign of Queen Mary and of King James VI till his accession to the
Crown of England* (1759), "says a hundred times that the King *forfeited* the
Estates of certain traitorous Lords instead of *confiscated*". In addition,
Mackenzie argues that English lacks what he calls a "personal *neuter* to
designate persons without reference to sex, as the word *it* applied to a child
whether male or female", and he draws his own conclusion that "*it* should
properly truly be applied to minimal things". Further examples lead him to
rather idiosyncratic explanations: "Beasts we refer to by *it*, though with some
exceptions when we wish to distinguish their sex or a person calls a *mare
she*." – "Of some the feminine is always used though the sex is known to be
male: a *hare* is always *she*, a *Fox he*, perhaps from a moral conclusion, the
extreme timidity of the one being a *female* and the cunning and desperate
endurance of the other a *male* quality." – "Machines are generally female, as
a *ship*, or a *mill*, from what cause I know not." – "The *sun* in almost all languages *male*, the *moon female*, though there are a few exceptions to this. The
appearance as well as the properties of these two avenues planets may have
induced this."

Further areas of Mackenzie's linguistic curiosity are English words for
scientific subjects and the Greek compounds "somewhat pedantically
introduced by persons learned in that language", "actions of the body and
emotions of the mind expressed by words of appropriate sound", Norman
French as introduced at the conquest and the Anglo-Saxon used before,
inaccuracy of expression, Highland or Gaelic language, place-names, and so
forth. Talking of place-names, Mackenzie refers to them as "descriptive of
their local situations" and "one of the best proofs of the language of the
ancient inhabitants". However, he adds by way of an anecdote that such
etymologies are not always to be trusted. A friend of his, "deeply skilled in
the Gaelic language", was asked about the derivation of the name *Balraiten*, a
place situated on Loch Lomond. Firmly convinced of his understanding of
the name, i.e. a place situated near which a great road passed, he took the
place-name for a corruption of *balrait*. In fact the name had nothing to do
with the Gaelic; quite on the contrary, "it was a corruption of *Bel retiro*, a
name given by a travelled Gentleman who was the owner of the place".

Like his friend Alexander Fraser Tytler, whose "Essay on the principles of
translation" was published in 1791, Mackenzie and the other literati of the

Scottish Enlightenment paid tribute to the art of translation. Mentioning Tytler, Mackenzie contemplated a "book on *Translation*" which, according to an entry in one of his notebooks, should be both "instructive and entertaining" and study the

> affinity between the situation of different people and their language, the different powers of words nearly synonymous, the connexion of their differences with the periods of their introduction to general use, the nationality of many words, and the local situation which invented or gave them currency.

This would amount to a "treatise on the *Philosophy of language*". It would be something different from Tytler's "Essay", "deservedly popular" as it is;

> ... a curious enough subject ... of a philosophical essay, such as Adam Smith could have written, not one confined to the comparison of the justness and accuracy of different translations, but a chart as it were of the mind, a view of its operations, a delineation of its feelings as growing into language, the different shades of their expression.

With his thoughts about language and translation Mackenzie was anticipating some central aspects of translation studies and analysis today. But he was also very much trapped in his own eighteenth-century world stressing that language exerts a great moral influence on society: "... names make virtue less respected and vice less blamed." And he gives the following example:

> Such are the words *gallantry* and *honour*, the first often measuring the most infamous conduct with regard to the wife or daughter of our neighbour; the second justifying murder and injustice. Say adultery or murder, and the sound carries something which is slightly affected by the words first above quoted.

Together with his letters, Mackenzie's notebooks, miscellaneous literary fragments, literary criticism, political reminiscences, observations on language, education, writers and their work represent Scottish Enlightenment attitudes and thought. They appeal to the principles of common sense, counselling man how to live virtuously in an emerging new society governed more and more by commercial considerations. In sum, they mirror the intellectual and social climate of the day, largely influenced by the impetus deriving from the Union of 1707 and the loss of a Scots parliament. At the same time they seem to anticipate twentieth-century contexts and perspectives, future and crucial patterns of thoughts and events.

> Of all the varieties of English which have developed within the British Isles, there are none more distinctive or more divergent from Standard English than some of those associated with Scotland. Indeed, the extent of the divergence in one of these varieties has led to a well-established use of the label, the 'Scots language', and to a spirited defence of all that such a label stands for. (Crystal 1995: 328)

The new Scots parliament of May 1999 will have to streamline Scotland's quest for cultural identity and reinforce the Scottish tradition in literature, language and society within the new political framework of Europe.

References

Broadie, Alexander (1993): "A nation of philosophers". Paul Henderson Scott, ed. *Scotland: a concise cultural history*. Edinburgh/London: Mainstream Publishing, 61-76.
Crystal, David (1995): *The Cambridge encyclopedia of the English language*. Cambrigde: CUP.
Drescher, Horst W., ed. (1989): *Literature and literati. The literary correspondence and notebooks of Henry Mackenzie, vol. 1: Letters 1766-1827*. Frankfurt am Main: Lang.
Drescher, Horst W. (1998): "Re-viewing the Scottish tradition in (British) literature". Barbara Korte/Klaus Peter Müller, eds. *Unity in diversity? British literature and culture in the 1990s*. Tübingen: Narr, 63-70.
Hansen, Klaus/Uwe Carls/Peter Lucko (1996): *Die Differenzierung des Englischen in nationale Varianten*. Berlin: Schmidt.
Lounger, The. A Periodical Paper, 1785-87. Edinburgh.
MacLachlan, Christopher (1998): Review of "Lives of the literati". *Scottish Literary Journal*, Supplement 49, 9-12.
Mirror, The. A Periodical Paper, 1779-80. Edinburgh.
NLS (National Library of Scotland): MSS 645, 34-96.
Scott, Paul Henderson, ed. (1993): *Scotland: a concise cultural history*. Edinburgh/London: Mainstream Publishing.
Strauss, Dietrich (1998): "Some reflections on Burns's command of English". *Studies in Scottish Literature* XXX, 77-89.

Joachim Schwend *(Leipzig)*

"Freedom is a noble thing" – Scottish independence rhetorics and the Referendum of 11 September 1997

I. The notion of Scottish independence, and in particular independence in Europe, has once again risen to the surface of political discussion after it received a new impetus from the Referendum in September 1997. In the debate about Scotland's future the nationalists began to hark back on their old claim which had been hidden under the general cloak of consensus during the YesYes Campaign. The Scottish nationalist discourse shows recurring patterns underlining the claim of Scotland to be a nation in her own right and thus to be qualified to acquire statehood once again after this was lost in 1707. The aim of this paper is to point out discursive formations and signifying practices within the nationalist discourse which result in typical and recurring representations and the subsequent creation of meaning. Meaning or knowledge is created according to certain patterns, and this knowledge results both in a cultural code and a power structure which leads to the differentiation between one's own position and the other. The terminology used in the discourse has remained very much the same through the ages. It is based on a whole system of a specific imagery, vocabulary, on knowledge and supporting doctrines. The historicisation which Foucault stresses is only partially applicable in the context of the Anglo-Scottish relationship, as the signs and the significations are frequently repeated. When looking into a sample of newspaper articles after the referendum of 11 September 1997 we find a well-worn "structure of attitude and reference" (Said 1994: 73). The aim of this paper cannot be to find out whether the statements are true or not, but to determine their significance. What is usually understood by 'truth', is nothing but representations within their individual context and historical framework, which rely very much on traditions, customs and specific vocabularies, and also on knowledge acquired and used for purposes of power: "power using knowledge to advance itself" (Said 1995: 336). Edward Said writes in *Culture and imperialism*:

> We live of course in a world not only of commodities but also of representation, and representations – their production, circulation, history, and interpretation – are the very element of culture. In much recent theory the problem of representation is deemed to be central, yet rarely is it put in its full political context, a context that is primarily imperial. (Said 1994: 66)

Culture is not so much a set of things, or 'commodities', but a process or a "set of practices" (Hall 1997: 2) and is concerned with the production and exchange of meaning. In the course of this paper relevant representations will be put in the political context, but the question whether we can follow Said and talk of an *imperial* context will remain more or less unanswered. Though Said's understanding of *imperialism* would fit the Anglo-Scottish relationship: "... 'imperialism' means the practice, the theory, and the attitudes of a dominating metropolitan centre ruling a distant territory" (Said 1994: 8). Representation must be understood as a dialogue, sustained by existing cultural codes, which allow variations in the meanings produced. The attempt to fix a certain meaning, Stuart Hall (1997: 166) talks of "preferred reading", must be seen in the context of a power struggle, which takes place in a nationalist framework.

Said (1994: 1) constructs the social framework of representations, when he says: "the 'what' and 'how' in the representation of 'things', while allowing for considerable individual freedom, are circumscribed and socially regulated." Following Hall's work, culture is about "shared meanings", about "values". People of the same culture communicate more or less successfully because they have the same or a similar set of values, they produce more or less the same meanings through language, things, "commodities" (Said 1994: 66), or signifying practices. A group of people create a "language of national identity, a discourse of national belongingness" (Hall 1997: 5). The meaning is not simply there, it is constructed in the nationalist discourse through representation, which "is *eo ipso* implicated, intertwined, embedded, interwoven with a great many other things besides the 'truth', which is itself a representation" (Said 1995: 272).

Representations have purposes and the meaning produced can change through the course of time due to usage and historical circumstances. The attempt to fix meaning is linked with a question of power. Hegemony in the sense of Gramsci is concomitant with power structures in civil society, it is important how the representation of foreign cultures is structured. "All cultures tend to make representations of foreign cultures the better to master or in some way control them" (Said 1994: 120). This implies once again the question of an 'imperial' context.

II.   As early as John Barbour's 14th-century epic *The Bruce* (1375), the emphasis in the nationalist discourse has been on the freedom the Scots had fought for. "A! fredome is A noble thing!" (Barbour 1870: 10). The definition of Scottish national identity began with and still relies on the antagonism between Scotland and England. Scottish nationalism is frequently negatively defined, in so far as it is anti-English. In the late 20th century it is still anti-

English and ever since Thatcher also anti-Conservative. In the "sanctioned narratives" (Said 1994: 380) of the Anglo-Scottish relationship the Wars of Independence have always played a major role, especially in the person of an outstanding enemy: Edward I, the so-called 'hammer of the Scots'. This ambiguous statement could describe the king who hammered the Scots into shape and united them for the battle against the 'Auld Enemy', or one could also see the hammer as a negative term: Edward pressed the Scots under the English yoke. In the secret national anthem of Scotland, *The flower of Scotland*, the text goes "we sent him [Edward I] homeward tae think again" (cf. The Corries 1991). This phrase expresses a feeling of pride, because the smaller nation was victorious over the more powerful, at Stirling Bridge the English were sent homewards to think again. The myths of the 'Auld Enemy' and the 'Auld Alliance' (established in 1295 and renewed in more definite terms in 1372) finally lost their relevance under Sir Walter Scott who tried to put an end to this bipolarity with the definition in us and them, home versus alien, when he said that the Scots and the English had fought 314 major battles and that enough was enough (Reid 1991: 25). Or as the text in *The flower of Scotland* continues: "those days are past now, and in the past they must remain, but we can still rise now, and be the nation again, that stood against him". The image of Edward I and his son Edward II is still alive and it is utilized in connection with Margaret Thatcher. In a letter to the editor a Glaswegian writes:

> I would like to express a personal debt of gratitude to Margaret Thatcher. Over 20 years, by her words and her actions, she did more to galvanise and unite the Scottish people than any other person since Edward Plantagenet in the late 13th century. (*The Guardian*, 9/13/1997: 20)

Father and son Plantagenet in line with Margaret Thatcher are the type of Southerners who help to hammer the Scots into a unified nation. The above mentioned nationalist narrative and the inherent rhetoric of blame have their specific array of heroes and villains who can be activated whenever needed. The nationalist discourse relies heavily on references to history.

> In Europe the normal basis for nationalism is the historic nation ... European nationalism is, therefore, in a sense always backward looking, always adverting to past glories, always apparently more conscious of the past than of the present. (Hanham 1969: 10)

The representation of history is one of the outstanding signifying practices in the Anglo-Scottish relationship. Said (1994: 18) writes: "More important than the past itself, therefore, is its bearing upon cultural attitudes in the present." The Scots look backwards to a glorious, but also gory past, hankering after the myth of the once great nation. Sir Reginald Coupland (1954: 1) writes that a nation is among other things "inspired by the memory of 'the great things done together' and the desire to do more of them". The time of heroic deeds is past, as we have left the primary period of military resistance, to refer to Said's definition. Looking back into history might help to explain things, but it will not solve any of the contemporary problems. The glorification of the past runs through the whole discourse ˉbout Scottish independence or devolution. The demarcation between the English and the Scots, whether real or imagined, has taken centuries of common history to come into existence. And there has always been a strong and a weaker element in the relationship between the two neighbours, Scotland as a rule being the weaker partner. The crititical voices are few and far between: Andrew Marr represents such a voice who sees Scottish history not through the glasses of romantic glorification.

> There was plenty of hewing, stabbing and poisoning, not to say fast-sickening, slow-starving and long-despairing ... Scottish kings were murdered or imprisoned, sometimes by their revolting children. Edinburgh stank. It rained. (Marr 1992: 15)

The Scots have been fighting for ages for Scottish nationhood, but here the difficulties begin. What do we understand by Scotland and the Scottish nation? The Scots are after all of Irish origin and have originally an Ulster background. As the Irish officer Captain Macmorris in Shakespeare's *Henry V* asks, "What ish my nation? Ish a villian, and a bastard, and a knave, and a rascal. What ish my nation? Who talks of my nation?" (476; III,2). It turns out to be difficult to give a succinct definition of the Scottish nation, if we fall back on traditional criteria such as common language, territory, history, culture.

The Highlands-Lowlands divide and the concomitant development-gap between these parts of what is usually called Scotland is only one among many bones of contention. Tom Nairn (1981: 165) talks of Scotland being two nations and of "the Anglophone reduction of Celtic society". In Jacobite songs the Highlanders are frequently abused as a band of thieves who are characterized by their dirt and rough living habits and by their "buttocks bare" (Donaldson 1988: 44). Once England stops being the outside enemy and the major point of comparison, internal differences of Scotland become more apparent. This is a recurring pattern in history and it became immediately apparent after the 1997 referendum, when the outlying regions claimed their own national self-awareness and sectarianism loomed on the horizon. Edinburgh suddenly moved from the periphery to the centre. The Highlands and Islands emphasized their own national identity in the debate about devolution. "Orkney pushes for its own referendum" is a headline in *The Scotsman* of

13 September 1997. The islanders want to decide on their own on a possible further devolution from Edinburgh to Kirkwall and they do not want to accept an Edinburgh dictate. They underline their strong Viking and Norwegian background and thus their own "strong sense of identity" (David Hartley in *The Scotsman*, 9/12/1997: 2).

There are two cultural codes between a highly anglicised culture in the Lowlands and a rather more Celtic or Viking culture in the Highlands and Islands. Contemporary nationalists such as P.H. Scott or Owen Dudley Edwards negate the divide and see the Scots as one nation, full stop. To the question whether the Scots are a nation there is only one answer for Edwards (1989: 13): "Of course they are. They were both a nation and a state until 1707". He does not feel obliged to go into more detail. Nairn sees the underlying problem and argues: "'identity' is what frustrated nationalities want and nation-states possess" (Nairn 1981: 172). This shows the dilemma, in which regions, provinces or self-declared nations such as Scotland find themselves. Rosalind Mitchison (1991: vii) talks of "separate histories of separate peoples within the nation states". She leaves it open whether she would accept this principle also for Scotland or whether she sees it only applicable in the United Kingdom context.

Visual signs, icons, which are linked with history, are used in the nationalist discourse to describe the identity of the nation or of what nationalists consider to be the nation. The cultural code fixes the relationship between signs and concepts or in the structuralist terminology the relationship between signifier and signified, the signified never being stable and established once and for all. Lord Macaulay writes in his *History of England* (1849-61): "before the Union, [the kilt] was considered by nine Scotchmen out of ten as the dress of a thief" (Macaulay 1986: 368). The Highland dress underwent definite and meaningful changes. It was forbidden in 1746 and resuscitated by Sir Walter Scott as part and parcel of his romantic vision of Scotland. The kilt has different connotations for an Englishman and a Scotsman, for a Lowland Scot and a Highlander. Meaning is not inherent in the thing as such, it is constructed within the discourse, in the "full political context" as Said (1994: 66) formulates. The kilt must be seen as one visual sign which changed its contextual reference through the ages depending on the ideological dimension and the place it occupied in a culture. Sir Walter Scott created the tourist image of the Scotsman in his Highland garb, the "dear, good, superior people" of Queen Victoria, painted as noble savages in their kilts by the Scottish miniaturist Kenneth Macleay (cf. K. Hamilton in *The Times*, 8/16/1986: 6). The kilt and bagpipes became an all inclusive Scottish characteristic and was not reserved to Highlanders. It probably was not by chance that *The Scotsman* of 13

September 1997 had a kilt advertisement by Macnoughtons of Pitlochry on the front page stating: "Tartan – The Traditional Choice". It is not so much the denotative as the connotative level on which signs such as the kilt work. Or as Roland Barthes puts it, the "level of the myth" (Hall 1997: 39). Myth-making is a central aspect in the nationalist discourse. William Wallace and the Braveheart-myth is a recent example. The Wallace-myth, just like Scott's usage of the kilt in George IV's visit to Edinburgh, is exploited for the tourist image of Scotland, of what is as a rule understood by 'Balmorality'. Most of the scenes of the film *Braveheart* were actually shot in Ireland with Irish soldiers playing the part of the Scots (cf. McArthur 1998).

Nationalism in a Scottish context has no *a priori* negative connotations. But nevertheless we can see the beginnings of a new terminology. The emphasis moves away from nationalism and towards a community feeling. Susan Bassnett (1997: xvii) underlines the importance to differentiate between "*nationalism*, with all its dangers of inherent racism and xenophobia, and *national consciousness*, which is an inclusive, not an exclusive concept and embraces racial, religious and ethnic difference".

Fredrik Brogger (1992: 36) links the concept of national identity with the idea of "dominant culture patterns" and refers to Gramsci's discussion of hegemony. He sees the continuing process of cultural domination and subordination as part of the nationalist discourse. The underlying idea is one of a continuing variation which could overcome the exclusive ethnocentric aspect of national homogeneity. Said has a similar approach and strengthens the continuous interchange between cultures:

> we need to go on and to situate these [identities] in a geography of other identities, peoples, cultures, and then to study how, despite their differences, they have always overlapped one another, through unhierarchical influence, crossing, incorporation, recollection, deliberate forgetfulness, and, of course, conflict ... The fact is, we are mixed in with one another in ways that most national systems of education have not dreamed of. (Said 1994: 401)

National consciousness in its inclusiveness takes into account variation through external influences and interdependencies. It is more suited to the age of globalisation and the notion of a united Europe which calls for transnational adjustments.

In the discussion of the referendum in September 1997 the importance of a national consciousness, i.e. of politics being in agreement with the Scottish people becomes increasingly clear and must be seen as a sign for 'national consciousness' beyond narrow nationalism. It is not the exclusive nationalist voice, but the idea of an inclusive consensus among all partners in the political arena of Scotland, consensus among Labour, the SNP and the Liberal Democrats, or to put names to the parties, of Donald Dewar, Alex Salmond and Jim Wallace, the "triumphurate", as it was also called (Alan Cochrane in *The Scotsman*, 9/12/1997: 2). The strongly nationalist voice, Alex Salmond and the SNP, is only one among several, even though still a powerful and carrying voice.

During the referendum the YesYes Campaign tried hard to speak with one voice, uniting Labour, SNP, and Liberal Democrats and to have a clear front towards the Unionist voice, mainly represented by the Conservatives and the odd Labour rebel such as Tam Dalyell of Linlithgow, in itself a very historic place. It certainly was no accident that the colours of the YesYes Campaign were the same red and yellow as in the royal flag of Scotland with the lion rampant. Ewen MacAskill writes in *The Guardian* (Sept 13, 1997: 4): "The Scottish lion has been let out and Labour might not find it that easy to prod him into a cage again." In the Declaration of Arbroath (1320) the Scots pledged their allegiance to the Scottish lion, and not to any king or lord. Allegiance to a symbol of the nation rather than to a personality. Hints of future problems considering the question where devolution will lead to are manifold. Fears among Labour begin to rise whether the SNP will finally succeed in bringing about independence and thus the break-up of the UK.

The simplifying binary oppositions which are so cherished by nationalists are gone. In the enlightened age of globalization and in a European age, new alignments have to be made across borders. A process of deterritorialisation is under way in a nationalist discourse and can also be seen in the Irish and Northern Irish context, preparing the ground for a new Europe, fit for the new millenium. Peter MacMahon calls for "A new Scotland for a new millenium" (*The Scotsman*, 9/12/1997: 1). Jan Nederveen (1993: 225) talks of "Europe's contemporary multicultural realities". The whole complex concept of multi-culturalism, if it is to be more than an empty phrase, does not fit in with narrow-minded nationalism of the old sort.

The fundamentally static notion of national identity is no longer applicable. The clearcut differentiation between cultures does not work any longer, cultures are hybrid and definitely not monolithic, they are not given and de-termined for all eternity, they do not imply privileged status for those who claim to have this national identity as opposed to those who are without it. Nederveen (1993: 229) argues: "Identity implies a relationship to what is different and thus a statement of boundaries ... They [identities] are projects rather than realities, mirrors of power and rhetorics of control." The Manichaen us-and-them opposition which divides between those who belong and those who do not belong cannot work any longer. Eve Tavor Bannet (1993: 29) describes the kind of society we should try to leave behind, a "hegemonic society where disciplinary practices exclude otherness, preclude singularity and silence difference". The hegemonic society and the concept of national pride build on the ideas of exclusiveness and superiority which have poisoned the Anglo-Scottish relationship for centuries. What is needed in a postcolonial age, and what most of the articles call for, is scope for cultural difference "by valorizing a plural decentered and non-identical conception of the subject" (Bannet 1993: 30).

Said criticized narrow-minded nationalism with its emphasis on identity: "Identity, always identity, over and above knowing about others" (Said 1994: 362). The understanding of a dominant metropolitan culture, as opposed to a peripheral and thus undesirable and subordinate culture has come to an end. This approach is no longer applicable in an age of the 'Europe of Regions', as the YesYes Campaign showed. The concept of a 'Europe of Regions' gained wider acceptance in the 1980s when centralisation and the so-called quangocracy in the UK acquired hitherto unknown strength under Margaret Thatcher. As one commentator wrote:

> Even Nationalism has changed with the advent of the European Union, an institution whose future will affect us all. Perfect independence is recognised as a myth. The world in which Scotland finds itself is interdependent, economically and culturally. (*The Scotsman*, 9/13/1997: 18)

Doreen Massey (1993: 232) talks of "A global sense of place". It is important to acquire knowledge about others, about Europe, to look beyond the saltires and the lions rampant and towards the blue flag of Europe and a new constitutional horizon for the UK. The knowledge about the other must, however, not be institutionalized, perpetuated, and taken for granted, but it must continuously be checked by empiricism. The danger exists that knowledge attains the

> self-reinforcing character of a closed system, in which objects are what they are *because* they are what they are, for once, for all time, for ontological reasons that no empirical material can either dislodge or alter. (Said 1995: 70)

The acquisition of a national consciousness must be seen as a pluralistic and continuing dialogue rather than a fixed and limited monologue which relies on anything like nationalist purity. Bakhtin's ideas about dialogue are relevant in this respect (Crawford 1997: 92).

This multiple identity implies also a new England and a new form of English self-awareness. Is it not common usage to say England when one means Great Britain or even the United Kingdom? Why did Elton John sing of England's rose and not of Britain's rose? Would William Blake have written of Britain's green and pleasant land? Katie Gramich (1997: 97) claims: "Britishness is a mask. Beneath it there is only one nation, England." It was

David Hume who in his essay "Of national character" in 1748 said: "the English, of any people in the universe, have the least of a national character" (Stanzel 1997: 7). This will certainly change within the near future as a new English self-awareness cannot be overlooked any longer. There is talk of Home Rule for England (cf. *The Scotsman*, 9/13/1997: 19). Hume did not mention the Scots as a nation in their own right, and this only two years after the catastrophe of Culloden. It is also significant that Walter Bagehot chose the title *The English Constitution* (1867) when he in fact talked of the United Kingdom constitution. It is probably the diffuse character of the term England or English which offers itself, if we do not fall back on an imperial explanation which goes hand in glove with Gramsci's idea of hegemony. The whole concept of national identity has to be redefined within the near future, placing it in a European framework and accepting the idea of multiple identities within this wider framework.

III. The future of Scotland was at the heart of the campaign, a future beyond centralisation, a future which will bring government closer to the people. The general tenor in the discussion of the referendum and during the period leading to the referendum has been one of modernisation, of the coming of a new age and a new millenium. Coupland (1954: 3) describes the new role a nation can play in a globalized world: "A nation's *raison d'être* is the contribution it can make to the welfare of the international community." Interdependence and globalization are the keywords, not brave hearts but "brave heads" are needed, as *The Sun* of 19 March 1997 claimed on the front page.

With a future Edinburgh parliament on the horizon one has to consider what it will look like. There is the danger of replacing one sort of aloof elite-government by another in the imperial context. One commentator in *The Scotsman* warns: "The referendum did not bring us the keys to the sweetie shop, nor did it exempt us from the need to survive in the global market place" (*The Scotsman*, 9/13/1997: 18). Scotland with its parliament will have to face reality after the champagne has been drunk in order to survive in the global market place. As Edward Said remarks, there are two sorts of "realities", namely the "reality out there" and the one in people's heads (Said 1995: 300). Jim McBeth voices a sceptical view when he writes: "It's going to be a lot harder than singing Flower of Scotland" (*The Scotsman*, 9/13/1997: 24). Singing the national anthem is one thing which is linked with tear-sodden anti-English nationalism, but building a new country needs more effort and hard work, and it needs above all consensus politics and the wish to get to know the other.

A new type of politician is demanded, an end to faction fighting and conviction politics. Nationalism at its moment of success must be changed into social consciousness, otherwise the future would not be liberation but an extension of the old imperialist system with new masters. The central government for Shetland and Orkney would no longer be London, but Edinburgh, just another type of core-periphery antagonism. The difference would only be marginal. "The old conflicts between regions are now repeated, privileges are monopolized by one people over another, and the hierarchies and divisions constituted by imperialism are reinstated" (Said 1994: 330). The decisive step which must be taken is the step towards a political and social consciousness, towards a "spirit of cooperation continuing in the work of the parliament when it is established", as Alastair Dalton wrote in *The Scotsman* of 12 September 1997: 3.

The SNP will have to prove that it is more than a single-issue party. The zealots and fundamentalists in the party will have to develop a pragmatist approach after the rhetorics of the campaign. Tom Nairn talked as early as the 1970s of "SNPism" and argued that it was "an ideological stance even more favourable to egomania than the normal theatre of Westminster politics" (Edwards 1989: 171). The SNP wanted to be neither left-wing nor right-wing, but "stood for 'New Politics'" (Marr 1992: 135) which meant more or less blaming the English for everything. Nairn described SNP sectarianism as follows:

> Its rigidly idealized picture is of a pure 'Scotland' embodying certain mythic social and psychological virtues regardless of class, race or creed – the nation of undefiled 'Scots' who, once awakened to their virtuous inheritance, will cast aside the false garb of Englishness and vote pure Nationalist. (Nairn 1989: 172)

Nairn expressed more or less 20 years ago the same ideas as in the relevant articles, namely that the SNP has to change and has to accept new responsibilities and be ready for compromise and consensus politics. Christopher Harvie (1994: 218) talks of a "greater sense of interdependence" which should be created in Scotland as part of a new feeling of national self-awareness. Confrontational and conviction politics is out, no matter whether it is cloaked by the Union Jack or the Saltire.

What is demanded is nothing less but a new type of politician who will forge consensus beyond party factions, "the new consensus style of politics" (John Penman, *The Scotsman*, 9/13/1997: 5). There will have to be only patriotic Scots left who invest all their energy in the betterment of their country. "We need people with something to offer their country, rather than people who want something – a salary – out of its parliament" (Cochrane, *The Scotsman*, 9/12/1997: 4). Said strengthens the call for a new type of government:

we begin to sense that old authority cannot simply be replaced by new
authority, but that new alignments made across borders, types, nations, and
essences are rapidly coming into view, and it is those new alignments that now
provoke and challenge the fundamentally static notion of identity that has been
the core of cultural thought during the era of imperialism. (Said 1994: xxvii)

The history of Scottish parliaments and Scottish politicians is not very
promising, so scepticism is justified and also widespread, but then on 11
September 1997 the new Scotland came into being. The demand is a large one
for politicians, a rehabilitation of politics, as Iain MacWhirter puts it (*The
Scotsman*, 9/12/1997: 7). If the Scottish politicians do not live up to the high
standard asked from them, parliament will end up as "the ineffectual tartan
talking shop that its detractors have always forecast" (MacWhirter, *The
Scotsman*, 9/12/1997: 7). The English can no longer be blamed then. "There's
no us and them anymore – only the new millenium" (MacWhirter, *The Scotsman*, 9/13/1997: 19). If the high hopes placed in the new parliament are
disappointed, it will be time once again for the Scots to say with a pinch of
masochism: "We can't do it rightly" (Marr 1992: 15), what Harvie (1994:
197) calls the "'we were rubbish hangover'".

IV. The main feature of imperialist expansion was an accumulation of power
which has characterized the Anglo-Scottish relationship up to 1707 or, some
might argue, up to 1997. Said sees this accumulation of power as "a process
that accelerated during the twentieth century" (Said 1994: 406). The Conservative Party, during the time of Thatcher in particular, accumulated power in a
centralised government and the proliferation and infiltration of quangos.
Everything was concentrated in London, if not in Downing Street 10, the
"power-swollen centre" (Marr 1992: 2). When Andrew Hunter, Tory MP for
Basingstoke, reacted to the result of the referendum with the exclamation:
"The people have spoken, damn the people." (*The Scotsman*, 9/12/1997: 1),
this only proved that he had not understood the signs of the times. The
reaction against Conservative politics of centralisation is apparent in the
decentralisation process set into motion by Tony Blair and New Labour. Blair
and his party are in harmony with the idea of the European Union and the
principle of subsidiarity. Decentralisation is not only a British feature, it is
European. New Labour, in contrast to the SNP – who want independence –
and the Liberal Democrats – who opt for federalism –, sees the preservation
of the UK by means of devolving power. They are in agreement with Enoch
Powell who stated a long time ago: "power devolved is power retained"
(Marr 1992: 122). Strange bedfellows, but Powell as a rule knew what he was
talking about.

Decentralisation means not only the shifting of power from one institution to another, it is also linked with respect for different cultures and with the idea of multiple identities. This works within a multinational state such as the United Kingdom, but it also works in a confederation such as the European Union. Respect for foreign cultures is the basis for a peaceful co-existence and mutual understanding. The idea is to overcome exclusive national identities which are defined as contrast to some other. As Said puts it:

> No one can deny the persisting continuities of long traditions, sustained habitations, national languages, and cultural geographies, but there seems no reason except fear and prejudice to keep insisting on their separation and distinctiveness, as if that was all human life was about ... It is more rewarding – and more difficult – to think concretely and sympathetically, contrapunctally, about others than only about 'us'. But this means also not trying to rule others, not trying to classify them or put them in hierarchies, above all, not constantly reiterating how 'our' culture or country is number one (or *not* number one, for that matter). (Said 1994: 408)

The call for consensus politics after the referendum and in the future parliament is the decisive claim. If the Edinburgh MSPs will not be able to achieve this consensus, the result will be comparable to the situation after the death of Robert the Bruce. In 1375 John Barbour wrote his epic poem to remind his countrymen what they could achieve if they were united and not lost in clannish faction fighting. The Scottish politicians will have to prove whether they can live up to the hopes which were placed in them by the overwhelming vote 700 years after the Battle of Stirling Bridge, or whether it will all end in typical Celtic fragmentation and internecine squabbling, with Scotland falling once again into the role of a "subsidy alcoholic – poor and too dazed by wee nips of intervention to rebuild its own prosperity" (Marr 1992: 113). The English might then fly the St. George's Cross, relax, and wash their hands off it all.

References

Bannet, Eve Tavor (1993): *Postcultural theory. Critical theory after the Marxist paradigm.* London: Macmillan.

Barbour, John (1870; 1st 1375): *The Bruce.* Rev. Walter W. Skeat, ed. London: Kegan, Trench, Trübner & Co.

Bassnett, Susan, ed. (1997): *Studying British cultures.* London: Routledge.

Brogger, Fredrik Chr. (1992). *Culture, language, text; culture studies within the study of English as a foreign language.* Oslo: Scandinavian UP.

Corries, The (1991): *The flower of Scotland.* MOIMC 002. Moidart Music Group Ltd. 1.

Coupland, Sir Reginald (1954): *Welsh and Scottish nationalism. A study.* London: Collins.

Donaldson, William (1988): *The Jacobite song. Political myth and national identity.* Aberdeen: AUP.

Edwards, Owen Dudley, ed. (1989): *A claim of right for Scotland.* Edinburgh: Polygon.

Gallagher, Tom, ed. (1991): *Nationalism in the nineties.* Edinburgh: Polygon.

Gramich, Katie (1997): "Cymru or Wales?: Explorations in a divided sensibility". Susan Bassnett, ed. *Studying British cultures.* London: Routledge, 97-112.

Grawford, Robert (1997): "Dedefining Scotland". Susan Bassnett, ed. *Studying British cultures.* London: Routledge.

Gray, Ann/Jim McGuigan, eds. (1993): *Studying culture. An introductory reader.* London: Arnold.

Hall, Stuart, ed. (1997): *Representation: cultural representations and signifying practices.* London: Sage Publications.

Hanham, Harold John (1969): *Scottish nationalism.* London: faber & faber.

Harvie, Christopher (1994; 1st ed. 1977): *Scotland and nationalism. Scottish society and politics 1707-1994.* London: Routledge.

Macaulay, Lord (1986; 1st ed. 1848–61): *The history of England.* Hugh Tevor-Roper, ed. Harmondsworth: Pengiun..

Marr, Andrew (1992): *The battle for Scotland.* London: Penguin.

Massey, Doreen (1993): "A global sense of place". Ann Gray/Jim McGuigan, eds. *Studying culture. An introductory reader.* London: Arnold, 232-240.

McArthur, Collin (1998): "Scotland and the Braveheart effect". Jürgen Kramer/ Bernd Lenz/Gerd Stratmann, eds. *Journal for the Study of British Cultures,* Vol. 5, No. 1, 27-39.

Mitchison, Rosalind, ed. (1991): *Why Scottish history matters.* Edinburgh: Saltire Society.

Nairn, Tom (1981): *The break-up of Britain.* London: Verso.

Nairn, Tom (1989): "The timeless girn". Owen Dudley Edwards, ed. *A claim of right for Scotland.* Edinburgh: Polygon, 163-178.

Nederveen, Jan (1993): "Fictions of Europe". Ann Gray/Jim McGuigan, eds. *Studying culture. An introductory reader*. London: Arnold, 225-231.

Reid, Alastair (1991): "... And the Auld Enemy". Douglas Dunn, ed. *Scotland. An anthology*. London: Collins, 25.

Said, Edward W. (1994): *Culture and imperialism*. London: Vintage.

Said, Edward W. (1995): *Orientalism*. London: Penguin.

Shakespeare, William (1977): "The life of King Henry the Fifth". *The complete works of William Shakespeare*. London: Murray Sales & Service Co., 465-494.

Scott, Paul H. (1992): *Scotland in Europe. Dialogue with a sceptical friend*. Edinburgh: Canongate.

Stanzel, Franz K. (1997): *Europäer. Ein imagologischer Essay*. Heidelberg: Winter.

Gerhard Leitner *(Berlin)*

The Aboriginal contribution to mainstream Australian English. A corpus-based study[1]

0. Introduction

Transplanted languages undergo significant changes as they are adapted to new environments and functions. Their speakers bring with them accents and dialects that are not found in such proximity in the home country, and those 'inputs' will gradually mix and level out the differences so as to create a new variety that meets the demands of the **new** society. The need of the immigrants to interact with speakers of indigenous languages and with immigrants from non-English-speaking countries will increase the changes underway. All levels of the language will be affected, but most of all it is its lexis. Over time, a new texture will emerge that reflects the needs of the new society and its demographic and social base. It may, but need not, become an endocentric national variety, an epicentre.

Indigenous languages play a considerable role in the transformation of the language since it is through them that migrants 'grasp' the new environment and adapt to the new situation. American English has gained expressions from native American languages, South African English from Bantu languages, Indian English from Hindi, Sanskrit, Persian, and other Indian languages. New Zealand English has been enriched from Maori, and English in Australia has borrowed from Aboriginal languages. The intensity of contact is most pronounced in the early or *formative* period since it is then that the language situation of the new society is most unstable and amenable to change. As for

[1] I am grateful to the Australian Research Council and Monash University (Melbourne) for research fellowship in 1995-96 that made it possible for me to do the groundwork for this and other research. Thanks go to Fairfax, who publish *The Age*, the *Sydney Morning Herald*, and the *Business Review Weekly*; to Herald-Weekly Times, the publishing company of the *Herald-Sun*, and to Kathy Woolley (Fairfax) and Kim Lockwood (HWT) for helping me to get the data and for comments. Colin Yallop (Macquarie University) and Michael Clyne (Monash University) kindly commented on an earlier version of this paper. As ever, I am particularly grateful to Brian Taylor (University of Sydney) for his numerous comments and corrections on several versions. Thanks are extended to Astrid von Enzberg, my research assistant, for her diligent work on the data. Earlier work was done by my former assistant Inke Sieloff.

English in the Australian colonies the impact of Aboriginal languages was strongest at the time of the foundation of each of the colonies and has been decreasing since the early 20th century (Leitner 1999). But it has not by any means been confined to that period, as new needs arose to deal with the socio-political problems in ethnically diverse societies and as the indigenous population is expressing its position in society more self-confidently.

Of the many themes that transplanted languages give rise to, I will look at the interaction of English with indigenous languages in Australia and explore the use of Aboriginal expressions and concepts (in English) that refer to Aboriginal issues in several newspapers over a period of several years. True, newspapers are a special kind of data, but it can be argued that mass media develop a *public idiom*, a variety that establishes a link between the general language and that of the sources or domains reported (Leitner 1997). A study of this or any other segment of lexis in the language of the media will highlight important aspects of the sharedness of lexical items and, by implication, bear upon the study of both variation and of mass communication.

I will begin with a review of the early contact situation that led to borrowing and the formation of English expressions for Aboriginal concepts. I will touch upon the contemporary situation. Sections two and three will survey what is known about their current role, elaborate on methodological problems, the nature of the data, and the interpretation of the findings. Section four will turn to the analysis of the newspaper corpus and compare the findings with those of the awareness study of Aboriginal expressions in Leitner/Sieloff (1998) to see to what extent they support one another and what they imply about m(= mainstream)AusE in general. Along with the interpretation of quantitative data, I will reveal lexico-semantic and related developments that signal the level of integration of these expressions in mAusE. I will conclude with an assessment of the findings within the broader research context.

1. The socio-historical context of language contact and word creation

While the medium-term effects of contact with indigenous Australians are nothing that modern Australia is proud of (Walsh/Yallop 1993; Troy 1993; Harris 1986), Arthur Phillip's brief was to establish amicability, based on domination, when he set foot on the Fifth Continent in 1788 "to endeavour by every possible means to open an intercourse with the natives, and to conciliate their affections, enjoining all our subjects to live in amity and kindness with them" (*Historical records of Australia*, Series I. Volume I. 1788-1796: 12; abbreviated as HRA henceforth). When the First Fleet entered Botany Bay,

Phillip went straight to the task of opening "an intercourse". Avoiding the large number of Aborigines that were watching them on one side, he opted for the less crowded other side:

> At last an officer in the boat made signs of a want of water, which was judged would indicate his wish of landing. The natives directly comprehended what he wanted, and pointed to a spot where water could be procured ... The Indians, though timorous, shewed no signs of resentment at the Governor's going on shore; an interview commenced, in which the conduct of both parties pleased each other so much, that the strangers returned to their ships with a much better opinion of the natives than they had landed with ... (Senior Officer Watkin Tench; quoted from Troy 1993: 33)

Note the ulterior motive behind the gestures. There was no need for water, but a desire to land and to make known the true intention, in the words of Tench, "to take possession of his [i.e. the King's, GL] new territory, and bring about an intercourse between its old and new masters" (from Troy 1993: 33). Contact began on a friendly level with each party feeling reasonably surprised at the friendliness of the other. The role of language was minimal but even during an early 'conference' the 'Indians', as Aborigines were sometimes called, used the *whurra*, a word that Tench takes to mean 'begone': "After nearly an hour's conversation by signs and gestures, they repeated several times the word *whurra*, which signifies begone, and walked away from us to the head of the bay" (quoted from Troy 1993: 33).

'Real' language was out of the question at that stage, the interaction was not intensive enough and remained on a rudimentary level. Governor Phillip turned to Captain Cook's glossary, which contained such words as *kangaroo*, *quoll* 'native cat', *bama* 'an Aborigine', and *boobook* 'owl'. They had been collected during Cook's stay at Endeavour River, near Cooktown in North Queensland, where Guugu Yimidhir was used. But Phillip had landed in the Dharuk-speaking region of Botany Bay. In February 1790 he reported to Lord Sydney that only two words in Cook's glossary were understood: "It is remarkable that of all the words given in the vocabulary by Captain Cook there are only two we have heard the natives make use of" (HRA 1788-1796: 161).

To fulfil the King's brief and reconcile the natives to their fate, a common language became ever more urgent, especially since the aggression by and against indigenous Australians had started to escalate. Late in May 1788, two men had been murdered by the Aborigines: "This was a very unfortunate circumstance, and the more, as it will be impossible to discover the people who committed the murder, and I am still persuaded that the natives were not the aggressors" (HRA 1788-1796: 48). Indeed Phillip later found that the murder of an Aborigine and the wounding of several others may have been the cause of that attack. Aborigines tended to respond in kind if there was a chance to. "The natives, though very friendly, whenever they are met by two or three people who are armed, still attack any of the convicts when they meet them in the woods", writes Arthur Phillip on September 28, 1788 (HRA 1788 -1796: 76). And yet, while they helped those who were 'lost in the woods' and guided the intruders to waterholes, they tended to keep at a distance. "The natives still refuse to come among us", Phillip laments in October 1788, and doubts

> whether it will be possible to get any of those people to remain with us, in order to get their language, without using force; they see no advantage that can arise from us that may make amends for the loss of that part of the harbour in which we occasionally employ the boats in fishing. (HRA 1788-1796: 96)

The natives saw no benefit in developing communication to a level that required a common language and preferred the intruders to *begone*, as Phillip writes to Lord Sydney: "they were friendly, but, as I have ever found them, since they find we intend to remain, they appeared best pleased when we were leaving them, though I gave them many useful articles" (HRA 1788-1796: 76).

As for the intruders the situation was different. It was not only the royal brief that was to be fulfilled, it was the need to survive in and, ultimately, exploit the new geo-physical and social environment. Eventually, Phillip felt forced to turn to kidnapping in December 1788, a method well-known from the slave trade:

> Not succeeding in my endeavours to persuade some of the natives to come and live with us, I ordered one to be taken by force, which was what I would gladly have avoided, as I know it must alarm them; but not a native had come near the settlement for many months, and it was absolutely necessary that we should attain their language, or teach them ours. (HRA 1788-1796: 145)

Despite initial problems, kidnapping produced the expected results. In 1790 Bennelong was captured, and he was eager and able to learn English. He is credited with an important role in interethnic communication. Phillip soon wrote to Sydney explaining what he had learnt about the customs and manners of Aborigines. He elaborates on tribal patterns, the naming of tribes, food collection, or cognitive abilities, such as counting. But while Bennelong may have acquired English, it seems unlikely the members of his and of other tribes did. As Troy and others have observed, what really developed was a jargon, an incipient New South Wales pidgin, that drew on both English and indigenous languages. It became the vehicle by which words could now travel either way, from indigenous languages into English and from there into indigenous languages. Aborigines often acquired words from other Aboriginal languages in the erroneous belief they were English, such as *gin* 'Aboriginal woman' or *kangaroo*. Borrowing into English illustrates the other direction, as words like *gunyah* 'temporary hut' show. *Jumbuck* 'young sheep' comes, like some others, from the pidgin English. Slowly Aboriginal words replaced descriptions of objects or practices that had been used before, as Phillip's correspondence with Lord Sydney illustrates at various places:

> no country can be more difficult to penetrate into than this is, tho' we always found *pools of water that had remained after the rainy season* (HRA 1788-1796: 30)

> In this journey I was surprized to find *temporary huts* made by the natives far inland, where they must depend solely on animals for food ... These *huts consist of only a single piece of bark*, about eleven feet in length, and from four to six feet in breath [*sic*!] (HRA 1788-1796: 30)

> they [the Aborigines, GL] wait in their *temporary huts* (HRA 1788-1796: 30)

One recognises the later loans, *billabong* and *gunyah*, respectively, which now changed the 'mental dictionary' of the varieties of English transplanted and introduced lexical expressions for the new world. Such change can be identified in other areas and some illustrations from the *Historical records of Australia* make the point:

> and I believe their numbers [of Aborigines, GL] in these *woods* must be small. (HRA 1788-1796)

> A soldier has been lately missing, who, I suppose, lost his way in the *woods* (HRA 1788-1796)

> The barracks ... will be covered with shingles, which we now make from a *tree like the pine-tree in appearance, the wood resembling the English oak.* (HRA 1788-1796)

Woods for 'bush' and the description of the tree soon to be called *she-oak*, is a possible loan from Irish Gaelic, as Taylor (1992) has argued.

There is no historical study of how invaders and settlers chose between different strategies to extend and adapt their lexicon. On the basis of the evidence from the *Historical records of Australia*, Dixon et al. (1990), and Ramson (1966) it looks as if paraphrase was a dominant early solution, followed by loaning. Word creation and semantic shift may be more prominent today since they use English lexis and manifest a greater degree of transparency. But gradually, the whole gamut of lexical solutions to problems that have arisen in interethnic contact and to the naming of the aspects of the new world must have been used, cf. table 1:

Table 1: Formal classification of Aboriginal expressions and concepts

Loans from indigenous languages	Loans from pidgins	Hybrids	Loan translation	English expression
corroboree	*jumbuck*	*koala bear*	*to point the bone at sb*	*outstation*
boomerang	*baal*	*coolibah tree*	*dreaming*	*bark painting*
dingo	*yabber*	*gin jockey*	*walkabout*	*native dog*

Despite the lack of precise historical information, it is obvious that words were borrowed from different languages for much the same referents. As other strategies, such as concept formation in English, could also be employed for those referents, a high level of *overlexicalisation* resulted. Thus, both *warrigal* and *dingo* refer to the 'native dog', which is itself a common expression, although the one stands for the 'wild dog', the other for the 'domesticated' animal in indigenous languages. The small, green parrot is called *budgerigar, lovebird, shell parrot, zebra parrot* and *warbling grass parakeet. Budgie* signals the positive connotations that are associated with this bird. Overlexicalisation was minimised when some expressions were eventually discarded, or became or remained regionally restricted. A few examples:

Table 2: Some regionally restricted words (based on Dixon et al. 1990)

Word	Regional currency	Paraphrase of meaning
budgeree	Australian pidgin	good, fine (colloquial)
cooee	esp. in the bush	a prolonged clear call, used in the bush to attract attention
Koori	NSW and esp. Vic.	name for Aborigines in south–east Australia
kylie	chiefly WA	a boomerang with particular kind of shape
mardo	chiefly WA	a yellow–footed marsupial mouse
pinkie	SA	a rabbit–eared mammal living in drier parts of Australia
nyunga	south–west of WA	name for Aborigines in south–west Australia
yolnu	north–eastern Arnhem Land	name for Aborigines in north–west Australia

The contact with indigenous Australians over more than two hundred years has led to over four hundred loan words, loan translations, hybrids, and English expressions. As the whole of the continent was explored, the need for loans or hybrids decreased but did not subside entirely, as recent loans like *Koori* 'south-eastern Aborigine' show. Occasionally, one finds in the press a new or old, but little used, indigenous word:

(1) We have had to use our own form of punishment to keep them in line. We've belted the bastards with a big *nulla-nulla*. (*The Age*, 2/27/1995, section Features)

But *nulla-nulla*, which is a club for belting, formerly used in inter-tribal strife, occurs as part of a quote from an Aborigine. In general, there has been a definite shift to the use or coinage of concepts in English to refer to Aboriginal issues in culture, politics, religion, etc. For some loans there are hybrids, such as *koala bear, dilly bag*, that are more transparent than the loan on its own.

2. Methodological aspects of the study of the currency of Aboriginal expressions

Anyone interested in the use of Aboriginal words and concepts in **current mAusE** faces the problem of searching for the needle in the haystack. Hundreds of newspaper articles or hours of broadcasting and of natural conversation may not reveal a single expression, if one discounts the few established ones like *koala, galah, kangaroo*, or others, like *dreaming, bark painting*, or *didgeridoo*, that occur frequently in specialised contexts. Articles like the following are rare. It reports on the conflict between mining and the preservation of Aboriginal culture. It uses Aboriginal expressions (see italics) and mixes mAusE with Aboriginal English (see both underlining and italics):

(2) *Dreamtime* pigeon stalls mining giant's plans
In the *Dreamtime*, an Aboriginal hunter in what is now South Australia went to catch a flock of bronzewing pigeons but one, Marnpi, escaped. The hunter threw his *boomerang* at the bird and injured it – but it continued to fly north ... its blood stained the ground ... Those 'bloodstains' of the *Aboriginal Dreamtime story* are now mineral deposits ... At Broken Hill, however, the clash of *Aboriginal culture* and 20th century mineral exploration has caused a 12-month stand-off between the Broken Hill *Aboriginal Land Council* and the zinc mining and smelting company Pasminco Limited ...
"It's not just the *Aboriginal people* who don't want the Pinnacles area mined, a lot of local people – *white fellas* – don't either", an *Aboriginal elder*, ..., Mr.

Badger Bates, said yesterday. "When we get up and say what *the old people*
told us, we *just been called* [omission of *have*, GL] *liars and everything*," Mr.
Bates said. "Twelve months ago the National Parks people got an anthro-
pologist in to talk to all the *Aboriginal people* ... and *he done* [use of *done*
for 'did'; similar to broad mAusE, GL] *a big report* ... None of us have seen
this report – ... and *old Aboriginal people just got* [omission of *have*, GL] to
sit down and *be called liars* the whole time." (*The Australian*, 7/25/1995,
section News)

Without any evidence on currency, Dixon et al. (1990) believe that Aboriginal
loans, loan translations, and hybrids are the most characteristic feature of
mAusE. The problem of currency, in use and awareness, is a neglected field,
although decisions on which expressions should be included or excluded from
dictionaries are routinely made by lexicographers. There are only two studies
on the issue of awareness or of what native speakers of mAusE know
(Ramson 1964; Leitner/Sieloff 1998). Both conclude that Aboriginal expressions are not widely known, a conclusion that, incidentally, applies to
other Australianisms.

Leitner/Sieloff (1998) find a mere ten of eighty-eight expressions to be
'universally known': *Abo, barramundi, billabong, blackfella, bunyip, dingo,
galah, kookaburra, wallaby* and *wombat.* Eleven items, viz. *Aboriginal beliefs, bark painting, brolga, coolabah* (*tree*), *corroboree, jumbuck, Koori, to
point the bone at, walkabout,* and *to yabber* were assigned correct meanings
by between 50 and 75 per cent of respondents. The majority has to be considered 'unknown', a category that includes *galah session, gibber, mallee* or
outstation. Neither that study, nor Ramson (1964) permit sweeping general-
isations. They are not representative of a wide enough range of speakers and
have inherent weaknesses in eliciting meaning, but they reflect trends that can
be confirmed by informal searches and the attitudes elicited from native
speakers. The results in the Leitner/Sieloff awareness study were arrived at by
self-reports in a decontextualised, somewhat artificial situation. Respondents
were asked to describe the meaning of an expression with a few hints as to
what a definition should look like. Answers required a reasonable ability to
define lexical meaning and may not reveal what speakers could have inferred
from contextualised expressions, such as example (1) above. To find out more
about speaker's actual competence, one could use a questionnaire where
expressions occur in an authentic context, permitting closed multiple choice or
free answers. Or one could study **real** language or corpora. Though a lot
speaks for the first alternative, it has its drawbacks. It may fail to elicit recent
meanings and uses of some item, witness *galah* 'common small cockatoo' and

'fool; simpleton'.[2] Also, with lexical items as infrequent as most of these are, it is not easy to find authentic samples. And, as comprehension may be related to age, interest, or other factors, it would be hard to design an 'all-purpose' questionnaire. The questionnaire approach, logically, presupposes the other alternative, the study of authentic uses in corpora. Unfortunately, such corpora are not available though there are a few computerised ones for linguistic analysis. There is an Australian replica of the two one-million word corpora each of British and American English (the so-called Lancaster-Oslo-Bergen Corpus of British and the Brown Corpus of American English). But the Australian corpus is not accessible and, like its models, it is not representative, given the small size, and outdated since data were collected before 1961.[3] A new one-million word corpus, a component of the *International Corpus of English* (ICE), will soon be ready for distribution, but again lacks the size for this segment of the lexicon and excludes texts where one would expect these items to be used, such as anthropological writings or lectures on ethnic affairs. Corpora of private or public spoken mAusE are non-existent. Only the Australian component of ICE will have 500,000 words of spoken mAusE (Peters 1987). With such a lack of computerised data, that alternative is not easy either. I, therefore, decided to use a specific kind of public, printed data, that of newspapers. But what is the relationship of the language of newspapers with the language in general? That is the question of the next section.

3. The *public idiom* of mass media

Clearly, it is not identical with written, non-public language or the printed language elsewhere. There is, and remains, a tension between newspaper language and the common, socially shared language used elsewhere, as this quote explains:

> Media are communication domains with specific communicative structures which are the cause of, broadly speaking, content becoming *public*, in other words becoming accessible as public knowledge and for public debate. The discourse in which content is couched has been defined as a *public idiom* (Hall 1978). It is not, and cannot be, homogeneous. What is more, each medium creates its own version. To quote from Hall: "The language employed will thus

---

[2] Definitions in single quotations are *verbatim* from the *Macquarie dictionary* (1997); definitions in double quotation marks are my own.

[3] It was compiled at Macquarie University, Sydney (Peters 1987). There is also a 100,000 word 'Melbourne-Surrey' corpus of Australian newspapers, which is distributed through ICAME, which is far too small for studies like this one.

be the newspaper's own version of the language of the public to whom it is principally addressed." (emph. in original; Leitner 1997:189)

Put differently, the function of the media consists in bridging an information gap between their sources and their readership. As they report and comment on any domain whatsoever, if there is anything that should be made public, they have to draw on the language of their sources, the *registers* of the reported domains. But since they address their message to a wide public, they have to rely on the linguistic resources of their readers. There is a third aspect, *viz.* the fact that each media has to produce a recognisable product. Media language, then, straddles the publicly known, general language, that of reported domains, and the media's own 'idiolect'. The *public idiom* is a compromise; it can never be homogeneous and it is always changing.

The notion *public* does not, of course, imply that every reader will be able to understand every article, far from it. There are differential competences and not overlapping interests. But *public* does mean that the readers informed in a particular segment of the reported domains will, with a high degree of plausibility, have access to the linguistic resources and the social background necessary for understanding. If they do not have that chance, the media have failed in their task. A few examples may be helpful at this point. Media report on such domains as hi-tech, business, arts, sports, or law. Each domain has its register, and if media are to be successful in making content public, they will have to translate these registers into a publicly accessible version without affecting content. They must balance out various pulls between the language of the source and the audience. Anyone who has watched or read newspaper reports on cricket, rugby, ski jumping, polo, or Australian Rules Football without being an addict will know what I mean. Comprehension is possible only if a sufficient amount of background is shared by the readers and the paper and if readers have had an experience with the technical register. If that cannot be taken for granted, media will aid comprehension with the provision of adequate background and by paraphrasing, if not translating, the terminology. In other words, audience needs are a powerful factor in shaping the public idiom.

To return to the main issue, the notion of public idiom in the Australian press. We will have to identify the items from the Aboriginal segment that are used. But can we infer from actual occurrence that they qualify as publicly shared? It looks as if we cannot. Often, highly technical terms from specific, reported domains do figure in the media's language. They are then translated or paraphrased for the benefit of the less informed audience to ensure comprehension. *Nulla-nulla* in (1) above is a case in point. The example shows that context, such as collocations, etc., give clues to at least partial understanding. Here are some further examples:

(3) The forest is also home to a population of *bobucks*, a cousin of the brushtail possum – the lowest-altitude population known for this species in Victoria. (*Herald-Sun*, 5/20/1995, section News)

(4) Dallas Albert Hill of Neurum, near Woodford, northwest of Brisbane, faces two charges of knowingly being concerned in the export of galahs, *Major Mitchell cockatoos* and *Gang Gang cockatoos.* (*The Australian*, 25/1995, section News)

Both deal with fauna. But while (3) paraphrases *bobuck*, (4) uses the terms as such, the hybrids indicate the general meaning. There are many words in the lexical segment studied here that are treated that way, such as the words for the different kinds of kangaroo, e.g. *bettong, potoroo, nabarlek, pademelon, quokka*, or hybrids like *nailtail wallaroo*, but also *Koori* or *Nunga* (see below). The word *lubra* is a derogatory, insulting word, but can also have a specific technical meaning to refer to an Aboriginal woman or wife. (It is not as heavily loaded as *gin*, however.)

(5) Biami, the most powerful of these ancestral beings, sent his *lubra* down from the high country to dig for food on the flat and waterless plain. He also sent his giant snake (the Rainbow Serpent) to keep an eye on her. She walked for many miles, dragging her digging stick behind her. (*The Age*, 4/15/1995, section Travel Age)

In other words, we will find in the public idom words that are by no means 'public', but are necessary because of the content of the article. They need, and often receive, explanatory context. In contrast, there are words that may be widely known but are not used, or naturally usable, in the public idiom, such as insults and swear words. They may become usable when they are legitimated in one way or another.

(6) Miranda was called a *f...g boong*. (*The Age*, 5/1/1994, section News)

(7) And the educated do not escape that easily. A group of Aboriginal students at Melbourne University is considering taking legal action against the university alleging discrimination, not for being called names but for the way their affairs are administered. "I'd rather be called a *boong* than what's going on here," says Mr. Gary Murray, spokesman for the Yuroke Students Aboriginal Corporation (*The Age*, 5/14/1995, section News)

(8) "*Boong ... Abo ... Coon ...* Go back to your own country ... Have another flagon," they said. (*The Age*, 9/3/1995, section News)

(9) By sheer luck, debate on the Racial Hatred Bill was deferred again in the Senate. Had the timing been different ... several million of us would be guilty of incitement to racial hatred – which under the proposed act carries a severe

jail term ... Into the compound with the rest of us *racist ocker dingoes*.
(*Sunday Herald-Sun*, 06/25/1995, section News)

It is interesting to observe the different treatment of *fucking* and *boong* in (6).
Both are heavily loaded swear words (Taylor 1995). And yet, *boong* and *coon*
in (8) seem to be less loaded than *fucking*; it may be worth noting here that
Miranda was from Sri Lanka, but dark skinned. Here is a similar example that
does not use Aboriginal expressions:

(10) No one had heard of pasta: mutton was fine if you smothered it with
enough pickles to kill the taste. Only *deros* drank wine. *Deros* were to be distinguished from the first wave of migrants, who were called *reffos*, and other
things. (*The Age*, 8/13/1995, section Coming Home)

Deros 'down and outs' drank wine, but southern European migrants, the
refos, did too, hence the combination of these words. But there were other
words for migrants, which are unprintable, like *fucking*. There are then words
that remain outside the style range of a paper for their association with the
very informal end of the spectrum or slang even. However, the Australian
press has a distinct bias for a high level of informality and the use of Australianisms, as (9) has shown. A few more illustrations:

(11) "[... suspended from the ceiling to keep it from the ants ...] Well, I
thought of *going* (fast) *like a Bondi tram*, and *having a head like a Mallee
root* (being very ugly). Any other offerings?" (glosses in original; *The Age*,
2/23/1995, section Today)

(12) Then, after much praiseworthy *brouhahaing* from the boys, he [= the
mythical Barbecue Man or Australian, GL] turns on the gas. (*Herald-Sun*,
9/16/1994, section Features)

Both articles re-create traditional aspects of Australian life. But an equivalent
bias towards what Seal (1999) calls the *Lingo* in Australia does not seem to be
found anywhere else in the supra-regional press in other English-speaking
countries. The notion of public idiom in Australia is wider, more inclusive,
more tolerant of the Lingo. It creates and reinforces a sense of Australianness
that must astonish a European reader not accustomed to this linguistic chau-
vinism. To quote from Seal:

> *The Lingo* [referring to the title of the book, G.L.] is about the development
> and power of that Australian vernacular ... It is also a celebration – though not
> an uncritical one – of the colour, cleverness and sheer vitality of the many
> linguistic forms that make up our Lingo. These include slang, insults, derog-
> ations, colloquialisms, similes and traditional wisdom, rhyming slang, the
> naming of places, houses, body parts, nicknames, BARRACKING, folk names

for flora, fauna and natural features, and many other informal uses of language. (capitalisation in the original; 1999: viii)

Note that the Lingo includes onomastics, which is normally outside of linguistics proper. Seal then turns to the socio-ideological function of the Lingo:

> Our Lingo carries and perpetuates prejudices of race, ethnicity, gender, and belief. It is a mire of malevolence and insult of an especially creative kind and it carries a large baggage of negativity, paranoia, and cultural loathing. It also carries our more cherished ideals of egalitarianism, sympathy for the BATTLER and the persistent yearning for a FAIR GO. Always it is witty, colourful, and playful, often most so when most abrasive. (capitalisation in the original; 1999: viii-ix)

As (9) implies, a Racial Hatred Bill would not only target ephemeral and easily eradicable aspects of language use, it would in fact be an attack on the ideological underpinning of the Lingo itself. And as that example (and others in section 4.1 below) shows, the aggressive, racist connotations are mitigated, legitimated even by context and the self-referential use. This analysis of the print media's public idiom will, then, have to address a wide range of linguistic issues associated with the Aboriginal segment of the lexis of mAusE. It will help to design more authentic elicitation techniques that are to explore what respondents know about such expressions and if and how they would use them in the general language.

4. The corpus and aspects of its analysis

I will now turn to a description of the corpus, its analysis and interpretation.

4.0 Corpus design

For several reasons, then, I decided to study the public idiom. I chose three daily newspapers over a period of four years and a specialised weekly magazine for a two-year period to see if usage differs between the general and the special interest press. For practical reasons I confined myself to papers available on CD-ROM: *The Age* (A), the *Herald-Sun* (HSu) (both from Melbourne), the *Sydney Morning Herald* (SMH), and the *Business Review Weekly* (BRW). Since *The Australian*, the only explicitly national daily, is not available on CD-ROM, while it is on the web, I excluded it. The software delivered with the CD-ROMs does not permit the counting of words or articles so that the exact size of a year's output is unknown. However, in a personal note Kathy Woolley (Fairfax) informs me of the number of articles in *The Age* and the *Sydney Morning Herald* per year and of the average length of articles by number of words per article. That permits reasonable estimates

of the overall size of the corpus. Over the four years studied, there were
451,336 articles and, given an average of 300 words per article, the total
number of words is around 135,400,800. If these figures apply to the *Herald-
Sun* as well, one would expect there to be another 60,000,000 words. The
Business Review Weekly with its 52-odd editions may have more than 20
million words. The total corpus will be well over 200 million words. And yet,
lacking precise figures or information on all word forms or lexemes, it is
impossible to make quantified comparisons. However, it is obvious that this
medium-term database is much larger than any that has been used before. It
should reveal what is stable in the public idiom and 'iron out' the bias introduced by day-to-day reporting. (We will see that this is not the case.) In order
to maintain a continuity of research and to have the opportunity to compare
the findings with Leitner/Sieloff (1998), I used the same expressions that were
studied there. Table 3 lists those features of the newspapers that are most
relevant for an understanding of this study:

Table 3: Some features of the papers selected

Titles	Circulation	Coverage	Status	Frequency	Approach	Year's used
Age	regional (Victoria)	general	broadsheet	Mon–Sun	formal-to-popular	1994–97
SMH	regional (NSW)	general	broadsheet	Mon–Sat	formal-to-popular	1994–97
HSu	regional (Victoria)	general	tabloid	Mon–Sun	popular (mainly)	1994–97
BRW	national	business	broadsheet	weekly	formal	1996–97

The characteristics must not be taken too literally. *The Age*, the *Herald-Sun*,
and the *Sydney Morning Herald* are sold across the nation, though the readership will diminish as one moves from Victoria or NSW into the States that
have their own state press.[4] But readers interested in national issues also turn
to *The Australian*. The distinction between tabloid and quality and the implied

---

[4]   The press situation is poor in all States and Territories. Queensland, for instance, has
the *Courier-Mail*, South Australia the *Adelaide Advertiser*, Western Australia the *West
Australian*. In Tasmania there is *The Hobart Mercury*, in the ACT there is the
Canberra Times. As for regional papers, one should mention the *Launceston Examiner*
in Launceston, Tasmania. The *Sydney Morning Herald* appears from Monday to
Saturday, the *Sun Herald* (from the same publisher) on Sundays. There is very little
press competition and some of the papers just listed are really rather provincial. The
papers used here, as well as *The Australian*, are the important papers nationwide.

relationship profiles are also less pronounced than in Britain. With the lack of diversity in the press and the domination of television, tabloids are widely read by the moneyed and the educated. 'Quality' papers have to take an approach that does not deviate entirely from the popular one of tabloids. The leaning towards the Lingo and traditional Australian content might well be a reflection of this, amongst other things. One would assume that there are fewer differences between the print media's idiom and the general language. The criteria in table 3, then, reflect Australian tendencies that must not be given a simple 'European' interpretation.

The corpus was searched for the occurrences of eighty-five expressions. The important ones are those that reflect an Aboriginal sense or can be related to, or derived from, it. They indicate the level of integration into the public idiom and/or into mAusE. The following cases were excluded:

(i) Occurrences of expressions as proper names. In fact, twenty-five items occurred also as proper names. To give a few examples: *jumbuck* (dairy product), *walkabout* (travel agency, film title, etc.), *dreaming* (festival title), *billabong* (surfwear company), *mallee* (regional name), *brolga* (airline), *lubra* (name of a rose), *warrigal* (place and street name), *waddy* (personal name), *dingo* (music band name; sports team; personal name), *kookaburra* (newspaper section; hockey team), *corroboree* (ballet name), *wallaby* (rugby team), *Koorie* (institutional name), *blackfella* (film title), *bunyip* (place name). An onomastic study of Aboriginal expressions would be interesting for its own sake, since they play such an important role in naming and as a constitutive part of the Lingo (see quote from Seal (1999) above). (ii) Occurrences of items in non-Aboriginal senses or ones that cannot be related to such a sense, such as *gin* for the drink, *outstation* as an outlying building on a station, or *women's business* as a mere genitive construction.

Most decisions were straightforward but there were some problematic cases. *Women's business*, for instance, is used in two constructions instanced in *women's business hoax* "women's business is a hoax", and *women's business lunches* "business lunches for women". The first type can have several senses: (i) "tasks or interests specific to, or claimable by, women, e.g. in Western-style societies", (ii) "the Aboriginal mythology to do with the limitation of knowledge to women", and (iii) a merger of the two that could be paraphrased as "specific types of important skills, knowledge reserved to women", as in the following examples:

(13) The council aims to develop and lobby on policy initiatives, develop and disseminate information, encourage *women's business* skills and work with global networks. (*Herald-Sun*, 7/11/95, section News)

(14) Proponents of *"women's business"* were asking us to accept that traditions "crucial for the reproduction of the Ngarrindjeri people" had completely escaped the notice of some of our most distinguished anthropologists. (*Herald-Sun*, 12/22/1995, section News)

(15) Don't think this secret *women's business* of Carmen Demidenko is a coincidence. These controversies over Carmen Lawrence, Helen (ex-Demidenko) Darville and the Hindmarsh Island *women's business* are connected in a disturbing way. In each case we have people who are held up as symbols of our new political orthodoxy – affirmative action, land rights, multiculturalism. (*Herald-Sun*, 08/29/1995, section News)

Senses (ii) and (iii) are relevant, (i) is not. *Blackfellow* is similar since it can refer to dark-skinned persons in general, not just to Aborigines. Some cases, then, required sense counts.

4.1 Frequency patterns

To turn to the quantitative findings and their interpretation. Overall frequencies are in table 4; they are ordered from most to least frequent expressions: [5]

Table 4: Totals of *The Age, Herald-Sun, Sydney Morning Herald* from 1994 to 1997

Rank	Age, HSu, SMH	Sum	Rank	Age, HSu, SMH	Sum
1	*Koori*	2,345	12	*walkabout*	342
2	*land rights*	1,167	13	*billabong*	334
3	*dingo*	1,161	14	*mallee*	295
4	*wallaby*	875	15	*coroborree*	204
5	*wombat*	832	16	*bark painting*	202
6	*barramundi*	613	17	*kangaroo court*	140
7	*dreaming*	464	18	*Abo*	120
8	*kookaburra*	441	19	*kangaroo route*	111
9	*traditional owners*	437	20	*bunyip*	108
10	*galah*	421	21	*mulga*	103
11	*women's business*	405	22	*bung*	98

---

[5]   To simplify the tables only one grammatical form, the singular noun or infinitive verb form, and one spelling are used; clippings and other forms are not mentioned. It would be interesting to study, for instance, frequencies and contexts of *kooka* for *kookaburra*, *budgie* or *budgerigar*, etc. Only the clipped form *Abo* was counted, since it is an offensive word, but the word *Aborigine* was not studied. The following expressions and clippings were not searched: *blackfellow*, *budgie*, *roo*, and *kanga*.

Table 4 continued

Rank	Age, HSu, SMH	Sum	Rank	Age, HSu, SMH	Sum
23	*blackfella*	94	55	*clever man*	1
24	*brolga*	86	56	*borak*	1
25	*outstation*	80	57	*baal*	1
26	*yolngu*	72	58	*yungan*	0
27	*marron*	65	59	*weet-weet*	0
28	*Aboriginal beliefs*	58	60	*wallaby jack*	0
29	*coolie*	53	61	*be a real dingo*	0
30	*coolabah (tree)*	47	62	*patter*	0
31	*boong*	43	63	*mulga wire*	0
32	*gibber*	32	64	*mulga mafia*	0
33	*jumbuck*	28	65	*mulga madness*	0
34	*paddymelon*	27	66	*marloo*	0
35	*to point the bone*	20	67	*kylie*	0
36	*wobbegong*	13	68	*koonac*	0
37	*tammar*	12	69	*kangaroo jack*	0
38	*gidgee*	11	70	*gunyang*	0
39	*dilly*	11	71	*gunyah*	0
40	*willy-willy*	9	72	*gin jockey*	0
41	*Nunga*	6	73	*gin*	0
42	*lubra*	6	74	*gilgic*	0
43	*waddy*	5	75	*dingo stiffener*	0
44	*to yabber (away)*	5	76	*bungarra*	0
45	*wonga-wonga vine*	4	77	*bumble tree*	0
46	*warrigal*	4	78	*bullan-bullan*	0
47	*kangaroo apple*	4	79	*boree shrub*	0
48	*bobuck*	4	80	*bora circle*	0
49	*bindi-eye*	3	81	*bondi*	0
50	*mungo*	2	82	*black velvet*	0
51	*galah session*	2	83	*bingy*	0
52	*mia-mia*	1	84	*billabonger*	0
53	*dillon bush*	1	85	*ballart*	0
54	*conkerberry*	1			

The grand total of all occurrences is 12,030. As the exact size of the corpus is unknown, an objective base-line for currency in the public idiom is difficult to define, but one might think, given the very large corpus and the specialised lexical expressions, that around fifty occurrences would be a mark of currency. Of the eighty-five expressions, only twenty-one occur more than one hundred times in four years. Another eight occur between one hundred and fifty times, ten at least ten times, and eighteen more only once or twice. If we confine attention to loans and discount the twelve English expressions and loan translations, we are left with twenty-eight items, above the ten-token mark out of the seventy in the list. That adds up to fifty-seven, which is very few indeed. It would seem that a study of the entire word list in Dixon et al. (1990) will not increase the total number of expressions above the baseline of fifty substantially (though it would reveal information on more items).[6]

A comparison of table 4 with the 'awareness level' (AL), Leitner/Sieloff (1998), cf. the first column in table 5, reveals that the findings do not match entirely, though they overlap reasonably well. The twenty-one expressions above the one hundred mark include nine of the 'universally known' items, with the exception of *blackfellow* in rank twenty-three. Another five are in the 50+ range, i.e. *Koori, land rights, walkabout, corroboree,* and *bark painting.* But five rank low in awareness, i.e. *women's business, dreaming, traditional owners, mallee,* and *kangaroo court* with only 24+. And *mulga* and *kangaroo route* are in the low 10+ range. There is a pronounced shift to lesser known expressions from rank fourteen in table 4. A look further down the table is also instructive. The 50+ level is found as far down as rank forty-four. While 'fully unknown' items (0 and 1+) tend to correspond to the ones in table 4 that are used barely or not at all, a few are used, i.e. *yolngu, marron, coolie,* and *tammar.* In contrast, a few items with 24+ are not used at all, e.g. *boree shrub, bumble tree, gin,* and *that man's a real dingo.*

Table 5: Aboriginal expressions studies with awareness level

AL	Words	Semantic paraphrase
75+	*Abo*	an Aborigine (derogative)
50+	*Aboriginal beliefs*	religious beliefs about dreamtime
0	*baal*	no, not
0	*ballart*	several kinds of shrub with cherry-like fruits
50+	*bark painting*	Aboriginal art of painting on bark
75+	*barramundi*	a northern Australian fish
75+	*billabong*	a waterhole
10+	*billabonger*	a swagman
24+	*bindi–eye*	several kinds of plants with barbed fruits
0	*bingy*	an Aborigine (obsolete)

---

[6] Of course, some well-known items not studied here would figure high, such as *kangaroo, koala, boomerang* or *didgeridoo.*

Table 5 continued

AL	Words	Semantic paraphrase
1+	black velvet	an Aboriginal woman as the focus of a white man's sexual desires
75+	blackfella	a black man; Aborigine
0	bobuck	a kind of owl
1+	bondi	a heavy club with knob on one end
24+	boong	an Aborigine (derogative)
1+	bora circle	place where initiation ceremony is held
1+	borak	nonsense, rubbish
24+	boree shrub	a kind of acacia plant
50+	brolga	a kind of crane
0	bullan–bullan	a kind of lyre–bird
24+	bumble tree	several kinds of shrubs bearing wild orange fruits
10+	bung	dead; broken, failed
0	bungarra	the sand goanna
75+	bunyip	a mythical animal
10+	clever man	an Aborigine with special skills in medicine
10+	conkerberry	a small shrub with edible fruits
50+	coolabah (tree)	several kinds of eucalyptus trees
1+	coolie	husband of an Aboriginal wife
50+	coroborree	a dance ceremony
10+	dillon bush	a salt-tolerant plant
10+	dilly	a bag or basket from woven grass etc.
1+	dingo stiffener	a dingo hunter
75+	dingo	native dog
24+	dreaming	spiritual identification with a place etc.
75+	galah	a kind of cockatoo
24+	galah session	[see text]
10+	gibber	a stone, rock; boulder
1+	gidgee	several kinds of acacia trees; a spear
0	gilgie	a small freshwater crayfish
24+	gin	an Aboriginal woman; wife
1+	gin jockey	so. who sleeps with an Aboriginal woman
10+	gunyah	a hut made of a tree trunk
0	gunyang	any of several plants, also called kankaroo apple
1+	be on the wallaby	itinerant station hand in search of work
50+	jumbuck	young sheep
24+	kangaroo apple	[see gunyang]
24+	kangaroo court	illegal court
1+	kangaroo jack	a jack to lift a car

Table 5 continued

AL	Words	Semantic paraphrase
10+	kangaroo route	the airlink to London
75+	kookaburra	a kingfisher
0	koonac	a small freshwater crayfish
50+	Koori	an Aborigine from the south–east of Australia
1+	kylie	a boomerang
50+	land rights	right of Aborigines to own their land
1+	lubra	Aboriginal woman (derogative)
24+	mallee	kinds of small eucalyptus bushes
0	marloo	red kangaroo
1+	marron	a large freshwater crayfish
10+	mia–mia	a hut made of a tree trunk, gunyah
10+	mulga	several kinds of acacia trees
1+	mulga madness	eccentric behaviour attributed to life in the bush
0	mulga mafia	a name for the National Country Party
1+	mulga wire	the grapevine
1+	mungo	a canoe made of bark
10+	Nunga	Aborigines in SA
24+	outstation	autonomous, outlying Aboriginal community
24+	paddymelon	kind of wallaby
0	patter	to eat (obsolete)
1+	tammar	greyish–brown wallaby
24+	be a real dingo	to behave cowardly
50+	to point the bone	to threaten, criticise
24+	traditional owner	Aborigines defined as a descent group that can make land claims
1+	waddy	a male Aborigine; a 'war–club'
50+	walkabout	a walk on foot to live in traditional manner
0	wallaby jack	a jack to lift a car
75+	wallaby	a kind of the smaller kangaroos
1+	warrigal	a dingo, native dog
0	weet–weet	a weapon and toy
0	willy–willy	a kind of whirlwind
10+	wobbegong	a kind of shark, also carpet shark
75+	wombat	a kind pf plant–eating burrowing animal
24+	women's business	knowledge confined to woman
10+	wonga–wonga vine	a climbing plant
50+	yabber (away)	to talk, ask
0	yolngu	an Aborigine in NT
0	yungan	a name for the dugong (fish)

If the public idiom strikes a balance between the general language and that of its sources, how do these findings fit? To begin with, one should recognise the overlap, which suggests that a large number of items are supported by either usage or awareness (in the group of respondents) or both. But what about the rest? Surely, one cannot conclude that low frequency items are outside the public idiom, as some, like *boong*, will not appear frequently and barely without contextualisation cues. So, has the awareness study failed to identify items that are actually used? Did it fail to sample a population that represents the readers of newspapers? Or was it unable to elicit the meaning of the items studied? A few reasons for the mismatches come to mind. Some lower range items amongst the top twelve, i.e. *Koori, women's business, traditional owners,* and *land rights*, are political terms and are, for that reason, likely to occur in papers. The notion of *dreaming* touches upon the political, as the text excerpt above has shown. Such terms are like the more technical ones in, say, cricket reports and presuppose a familiarity with that register. They are clearly a part of the public idiom. But *kangaroo route, mallee, mulga,* and *bung* must be seen in a different light. *Mallee* and *mulga* are flora terms, *bung* is one of the few adjectives with the meaning of 'not in good order' and belongs to the Lingo. So does *kangaroo route*, the description of the air route to Britain, that occurs in Australian-centred texts. No plausible explanations come to mind for the remaining items, but Leitner/Sieloff mentioned a few ideas:

> Recent loans, for instance *Nunga*, have not yet entered the common vocabulary. Even expressions like *outstation, dreaming, Koori, Aboriginal beliefs, women's business,* or *walkabout*, which are in much use, do not appear to be generally known ... A number of expressions, particularly from the cultural domain, were more widely known with increasing age. Thus, a large part of the youngest group (13-17 years) was unaware of the meaning of items like *land rights, women's business, dreaming,* or *to point the bone at sb.* (1998: 167)

If one combines this conclusion with the findings reported here, one cannot fail to see that age is a factor (and that the awareness study did not reach out to a representative sample of native speakers). The public idiom of these print media is for an adult, not an adolescent, readership. It will differ because it has to do with politics and domains that are not so relevant to adolescents. If one assumes that maturation leads to a widening of interests, one will see that interest may turn out to be another, often overlooked factor. (One should study effects of social class and living environment in this connection.) But a considerable number of items will remain unaccounted for.

It may be helpful now to add in the frequencies and rankorders from the two-year output of the *Business Review Weekly*. Table 6 highlights some facts about the language of a specialised magazine. The first is that seventeen items are amongst the top twenty-two in table 4. Print media share a strong consensus on the lexicon. But differences in content correlate with differences in the choice and frequency of lexical items and items that relate to the economy, such as mining, and politics come out on top, i.e. *land rights* and *traditional owners*. The third point concerns the low rank of *Koori*, which may reflect the fact that it is a regional word for Aborigines in the south-east. Given that the three of the papers studied are from the south-east, one would expect it to be used often. While this is true of *The Age* and the *Herald-Sun*, it is not for the *Sydney Morning Herald*. Its low frequency in the national press is confirmed by the *Business Review Weekly*. Finally, like the other papers the *Business Review Weekly* uses words that rank low in the awareness study.

Table 6: Tokens and articles in the *Business Review Weekly* (1996-1997)

Rank	BRW	Tokens	Articles
1	*land rights*	15	21
2	*traditional owners*	7	8
3	*barramundi*	5	5
4	*wallaby*	5	6
5	*wombat*	5	5
6	*bark painting*	3	3
7	*dreaming*	3	3
8	*Koori*	3	3
9	*walkabout*	3	3
10	*dingo*	2	3
11	*kookaburra*	2	2
12	*mallee*	2	2
13	*Aboriginal beliefs*	1	1
14	*billabong*	1	2
15	*bung*	1	1
16	*bunyip*	1	1
17	*coolie*	1	1
18	*galah*	1	1
19	*gidgee*	1	2
20	*kangaroo route*	1	1
21	*marron*	1	3
22	*paddymelon*	1	1

The comparisons so far lead to other questions. One is: Is there evidence of a paper's own version of the public idiom, as mentioned earlier? And are there noticeable differences between yearly outputs? Table 7 shows which expressions occur in all dailies, in pairs of two papers, or in just one. The fully shared items are grouped according to the range they occur in. Thus, range one to ten comprises seven items that are in rank one-to-ten in all papers. *Kooka* (abbreviation from *kookaburra*) is in the next range as it has rank eleven in the *Herald-Sun. Bunyip* is in 'twenty-one to thirty', because it has rank twenty-three in *The Age.* Ranking differences increase above rank twenty, but they are minor. (Figures after each item indicate the rank it has in each paper.)

Table 7: A break-up of items by media outlets over four years (figures indicate ranking in each paper)

AGE–HSu–SMH				
Rank 1–10	Rank 11–20	Rank 21–30	Rank 31–40	Rank 41–50
Koori 1–1–4	*kooka* 8–11–9	*k'roo route* 18–23–20	*Ab'al beliefs* 27–33–26	*gidgie* 34–45–41
land rights 2–3–1	*trad'al owner* 9–14–7	*bung* 19–20–28	*boong* 29–35–29	*willy–willy* 42–38–48
dingo 3–2–2	*billabong* 12–12–11	*mulga* 20–21–21	*coolie* 30–37–23	*lubra* 46–46–37
wallaby 4–4–5	*mallee* 13–10–15	*Abo* 21–22–16	*coolabah tree* 31–27–31	*pademelon* 47–28–32
wombat 5–5–3	*walkabout* 14–8–13	*blackfella* 22–24–19	*gibber* 32–31–34	*wobbegong* 48–36–35
barra 6–7–6	*corroboree* 15–15–14	*bunyip* 23–19–17	*jumbuck* 33–32–33	*nunga* 51–39–39
galah 10–9–10	*k'roo court* 16–17–18	*brolga* 24–18–27	*point the bone* 35–30–40	
	bark paint 17–16–12	*outstation* 25–25–25	*tammar* 37–40–36	
	yolngu 26–29–22	*yabber* 43–48–49		
	marron 28–26–24			
	women's bus 11–6–30			

Gerhard Leitner

|

AGE/HSu	AGE/SMH	HSu/SMH
waddy	*k'roo apple*	*bindi–eye*
40–43	39–45	44–37
bobuck		
44–41		

|

AGE	HSu	SMH
wonga–wonga vine 38	*mungo* 42	*mia–mia* 36
warrigal 41	*warrigal* 47	*clever man* 41
galah session 45		*dillon bush* 43
baal 49		
borack 50		

Of the fifty-five expressions used in the dailies, as many as two-thirds are fully shared, four occur in two papers, ten in one. There is not a big difference in the total number of expressions that are used in the papers. It is not surprising that the *Business Review Weekly* differs, but it does not add a single item of its own to the ones used elsewhere. A number of Australianisms do not occur at all. *Kangaroo jack* 'jack to lift a car', *dingo stiffener* 'dingo hunter' are cases in point. (For *dingo stiffener* a more frequent expression was *dingo trapper*, possibly a part-Americanism.) *Mulga wire* 'bush telegraph' and *billabonger* 'swagman' have not been found either. *Baal* 'no' and *galah session* 'a transmission time set aside for outback women to talk with one another by radio' are in a very low frequency range. *Gin* and *black velvet* both for 'Aboriginal woman' and *gin jockey* 'a man who sleeps with an Aboriginal woman' are not used, although their racist and derogatory connotations may account for that. These observations suggest that the consensus comprises the words that can be used and the ones that cannot. Maybe one should take low levels of usage (below 10) or non-occurrence to signal the development of a historical layer.

There is little evidence for the idea that the papers use the expressions in this lexical segment as a resource to create their own version of the *public idiom*.

But there are frequency differences, which require some comment. *The Age* has 4,410 tokens, the *Herald-Sun* has 3,979, and the *Sydney Morning Herald* 3,641. Put differently, *The Age* accounts for 36.7 per cent of the grand total of 12,030, the *Herald-Sun* for 33.1 per cent, and the *Sydney Morning Herald* for 30.3 per cent. These proportions, together with the observation from table 7 that *The Age* uses the greatest number of different expressions, tend to suggest that it is *The Age* that supports Aboriginal expressions most. But when we turn to measure the proportion of tokens accounted for by the baselines of one hundred, fifty, and ten occurrences introduced above, a common trend comes to surface again. The one hundred mark accounts for 82 per cent of all tokens, the fifty mark for 89 per cent, and the ten mark for 99 per cent, and these percentages are much the same for all papers. In other words, frequency differences between individual items are ironed out for the set. And that, I think, indicates the force of the underlying consensus and that the differences between individual expressions are not strong enough to warrant one to speak of 'house styles'.

Turning to differences across years of output, I cannot go into the same level of detail with all the papers, but shall use *The Age* as my primary example. Diagram 1 (cf. Appendix) has those items that occur twenty or more times in any one of the four-year time-span.

The diagram accounts for 3,774 of the total of 4,410 tokens, or 76.5 per cent. But that figure hides significant fluctuations. The average per year would be 21.5 per cent, but observed percentages vary between 18.5 per cent in 1996 and 27.3 per cent in 1995. Eleven of seventeen words occur in all years, two in three, two in two years, two in only one. (Bear in mind that the diagram is confined to items with a frequency of 20+.) How do we account for such gross fluctuations? Are they mere chance or related to some theme? A good deal of the differences is indeed triggered by the events of the year, as journalists might say. An excellent case is *women's business*, a word that has been mentioned on several occasions. It peaked in 1995, when a Royal Commission in South Australia investigated a controversy about a bridge project that would connect Hindmarsh Island, near Adelaide, with the mainland. Aboriginal groups claimed that the bridge would violate sacred land. Knowledge about the spiritual link was confined to women, hence the use of the term. The *Herald-Sun* and *Sydney Morning Herald* also used the word most frequently in 1995, while frequencies in the other years were significantly lower, always well below the 20+ benchmark used here.

A pattern of a different kind comes from *land rights*. The word is connected with the debates about the Mabo agreement that gave Aborigines the
right to the land of their ancestors, provided they could establish a direct link.
It also occurs in disputes about mining explorations or the shift in political
priorities after the Liberal National Party defeated Labor in 1996. *Land rights*
peaked in *The Age* in 1994 and 1996. The *Herald-Sun* and the *Sydney
Morning Herald*, in contrast, had high figures in 1997. The *Sydney Morning
Herald* also had high frequencies ⁚ ᵢ 1995, as mentioned earlier. Why did that
expression soar in one paper in two years and in the intervening years in the
other papers? A similar case can be made if we look at the most frequent
words in each paper. *Koori* has the highest totals in *The Age* (1,131) and in
the *Herald-Sun* (941), but only 273 in the *Sydney Morning Herald*. The most
frequent words in that paper are *land rights* with 498 tokens, followed by
dingo and *wombat*, and *Koori* in fourth place, whereas they rank lower in the
Victorian papers.

Before turning to a few ideas that bear upon such fluctuations over the
years and between the papers, I should mention another observation, *viz.*
frequencies-per-article. Some items are noticeably more frequent in some
articles than in others. Once more *women's business* is a good case. It occurs
eight times in one article in the *Herald-Sun* (12/22/1995) and seven times in
two (*Herald-Sun*, 12/22/1995 and 12/30/1995), so that 10 per cent of all
tokens is accounted for by a mere three articles. And all were about the
Hindmarsh Bridge dispute. *Dingo* occurs nineteen times in an article of *The
Age* (12/12/1996) and twenty-one times in another (*The Age*, 12/16/1995).
Both articles are about the 'Chamberlain Case', which was about the killing of
a baby. It was alleged that a dingo killed the Chamberlain's baby. A final
example, *dreaming*, is found eleven times in one article in *The Age* (12/
2/1996). In contrast, other reasonably frequent expressions never have such a
concentration in one article. *Bung* is a case in point. There are forty-eight
tokens spread over forty-eight articles. The ninety-seven occurrences of
walkabout occur in ninety-four texts, *kangaroo court*, which is not an Aus-
tralianism, although often used in Australia, occurs fifty-two times in forty-
seven articles, and *jumbuck* has twelve tokens in eleven articles.

How can such differences be explained? From a media angle, one must re-
emphasise the effects of the 'events of the day' upon the choice of expressions. I have given information on such events that can be identified in
connection with some items mentioned. In this context it is fascinating to see
how a word can spread beyond its immediate function. The passage quoted in
(15) above unites three scandals, *viz.* (i) author Helen Demidenko's lie about
her identity when she won a prize for an allegedly auto-biographical novel, (ii)
that of Carmen Lawrence, former Premier in Western Australia, who was

accused of lying in a political matter that led to the suicide of a civil servant, and (iii) the Hindmarsh women's business, that was claimed to be a hoax. It is hard to overlook the ideological significance of the word *women's business*. And yet, the word practically disappeared from the linguistic scene after 1995.

But though one may be able to relate some such differences to the events of the day, are we safe to conclude from non-occurrence or low frequencies in one year that the events of other years never made it necessary to use such words? Do 'stories' alone explain such differences? Or do they also signal a paper's editorial positions? It is hard to find convincing explanations, but one should not jump to easy explanations if a word peaks or slumps in one year without carefully studying the overall editorial content.

Corpus linguistic, but also descriptive, studies tend to ignore the significance of the content of their sources, taking it for granted that high frequencies signal 'high relevance' in the language. Undoubtedly, this is not the right option to choose. A cursory look at the available English language corpora reveals such gross imbalances in some samples, even if it is true to say that some of their effects are 'ironed out' somewhat because the data come from a wider range of sources. They are particularly significant in special purpose corpora like this one so that the relationship between the public idiom and the general language needs careful consideration. A more even picture would probably appear if one were to look at long-range corpora from over many more years.

4.2 Lexical semantics and grammar

A good deal of information on lexical semantics, style range, and lexico-grammar of some items was included above, since it was impossible to talk about frequencies without a consideration of context. But more can be said. A generalisation to begin with. Most expressions have remained within the semantic domain in which they originated (Leitner; in progress). Not many expressions from fauna, flora, politics, or culture have spread beyond their original meaning and uses. But some have, and I will turn to those that have done. I will begin with style and register, before I turn to semantic developments.

4.2.1 Style and register

An association with some style, register, in particular with the Lingo (Seal 1999), or even a regional dialect, can be indicative of integration and institutionalisation within mAusE.

(A) Terms for Aborigines, i.e. *Koorie* (south-east of Australia), *Nunga* (South Australia), *Yolngu* (north-western part of Western Australia). They are recent loans from indigenous languages for modern, self-defined groups of indigenous Australians; they do not reflect pre-colonial tribal affiliations. There are a few names for smaller groups, such as *Mutitjulu* for some Central Australian Aborigines and *Ananga* for the area around Uluru, as (16) shows. They are even less widely known. The following quotation clarifies the social errors that can be made when these terms are used wrongly:

(16) "Then it was our turn to misspell the name of the *Mutitjulu* community of central Australia, who are not the 'Mutijuli'. We put our foot in it again by referring to them as a *Koori* community which, writes our Darwin correspondent Chips Mackinolty, is as offensive as calling a Canadian an American. Around Uluru, the people are known as *Anangu*. (*Koori* refers to the Aboriginal people of southern NSW and Victoria)." (*Sydney Morning Herald*, 11/16/95, section News & Features)

Such terms are both specific and regional. The regional restriction of *Koorie* is well-known and highlighted by the national *Business Review Weekly*'s frequency. But it is worth noting that it occurs by far more often in the Victorian papers than the *Sydney Morning Herald* and so it may be even more restricted regionally.[7] *Yolngu* and *Nunga* trail far behind in all papers, although *Yolngu* is used somewhat more in the *Sydney Morning Herald* and has, as table 4 has shown, as many as seventy-two occurrences, a figure that is in stark contrast with the findings in Leitner/Sieloff (1998), where it was found to be 'unknown', i.e. in the zero per cent group. *Nunga* was in the 10+ awareness range (cf. table 5).

It was interesting to check the application of these terms to specific groups. The three dailies were searched for the occurrences of *Aborigine, Koori,* and *Nunga*, which is the South Australian term, in connection with the Hindmarsh issue. The *Sydney Morning Herald* preferred the term *Aborigine* in this context. When *Koori* was used, sparingly, it was restricted to indigenous Australians in the Southeast. *The Age* and the *Herald-Sun*, in contrast, did extend the reference of *Koori* occasionally to include South Australian Aborigines:

(17) *Koori* Probe Face (6/9/95, section News)

(18) *Koori* Hoax claim (5/20/95, section News)

(19) *Koori* elder denies hoax (5/22/95, section News)

(20) "We audition every 15 minutes for 10 hours over days and reckon we see everyone. Some *Aboriginal* actors are fantastic, but they are *Koori*, or

---

[7]   *Koori* is a recent loan from the 1980s (Eagleson 1982). It peaks in both *The Age* and the *Herald Sun* in 1994 and 1995, accounting for about 69 per cent and 62 per cent of occurrences, respectively. Frequencies in the *Sydney Morning Herald* are more even.

Torres Strait Islanders. We need South Australian *Nungas* and the look is totally different. A major blow." (direct quote from an Aboriginal producer; *Herald-Sun*, 6/15/95, section Entertainment)

There was no occurrence of the correct term *Nunga*. What seems to have been done in *The Age* is that the proper term was perceived as outside the media's idiom and was replaced by the commonly used one, i.e. *Aborigine*, and occasionally by the term *Koori* that reflects a local shade of meaning.

(B) Insults and swear words, such as *Abo, boong,* (some uses of) *galah,* (the dominant use of) *lubra,* and *gin.* As mentioned in section three, they can be used if they can be legitimated. Thus, *boong* and *Abo* are well represented despite their offensive connotations but do not occur within straightforward editorial matter. If contextualisation cues are provided, such as direct quotes, apparent one-word quotes, or narratives that reflect the world they narrate, they do occur. (cf. also (6) to (9) above)

(21) Hawke reports Farmer [an Aussie Rules player] telling mates who chided him for not buying a drink: "The difference between me and these blokes is that when I retire from football I'm just another *boong*." Only nonentities would think that, even in Perth. (*The Age*, 9/9/94, section Sports)

(22) ENOUGH is enough! Most of us deplore racism. But where was the uproar when a high-profile Aboriginal activist interviewed on TV described the re-opening of Northland High as "not bad for a *bunch of Abos* and white trash". (*Herald-Sun*, 05/24/1995, section Letters-to-the-Editor)

(23) It was common then to describe Australia's neighbors in racist terms; and, to him [a very prominent war-time journalist, GL], the Timorese were *boongs* and *fuzzy wuzzies*. But he also spoke of them with unusual affection and admiration, and would point in an atlas to where he had served as a commando and tell of the people he had "left behind". He had regrets. (*The Age*, 6/6/94, section Features)

Unlike examples (6) to (9), (21) and (22) show the legitimate use of these terms in direct quotes from Aborigines themselves. (23) illustrates the point mentioned in section three that the effect of offensive words is mitigated if it is clear that the speaker is one of those who is a potential member of the referent group, would be a speaker of the Lingo or, put differently, be a speaker of *ocker*.

One should also recall that example (6) showed the differences in loading in some words. In this context, I might add that Leitner/Sieloff (1998) found that only half of the respondents thought *Abo* was offensive, half thought it was just slang. That might explain why *Abo* occurs so often, even though it remains outside the top range in table 1. In contrast, *boong* was considered offensive by all respondents and yet it is used remarkably often in *The Age* and the *Sydney Morning Herald* (seventeen and eighteen occurrences). Other racist words, such as *gin, black velvet* do not occur. One wonders why. *Lubra* occurs a few times with racist overtones, but once in the legitimate sense (see example (5)).

(C) Items from the informal spectrum, i.e. *bung, bunyip,* (uses of) *dingo, galah session, kangaroo court, kangaroo route, walkabout* in the extended, non-Aboriginal sense. Like insults, their occurrence reinforces the bias of the public idiom towards the colloquial and informal. A few excerpts from articles illustrate that point:

(24) Brumby, for his part, said on Saturday at Footscray's lunch that the AFL was "like a *dingo*" and that the "AFL's job is not to *white-ant* existing teams". Clearly, Brumby was in a zoological mood. He may well have had *salmon* as an entree followed by *quail*. (*The Age*, 6/29/1994, section Sport)

(25) Earlier, Mr Qureshi stormed out of the courtroom saying it was a *kangaroo court* and accusing Pakistan's Christian minority of working with Indian-born writer Salman Rushdie, who is under an Iranian death sentence for offending Islam. (*Herald-Sun*, 2/24/1995, section News)

(26) There was a certain amount of *bunyip* Shakespearean diction in *Austrillyria*: Viola rhymed with Rylah. Cutting and making free with Shakespearean deadwood is to be commended, but some of the quick disappeared in the process. (*The Age*, 05/15/1995, section Arts & Entertainment)

Example (24) has the meaning of *dingo* as 'simpleton' and embeds it in a highly creative context, along with the verb *ant-eating* and the nickname *salmon* for the well-known Aussie Rules player Fish. Once again, one cannot fail to see the association of the print media's public idiom with the Lingo.

(D) But some very typical Australianisms are surprisingly infrequent, witness *gibber, dillon bush, to yabber, baal*. I did not include *bogey* (or *bogey hole*), a 'waterhole for swimming', in the study but am told that it too does not occur often. What seems to be happening is that a number of items are becoming archaisms. And yet, it is conceivable that local Australian topics will lead to the occasional use of these words. (cf. also section five below)

To conclude. As I mentioned in section three, I was interested in the occurrence of Aboriginal expressions that retained an earlier Aboriginal meaning or could be related to one. I ignored proper names. A number of such expressions are so integrated that it would be interesting to make semantic counts as to whether the original or the derived meanings are more frequent. Cases in point are *bung, bunyip, corroboree, dingo, galah, to walkabout*. In many cases an Aboriginal expression is almost the only one for a given referent, witness *budgerigar, galah, kangaroo, wombat* or *wallaby*; they, therefore, occur in all styles and are really an indispensable part of (standard) mAusE. Though infrequent, *to yabber*, too, is well integrated but used as a colloquialism, like the clipped forms of some words, such as *barra* (from *barramundi*), *budgie*, or *kooka*; they express the close association with informality and slang. I could also show the relatively frequent use of swear and racist words in the public idiom, which confirms Seal's point about the strong socio-ideological functions of the Lingo. Other words are limited to formal styles, witness *Aboriginal beliefs, land rights, dreaming, traditional owners, bark painting, outstation*, or the names for Aboriginal people. There is no reason to suspect that they would be less well established in the public idiom.

4.2.2 Lexical semantics and lexico-grammar
I will now continue with lexical semantics and lexico-grammar to show recent developments inside mAusE. But recall what I said earlier, the majority of expressions have remained within their original domain. I will, therefore, confine myself to a few individual expressions and continue to use the *Macquarie Dictionary* (1997) as a yardstick.

(A) The noun *dingo* designates the 'Australian wild native dog' but it occurs in several interesting uses described in the *Macquarie*. Here are some examples that show features that have been ignored there:

(i) as a premodifier in compound nouns where it reinforces the negative meaning "rubbish, bullshit", such as in *dead dingo's donger* [*donger* is a slang word for penis, GL], or in this example:

(27) "Anyway, do we care? Nup. Nothing but a bunch of Pommy and septic galahs talkin' a load of *dingo poop* and gettin' their undies in a knot" (*The Age*, 11/26/1995, section News)

(ii) in the compound *dingo fence* 'a fence to keep dingoes out of a particular area' but with (i) an extended reference that includes rabbits and other animals, and (ii) a metaphorical sense that refers to a fence that is to bar unwelcome intruders, in politics etc.:

(28) "It's a constant wonder what S and T exactly thought they'd find at a *dingo fence*. I mean, it's a big fence to stop dingoes and rabbits getting to the other side." (*The Age*, 11/2/1995, section News)

(29) Acknowledging that his relationship with Mr. Keating was 'testy', Mr. Goss said he would not "put the *dingo fence* up" to keep the Prime Minister away from the state (*The Age*, 12/11/1995, section News)

(iii) as the verbs *to dingo* and *to dingo on* (both in the *Macquarie*); both verbs permit inanimate objects; *to dingo on*, then, seems to mean much the same as the transitive verb *to dingo*:

(30) The Government, with an election in the offing, would simply *dingo* the fiscal challenge. (*The Age*, 3/22/1995, section Front Page)

(31) Unfortunately, the Commonwealth *dingoed on* essential issues like ports and shipping reform and labor market reform. (*The Age*, 4/13/1995, section Front Page)

(B) The noun *walkabout* refers to a spiritual foot walk to renew contact with traditional Aboriginal life. Its uses have been extended so that it can refer to an 'inspection walk' or 'a walk in the crowd of admirers by a celebrity'. It also occurs in the complex verb *to go walkabout* in the Aboriginal sense or extended ones, *viz.* 'to be misplaced or lost' and 'to go on a walk'. The following examples illustrate (i) the verb with inanimate subjects, (ii) the noun that refers to a fixed path, rather than one chosen haphazardly as a nomad (however, like the Aboriginal sense, the path may have a specific purpose), and (iii) the noun referring to an extra-marital affair (an 'ab-erration' from the normal):

(32) "So more than £100,000 ($211,060) *has gone walkabout*," she said. (*The Age*, 2/1/1995, section Front Page)

(33) or, in those cases where one machine's floppy drive is faulty or *has gone walkabout*, to use those of the other machine. (*The Age*, 6/8/1995, section Front Page)

(34) [of a space project, GL] you can also *go walkabout* in a personal manoeuvring unit. (*The Age*, 24/11/1995, section Front Page)

(35) It comprises a *walkabout* route around the Central Business District, with the express aim of revealing city vistas that are always there, but seldom regarded. (*The Age*, 28/10/1995, section Employment)

(36) a sixfold increase in training frequency ... has helped her to curb her tendency to go on a mental walkabout during matches. (*The Age*, 16/4/1995, section Front Page)

(37) Last year, it was Charles admitting he had *gone "walkabout"*, while the latest episode of this royal version of Melrose Place has the Princess of Wales in a relationship with James Hewitt which, to use the BBC euphemism, "went beyond close friendship". (*Herald-Sun*, 26/11/1995, section News)

In fact, this word has made its way well into mainstream international English, with regular occurrences in British English. That extension of sense blurs totally its mythological reference to traditional Aboriginal life.

(C) The compound *women's business* has been illustrated extensively above in its Aboriginal and mainstream sense. When exactly *women's business* or *men's business* gained currency is unknown. The judge in the Hindmarsh case reacted with scepticism when the term suddenly occurred in the objections against the construction of the bridge, although she did not imply that the term itself was a novel one:

(38) And in a later summary of her findings, the judge said: Not only was the *women's business* unknown and unrecognised in the literature of the Ngarrindjeri people, the existence of the *women's business* was not known to other Ngarrindjeri women. (*Herald-Sun*, 12/22/1995, section News)

Once introduced in this highly critical context, its use peaked, but the formal identity with the mainstream English word led to trivialisations, such as the following, which comes from the same text as (12) above. It is a parody on the Australian habit of barbecuing:

(39) Barbecuing is a secret ceremony viewed only by the male members of the tribe. Female members are sent away to occupy themselves with *women's business*, such as making the salad. (*Herald-Sun*, 9/16/94, section Features)

It may be pertinent here to add a few remarks on the coverage in *The Australian national dictionary*. There is, in fact, neither an entry for *women's business*, nor for *men's business*, but there is one for *business* described as 'traditional lore or ritual; the exercise of this'. The first quotation is as late as 1943, and is a direct speech quote by an Aborigine and contains the compound *blackfellow business*, cf. (40a). The same entry illustrates *sorry business* "mourning ceremonies" with an example. Example (40b) below, also from *The Australian national dictionary*, shows the use of *business* in an Aboriginal sense:

(40a) That not proper wind, but *blackfellow business*. (1943; *The Australian national dictionary*)

(40b) "Do they also own the business and the story to that place?" (quote from a land claim case, 1978; *The Australian national dictionary*)

One might treat the occurrence of the meaning of (40b) either as contextually derived from compounds (ellipsis), such as *women's business, men's business*, or from *sorrow business* 'mourning', or else as a quote from a register outside the public idiom. This use requires extensive contextualisation. Both the *Macquarie* and *The Australian national dictionary* opt for that explanation and add the restrictive label 'Aboriginal English', which is, it would seem, more than warranted. The newspaper corpus, too, contained compounds like *men's business*, see (41), or *traditional business* (42). The use of the simple noun *business*, as in (40b) above, could not be found by browsing the 20,000-odd tokens of *business* in the corpus. One would assume it to be used in that sense somewhere.

(41) It also needs to be able to protect the process against the possibility of fraudulent applications and to be able to properly examine secret *men's* and women's *business* in a manner that stands up to scrutiny by the mainstream legal system. (*The Age*, 12/23/1995, section Opinion)

(42) The Wik people's main argument seems simple enough: they're quite happy to co-exist with pastoralists, as long as they do not lose the right to go about their *traditional business* on the land. But nothing is quite so simple in the High Court – not with 60 lawyers involved, and nervous States declaring the whole matter has enormous ramifications for the nation. (*Sydney Morning Herald*, 6/12/96, section News & Features)

(D) *Galah* 'a common small cockatoo' and '*Colloquial*: a fool; simpleton' is one of the more frequent items in all papers. The *Macquarie* describes the compound *galah session* as '*Colloquial* a time set aside for the women of isolated outback areas to converse with one another by radio'. Here are some examples that (i) show these meanings and (ii) add to them, particularly the phrase *to make a galah of oneself*:

(43) Noddy has ceased to be. He's expired. He's gone to meet his Maker. He's a late *galah*. He's bereft of life. He's an *ex-galah*. (*Sydney Morning Herald*, 1/17/95, section News & Features)

(44) So as not to *make a complete galah* of yourself you'd have to engage in a modicum of training but I doubt if I could eat that much breakfast cereal. (*The Age*, 11/7/1994, section Front Page)

A count of the frequencies of the two senses, *viz.* (i) the fauna one and (ii) the transferred metaphorical one, in *The Age* 1994 showed that sense (ii) outdid sense (i), following a quip by the then Prime Minister Keating about critics of his micro-economic reform plans, with thirty-nine as against eight instances. But in 1995 the balance was (again?) in favour of sense (i), although there was considerable evidence for (ii).

(E) *Dreaming*, described as 'an Aborigine's awareness and knowledge of the dreamtime' and 'a division of an Aboriginal people, based on totemic allegiance', has undoubtedly acquired looser connotations that enable it to be used with reference to white people, events, and the like. It seems to be a blend between the original meaning and a romantic interpretation of the English noun. *The Australian national dictionary*, once again, shows that it is a recent concept with the first quotation from 1943.

Here are some illustrations of its extended use that show how deeply cultural this word has become in mAusE:

(45) For as long as I can remember, the Murray River has been a sort of white man's *dreaming*. It first entered my consciousness during dull geography and history lessons at school (*The Age*, 7/8/1995, section Front Page)

(46) "But I'd have been very sterile if I had been born in a hospital," swears Lawford now. "That open space became part of my *dreaming*." (*The Age*, 5/15/1995, section Front Page)

(47) We are becoming a spiritually impoverished folk. Our students are offered no *dreaming*. Our prospective citizens are never exposed to any systematic tellings of the history of Australia and Australians. (*The Age*, 8/21/1995, section Front Page)

(48) Tom Petsinis' *Inheritance* is a gallant attempt to write the ancestral poem. Its goal is to ground the emigrant, conjoin aboriginalities, as it were Macedonian/Australian, Grandmother/Earth and to translate nostalgia into self-sustaining *dreaming*. (*The Age* 1997)

Unlike the examples for *walkabout* and *women's business*, the ones here reflect a serious attempt to incorporate Aboriginal spirituality into modern interpretations of multicultural Australia.

There is some evidence, then, of lexico-grammatical and lexical semantic developments after a word has been borrowed or coined in other ways. But the most striking picture of newspaper language is that it reflects mainly the common meanings of the words, along with their associations with styles and registers.

5. Discussion

The broad theme of this paper was the changes that occur when languages are transplanted. I confined myself to the role of indigenous languages and, more narrowly still, to Aboriginal words and concepts and continued the theme of Leitner/Sieloff (1998), which dealt with what speakers of mAusE knew about such expressions. But I employed a complementary technique in this paper: I have here analysed **real** language, the output of four newspapers over several years. Such a line or research, I maintain, logically precedes any further attempt to elicit speakers' knowledge in this low-frequency segment of the vocabulary. I will conclude with a few remarks on the maintenance of such expressions in the language, the role of indigenous languages and concept formation, and on implications for corpus linguistics.

As in Leitner/Sieloff (1998), I have come to the inescapable conclusion that these expressions are not in general use, nor are they widely known. If we assume that the total corpus is in the order of 200,000,000+ words, a total number of occurrences of around 12,000 (= below .1 per cent) is small indeed. The view expressed by Dixon et al. (1990), that they represent the most epicentric feature of mAusE, cannot be accepted as a statement about today's language. At most it reflects a historical stage. But this study does reveal a very strong consensus on two aspects. There is, for one thing, a small set of expressions that are used and, for another, the items in this set are rank-ordered (if not used to the same extent) in much the same way over a four-year period in all papers. Thus, of the eighty-five items tested fifty-five oc-curred, the others did not. Twenty-nine occurred more than fifty times and, if one lowers the baseline, thirty-five did more than twenty times. Over two-thirds occurred in all papers. The items covered the entire spectrum of formality, informality, slang, special registers and 'technical' words. This smaller set could, if one so wishes, be called characteristic of the public idiom.[8] But within the consensus, there is a level of variation between the papers and across the years of output. Some of this is related to focal issues and coverage, some, marginally, to the 'house style'.

Now, if one can go by the newspaper language, one cannot fail to notice that these expressions are not well maintained in actual language. But there is some reason for optimism. A few expressions showed that papers do not hesitate to introduce novel terms that they explain, paraphrase, teach, for short. That apart, the drift of this study and Leitner/Sieloff (1998) is the same, but disagreements on details require comment. How come that papers use some less well-known items amongst the top twenty-five? How come that quite well-known ones rank so low? It seems that age and interests may help understand the differences. The majority of respondents in Leitner/Sieloff (1998) were adolescents. Informants at university level seemed to have a better understanding of such items as *land rights*, *women's business*, or *dreaming*, which were among the more widely used items in the newspaper

---

[8]   While the findings are significant for the print media's practices, the notion of *public idiom* still remains somewhat elusive. To argue that it is identical with what is found in the output leaves one with a vacuous definition; all words of a language can occur, if there is a reason. It is difficult to draw a line with frequencies. It is, as was shown, neither possible to exclude low frequency words (for they may occur for reasons of style or content), nor to argue that high frequency words in the set are undoubtedly in it. They may be over-used for a time.

corpus. The newspaper idiom is for a mature readership that may, but need not, have developed this lexical segment better. The findings from the *Business Review Weekly* support this interpretation. It only uses twenty-two items and does not add a single expression not used in the dailies. In other words, general and special interest print media seem to share a core of the public idiom. One might go a step further and suggest that the findings reported here and those in the earlier awareness study point to a shared set of Aboriginal expressions and concepts amongst adults.

A note is worth making on the maintenance of Australian lexis generally. It has been observed elsewhere that mAusE has been losing some of its more typical Australianisms at a fast pace. The loss of Aboriginal items seems to be a part of a wider and far advanced process. To quote a survey reported on in *The Sunday Age*:

> girls and boys aged 11 to 16 found that some traditional Australian slang terms like drongo, sheila and dingbat were still widely recognised but rarely used in conversation. Other terms, such as wowser, furphy, and come the raw prawn appear to be almost extinct. (1/30/1994, section News)

The author quotes approvingly the poet Wallace-Crabbe, who attributes it all to American:[9]

> The decline has been going on a long time but it has been accelerated by a campaign to sell American basketball. Australian kids are now confused about their own identity. If something is American it is real. Even Australian soaps on TV tend not to use Australian slang terms because they sound old-fashioned. We are simply the victim of American cultural imperialism. Some countries are powerful, others are victims. (*The Age and Sunday Age*, 1/30/ 1994, section News)

Things may not be so simple, unless we know more about the details of that loss. But if Fowler's (Whorfian) claim that the "[V]ocabulary can be regarded ... as a representation of the world *for* a culture" (1991: 82) and that "the validity of a system of nomenclature is constantly reaffirmed by usage" (1991: 56), can be taken seriously, losses amount to more than the disuse of some words. They change the underlying cognitive representation of the Australian reality, they affect, as Wallace-Crabbe maintains, people's identity. And the media's practices fail to re-affirm what has been seen as the most typical vocabulary of mAusE. If one sees any value in maintaining this lexical segment, the media and textbook writers for children should, then, feel a

---

[9] That study also found that the meaning of *galah* was described as "idiot, loser" by 8-12-year-olds, as "loser" by 13 to 17 year-olds, and, interestingly, as "player, live" by those between 18 and 22, a connotation neither mentioned in the *Macquarie*, nor found in the papers.

responsibility to contextualise such expressions so that they get passed on to the younger generation. In other words, as losses are part of a wider process of social and linguistic change the task to maintain the Aboriginal expressions and concepts may be an uphill struggle.

To turn to the role of indigenous languages today, including contact languages. Section one surveyed the contact period and the fact that many words were adopted during the formative period of mAusE. Borrowing and related processes have been going on, and even now there is the occasional loan, as (16) has shown. But most concepts today are semantically derived from English words or are formed by means of English words. They are easier to understand, and yet their apparent transparency leads to mis-communication, as Harkins (1994) has argued. A process that has been observed in this study is that formal identity with ordinary mAusE words or the ease of morpheme analysis may trigger trivialised uses, such as were found with *men's business, dreaming* or *walkabout*. In contrast, the uses of *dreaming* pointed to a quite serious concern with spiritual issues. Moreover, this study has shown that, while indigenous languages do not play a significant role for mAusE at all, Aboriginal English may do. The rise of new meanings of *business* (and derivatives), and others, such as *elders, traditional*, etc. do point to this 'new player'. The increased self-confidence of Aboriginal Australians may well impinge more and more on mAusE.

To conclude with a comment on corpus linguistics and particularly on the problem of corpus design. Though the study of newspaper output has revealed a powerful consensus inside the media, differences between the papers and from year to year must not be ignored. We have seen that only a limited amount of the variation in this lexical segment might be relatable to a paper's approach, even to a 'house style'. Other differences, such as the frequencies of *women's business* or *dingo*, were presumably triggered by the events of the year and the editorial weight they are given. So there is a lesson in that for corpus linguistics. If such frequency differences show up between papers and from year to year or even from month to month, they may well introduce a bias into even very large corpora. Words, such as *women's business*, may end up as 'generally significant', although they are only used for short periods. Even very large corpora may collect chance frequencies whose real meaning can only be revealed through long-term research and a sound understanding of editorial practices regarding the events reported. To really establish the general significance of some expression, then, one will need to sample longer periods still that iron out such discrepancies. Such imbalances may, of course, be larger in, relatively speaking, more homogeneous 'special purpose corpora', such as this one, but they will not disappear entirely from 'general purpose corpora' either (for the technical terms, see Leitner (1992)).

While this study brought to light interesting facets of the special public idiom and suggested correlations with mAusE at large, it can only be one step towards a fuller understanding of the currency and dynamics of the set of Aboriginal expressions and concepts. There is room for complementary techniques. One would have to design corpora of special interest magazines, such as music, gardening, investigate the differences between the cities and the country, between age groups and gender and their interaction with interests or living styles. Based on corpus studies, contextualised elicitation techniques could be developed to explore better what speakers actually know, but also what attitudes they have towards certain expressions.

References

Australian national dictionary, The (1988). Melbourne: OUP.

Collins, Peter/ David Blair, eds. (1989): *Australian English. The language for a new society.* St. Lucia, Qld: UP.

Dixon, Richard M.W. et al. (1990): *Australian Aboriginal words in English. Their origin and meaning.* Melbourne: OUP.

Eagleson, Robert (1982): "Aboriginal English in an urban setting". Robert Eagleson/Susan Kaldor/Ian Malcolm, eds. *English and the Aboriginal child.* Canberra: Curriculum Development Centre.

Fowler, Roger (1991): *Language in the news.* London: Routledge.

Harkins, Jean (1994): *Bridging two worlds.* St. Lucia, Qld: UP.

Harris, John (1986): *Northern Territory pidgins and the origin of Kriol* [= Pacific Linguistics C89]. Canberra: Australian National University Press.

HRA = *Historical records of Australia* (Volume I, 1788-96). Canberra: The Library Committee of the Commonwealth Parliament.

Leitner, Gerhard (1992): "International corpus of English: Corpus design – problems and suggested solutions". Gerhard Leitner, ed. *New directions in English language corpora.* Berlin: Mouton-de Gruyter, 33-64.

Leitner, Gerhard (1996): "Australiens Sprachökologie". Rudolf Bader, ed. *Australlien. Eine interdisziplinäre Einführung.* Trier: Wissenschaftlicher Verlag Trier, 215-262.

Leitner, Gerhard (1997): "The sociolinguistics of communication media". Florian Coulmas, ed. *Handbook of sociolinguistics.* Oxford: Blackwell, 187-204.

Leitner, Gerhard (1999): "Der Beitrag der Sprachen der Aborigines für das australische Englisch". Rudolf Bader, ed. *Australien auf dem Weg ins 21. Jahrhundert.* Tübingen: Stauffenburg.

Leitner, Gerhard (in progress): *Australia's many voices. English, indigenous, migrant, and contact languages.*

Leitner, Gerhard/Inke Sieloff (1998): "Aboriginal words and concepts in Australian English". *World Englishes* 17 (2), 153-169.

Macquarie Dictionary (1997). Macquarie University: The Macquarie Library. [1st edition 1981]

Peters, Pam (1987): "Towards a corpus of Australian English". *ICAME Journal* 11, 27-38.

Ramson, William Stanley (1964): *The currency of Aboriginal words in Australian English* [= Occasional Papers 3]. The University of Sydney, Australian Language Research Centre.

Ramson, William Stanley (1966): *Australian English. A historical study of vocabulary, 1788-1889.* Canberra: Australian National University Press.

Seal, Graham (1999): *The Lingo. Listening to Australian English.* Sydney: University of New South Wales Press.

Taylor, Brian (1992): "Syntactic, lexical and other transfers from Celtic into (Australian) English". Geraint Evans et al., eds. *Origins and survivals: Proceedings of the First Australian Conference of Celtic Studies* (held at The University of Sydney, 5-9 July 1992). Sydney: University of Sydney Centre for Celtic Studies, 47-70.

Taylor, Brian (1995): "Offensive language: a linguistic and sociolinguistic perspective". Diana Eades, ed. *Language in evidence.* Sydney: University of New South Wales Press, 219-258.

Troy, Jakelin (1993): "Language contact in early colonial New South Wales 1788 to 1791". Michael Walsh/Colin Yallop, eds. *Language and culture in Aboriginal Australia.* Canberra: Aboriginal Studies Press, 33-50.

Walsh, Michael/Colin Yallop, eds. (1993): *Language and culture in Aboriginal Australia.* Canberra: Aboriginal Studies Press.

Appendix

Diagram 1: The Age (1994–1997): 20+

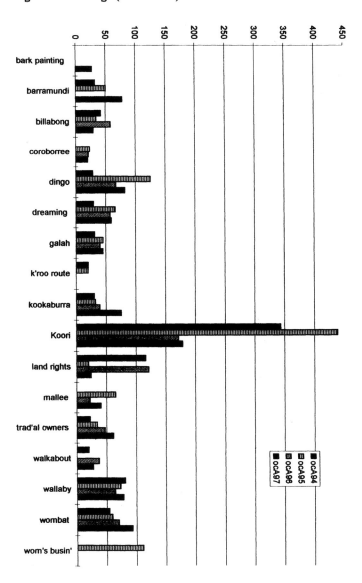

Norbert Schaffeld *(Jena)*

Staging the rehearsals: theatrical patterns of the play within the play in contemporary British, Australian and Canadian metadrama

1. Introduction

The theatrical subversion of realism within English drama has been a popular device since the Renaissance and its propensity for staging the play within the play. Skakespeare's *Hamlet* is the most famous example. While this form of theatricalism was readily adopted by the 18th century taste for dramatic burlesques, the second half of the 20th century witnessed a much more subtantial interest in the foregrounding of theatre in performance (cf. Cohn: 1991: 95f.). Yet, the range of this mode of presentation is broad. Due to the specific nexus between the frame play and the inset play, a number of further subgenres take shape, which can then be categorized in terms of both structure and content. In a somewhat simplified labelling one can distinguish between the integration of elements taken from popular theatre, i.e. music-hall features, pantomime and standup comedy, into serious drama, the self-reflexive play with some tentative scenes enacted on stage, and the familiar or fictional plays within plays. There can hardly be any doubt that the latter variant has become a hallmark of contemporary British playwrights. Dramatists such as John Arden, Alan Ayckbourn, Peter Barnes, Alan Bennett, Howard Brenton, David Edgar, Michael Frayn, Tom Stoppard, and Timberlake Wertenbaker have repeatedly explored the theatre on theatre with a metadramatic thrust that moves between farce and social criticism.[1]

If from a different footing, post-colonial drama has displayed an even greater interest in metadrama while coming to terms with the European 'classics', especially and not surprisingly with William Shakespeare's *The Tempest* (cf. Gilbert and Tompkins 1996: 25–35). As a general rule, the dual aspect of rewriting the canon comprises the regional revision of the originary text and the deconstruction of its received authority. This "canonical counter-discourse" (Tiffin 1987: 22) has found a stronghold in the theatre where a

---

[1] For a substantial discussion of the genre see Boireau (1997).

revisionist performance can focus on the gap between the canonical text and its distant reenactment. Helen Gilbert and Joanne Tompkins (1996: 18; emphasis: HG and JT) have stressed the advantages of the genre:

> Those plays which do articulate oppositional reworkings of the European canon almost always incorporate performative elements as part of their anti-imperial arsenal. As a genre, drama is particularly suited to counter-discursive intervention *and* equally useful for its expression, since performance itself replays an originary moment. In other words, the rehearsal/production of a play is a continued reacting – which may or may not be interventionary – of and to an originary script.

Among the numerous plays whose counter-discursivity addresses the problematic encounter between local contexts and imported texts, those dramas are the most rewarding which articulate a self-reflexive discourse through plays within plays and interventionary frameworks. In this respect, Murray Carlin's *Not now, sweet Desdemona* and Derek Walcott's *A branch of the Blue Nile* not only question the received theatrical programme of the metropolis and the corresponding performance conventions, they also embark on a new performance aesthetic that observes the cultural and political implications of the indigenous context.

In what follows, three metatheatrical plays from Britain, Australia and Canada form the material of a comparative approach which tries to probe into the diverse ways in which theatricalism can be employed. As each comparison necessitates a common ground on which to operate, the dramas were selected on the basis of five criteria. First, they have to stage familiar or fictional plays within plays. Second, their frame should largely be characterized by an ongoing rehearsal or performance praxis self-reflexively accompanying the staging of the inner play. Third, the three plays under scrutiny should cover diverse regions of the English-speaking world. Fourth, they should have met with considerable public or critical acclaim. And, finally, just to comply with the notion of contemporaneity, each play was to have premiered during the last three decades. Thus, the text corpus of the present paper embraces Timberlake Wertenbaker's *Our country's good* (1966a; first performance 1988)[2], Mudrooroo's *The Aboriginal protesters* (1993a; first performance 1996), and David French's comedy *Jitters* (1986; first performance 1979).

---

[2] Timberlake Wertenbaker is an American-born dramatist, who now lives and works in London.

2. The humanizing effect of the theatrical experience

The process of appropriation, i.e. the partial acceptance of a British cultural export, can at times encourage the articulation of a new social identity based on a common humanistic outlook. In this vein, Timberlake Wertenbaker's (*1944?) *Our country's good*, which was first performed at the Royal Court Theatre, London, in 1988 not only appeals to Britain's cultural heritage, it also presents one of its key manifestations, the theatre, as a means of emancipating people. Wertenbaker's play is set in New South Wales in the years 1788–1789, where convicts rehearse George Farquhar's *The recruiting officer* (1706) to celebrate – at Governor Phillip's behest – the birthday of King George III. What looks like the implausible gimmick of the playwright's imagination, nevertheless, has its origin in historical fact. Farquhar's Restoration comedy was indeed performed by a convict cast in 1789 (cf. Hughes 1987: 340). Some two hundred years later, Thomas Keneally took up the story in his novel *The playmaker* (1987) and it is from this account that the narrative spine of the contemporary British play is adopted.[3]

In her attempt to construct the past as a compelling example for the present, Wertenbaker reshapes historiographic evidence in at least two respects. First, she overcomes the patterns of conventional historical discourse "by installing speaking subjects from the ranks of the silenced and the oppressed" (Sakellaridou 1993: 308). And second, she modifies some of the historical agents, notably Governor Phillip, in order to keep their timeless outlook alive in the present of the theatrical encounter. To be sure, the historical accounts hardly ever fail to mention the humane qualities of Phillip's rule, but in Wertenbaker's version he becomes the larger-than-life embodiment of the Enlightenment. He is just, benevolent and a strong believer in the societal merits of education. Where most of his officers favour acts of severe punishment as deterrents, Phillip even refers to Plato's *Meno* to substantiate the innate qualities of human beings. According to him, education can eventually be accomplished through culture and it is here that Phillip's views on the theatre question the everyday spectacle of the floggings and hangings, in short, the theatre of non-mimetic violence. The metadramatic stance that runs through Wertenbaker's play underlines both the reformative effect of acting and the creation of a homogeneous community, which, though first created in the theatrical medium, might outlive the relatively short time span of artistic illusion. Confronting the critical voices among his officers, Phillip argues:

---

[3] For a detailed comparison between the play and the novel, which focuses on colonialism and its discourse of power, see Wilson (1991) and Davis (1993).

PHILLIP: The theatre is an expression of civilization. We belong to a great country which has spawned great playwrights: Shakespeare, Marlowe, Jonson, and even in our own time, Sheridan. The convicts will be speaking a refined, literate language and expressing sentiments of a delicacy they are not used to. It will remind them that there is more to life than crime, punishment. And we, this colony of a few hundred, will be watching this together, for a few hours we will no longer be despised prisoners and hated gaolers. We will laugh, we may be moved, we may even think a little. (Wertenbaker 1996a, I.vi: 206)

As the play develops, art – seen as the place of humanist refuge – is constantly exposed to the danger of being crushed by the harsh realities of the prison camp. For in spite of the Reverend's agreement to the production of Farquhar's play, given on the understanding that it does not encourage loose morals, the rehearsals themselves turn out to be a tightrope affair. From the perspective of the audience the most memorable and moving scenes are those in which the brutality of the system interferes with the theatrical project. In these crucial moments, when, for example, the screams of their flogged mates are heard off-stage, the convict actors quite naturally tend to lose their lines of refined speech, but the cast will not be put off for long. Even the imminent death penalty for some of its members does not seem to impair the dedication with which the doomed take part in the rehearsals. Quite obviously, the convict stage gradually accomodates a new community, which is able to re-establish both cultural and societal links. When Wertenbaker's play opens, convicts and officers alike express a profound sense of exile and historical as well as cultural displacemet (cf. Middeke 1997: 227). Yet, it is with their involvement in the theatrical production and the essential, if temporary, role play that the convicts compensate the twofold denial of nation and status. Where the cultural transplant of Farquhar's text alleviates the condition of enforced exile, the casting eventually subverts social hierarchies. Liz Morden, for instance, who is described by Governor Phillip as being "Lower than a slave, full of loathing, foul mouthed, desperate" (Wertenbaker 1996a, II.ii: 245), will play the part of Farquhar's Melinda, thereby winning a linguistic and social self-confidence that earns her the respect of the cast. In a more general way, the rehearsals mark a period of communal transition which in pointing towards the restrictions imposed by gender partially removes hierarchies among the convicts and the emotional boundaries between this group and some of the more cooperative officers. Over and above that, it is interesting to observe how Wertenbaker's drama actually invests a marginalised class with historical agency. When during rehearsals, Major Ross and Captain Campbell, who still disapprove of the performance, begin to insult and humiliate the actors, the convicts drop their initial paralysis and literally resist by acting:

But Sideway turns to Liz and starts acting, boldly, across the room, across everyone.

SIDEWAY [as Mr Worthy]: What pleasures I may receive abroad are indeed uncertain; but this I am sure of, I shall meet with less cruelty among the most barbarous nations than I have found at home. (Wertenbaker 1996a, II.v: 252)

Here, within the new context, Farquhar's subtext provides an eloquent piece of non-violent resistance, which disrupts the brutal display of power by purely theatrical means. For a brief interlude the convict actors have experienced a scene of mutual responsibility, whose human impulse reaches well beyond the arbitrary particulars of place and time.

Up to now, *Our country's good* has remained the most well received of Wertenbaker's plays (cf. McDonough 1996: 412). After its opening at the Royal Court Theatre, it was soon transferred to the West End and has seen quite a number of productions in Canada, the United States and Australia. The drama was even put on at Blundeston prison, Britain, performed by the inmates with – as Wertenbaker (1996b: 163) observes – "an intensity and accuracy playwrights dream of". In view of this reception and bearing in mind the play's major concern that against all odds, art can indeed restore humanity, a final remark on the title should be made. In *Our country's good* it is one of the convicts, John Wisehammer, who speculates on the word 'country':

WISEHAMMER: Country can mean opposite things. It renews you with trees and grass, you go rest in the country, or it crushes you with power: you die for your country, your country doesn't want you, you're thrown out of your country. (Wertenbaker 1996a, I.x: 224)

To be sure, at least as far as the convicts are concerned, 18th century Britain got rid of their criminals in what they took to be the interest of the country's good. As a contemporary piece of art, however, which strongly expresses the theatre's humanist concern, the play amounts to a subtle criticism of Margaret Thatcher's cultural policy. In view of severe cuts in arts funding in the 1980s (cf. Humphrey 1990), Wertenbaker's play no doubt demands the recovery of public support for the theatre, whose intrinsic reformatory merits are – a pun on the title – for the country's own good.

3. The metadramatic frame and counter-discursive intervention

Contrary to Wertenbaker's approach, which sees the canonical transplantation of the theatrical practice as a tool of emancipation, Mudrooroo's metadrama with the longish title *The Aboriginal protesters confront the Declaration of the Australian Republic on 26 January 2001 with the production of 'The commission' by Heiner Müller* finally rejects the **planned** import of European culture and thought. The play was first workshopped in 1991, in collaboration with the dramatic adviser and translator Gerhard Fischer, and saw its premiere at The Performance Space as part of the Sydney Festival in January 1996. The public and critical response was so marked that it did not go unnoticed overseas, especially in Germany, which two weeks after Müller's death was predisposed to showing a growing interest in the world-wide reception of one of its most famous contemporary dramatists (cf. Michaelis 1996: 51). Theatres in Weimar and Munich invited the Australian playwright and his Aboriginal performers, but it was during those months that a public debate suddenly got underway seriously questioning Mudrooroo's Aboriginal ancestry. Victoria Laurie's article in the *Australian Magazine* confronted its readers with the details of a private research undertaken by Mudrooroo's older sister, Betty Polgaze, who now claims that the antecedents of the family were Anglo-Celtic on their mother's side and African American in their father's (cf. Hughes 1998: 22). The contents of this revelation triggered off some harsh criticism, especially from the Aboriginal community, whose leading literary as well as academic authority Mudrooroo had been. Yet, to be fair, the case of Mudrooroo is neither a fraud nor a literary hoax. In an objective and helpful essay, Gerhard Fischer has cast some light on the matter (cf. 1998: 223–235). According to Fischer (1998: 227; emphasis: GF), Mudrooroo never willfully fabricated an identity, rather he "became an Aborigine, or better: *was made one*, primarily through the reactions of people around him". Mudrooroo, who adopted his Aboriginal pen name Mudrooroo Narrogin in protest against the Australian Bicentenary in 1988,[4] was born as Colin Johnson in 1938. The boy did not know his father because he had died a few months before his birth. When Colin was nine, his mother, who had to cope with the lean time of the Depression, sent him to a Christian Brother's orphanage. It must have been during his early childhood, the years at the orphanage and, later on, at Fremantle Gaol, that society classified and stigmatized the fatherless boy of darker skin as an Aborigine, with the consequence that the youth increasingly identified with his Aboriginal peers. From today's perspective, the relationship between mother and son might have been the tie to solve the problem, yet, since it was cut, any further argumentation verges on pointless hypothesis. Within the field of literature, however, the most crucial question still remains to be solved. It is again Gerhard Fischer who puts it all in a nutshell. "Can one," he asks, "be an Aboriginal writer and not of Aboriginal descent?" (Fischer 1998: 233) What for a European reader appears to be a minor issue,

---

[4]   While Narrogin is a place in Western Australia, Mudrooroo refers to an Aboriginal
       name for the paperbark, indicating the writer's material or his working totem.

since literary evaluation should not follow any ethnographic label, turns out to be a serious matter of dispute among indigenous writers in Australia and their idea of the authentic Aboriginal voice. Admittedly, this paper is based on a perspective from without, but still it would like to argue that Aboriginality cannot simply be addressed by documenting biological inheritance (cf. Hughes 1998: 23). This approach is after all reductionist in nature and it fails, as Hughes clearly sees (cf. 1998: 24), to take in an experiental identity formation which is not so much the product of the family tree but – I would like to add – the outcome of white discursive control locating the body as the site of inscription. If on the basis of physical differences, Mudrooroo was constructed as the other, thus becoming an excluded subject belonging to a collective 'they', which in the Australian context of the day spelt Aboriginal, his wholehearted identification with and his outstanding support of the community should qualify him for a belated adoption (cf. Fischer 1998: 234f.). It is against this background that I would like to discuss Mudrooroo's play in terms of Aboriginal or Black Australian theatre.

Mudrooroo's *The Aboriginal protesters* is structured as a play within a play, in which a group of Aboriginal lay performers rehearse Heiner Müller's *Der Auftrag*. While the highly intertextual German drama with its references to the work of Anna Seghers, Georg Büchner and Bertolt Brecht is at last performed at full length, the frame play, which is also enriched by elements of Aboriginal dance theatre, centres around the numerous problems of the actual dress rehearsal. Within the imaginary reality of the frame play, that is, the eve of Australia Day 2001, the cast initially intends to present *Der Auftrag* the next day to protest against the proclamation of a Republic that is not willing to grant Aboriginal sovereignty. Both Australian and German TV stations will cover the event and it would be a great opportunity to draw national and international attention to the plight of the First Australians. Yet, the idea of performing Müller's postmodern drama as a critical contribution to the festivities of the Australia Day will never be realized. At the end of the staged rehearsal, after much debate on the casting, the significance of Müller's work and the political effect of the theatrical enterprise, the majority of the performers come out against the project. By that time, however, the actual audience of this theatre on theatre has already seen the unabridged English version of Müller's play.

As a didactic historical drama, *Der Auftrag* combines three plots. First, there is the story of three emissaries of the French Revolution who are sent to Jamaica in order to launch a rebellion among the slaves. Second, the subplot of Antoine, the master mind behind the mission, focuses on the disillusion of a former revolutionary. And third, the almost Kafkaesque soliloquy of a man in the elevator who suddenly finds himself lost in the surreal landscape of Peru as a symbol of the European without a commission or task. Within the framework of these layers, Müller's thematic scope comprises the betrayal of the revolution and its promise of justice, liberty and equality, the ideological relationship between Europe and the Third World, and, finally, the need to come to terms with history at a time of political stagnation or even regression. Of the three emissaries only Galloudec and Sasportas remain true to their vision, while Debuisson wants to change to that side where he could welcome the comforts of irresponsibility as a kind of personal liberation. Though Sasportas, the ex-slave, dissociates himself from the Napoleonic betrayal of the European revolution, he nevertheless intends to follow his own rebellious course, arguing that "as long as there are masters and slaves we cannot be released from our mission" (Mudrooroo 1993a: 114). Whereas Müller's portrayal of the Black hero is often discussed with reference to Fanonism and the theory of *négritude* (cf. Vaßen 1991: 151f.), critics such as Gerhard Fischer find fault with an overall image that is pre-modern, simplistic as well as reductive. In this vein he points out that

> Müller does not allow for a complex Black identity. Instead, he defines his hero simply with reference to his supposed revolutionary mission; 'the home of slaves is revolt' ... which in turn is linked to a concept of a natural or 'Black' revolution that is set apart from the experience of European revolution dominated by enlightenment and rationality ... It is an interesting aspect of Müller's Eurocentric thinking that he refuses to endow his Black hero with a sense of *mortal fear* and an awareness of his own individuality in the face of death, a striking contrast to the portrayal of European revolutionaries in Müller's plays. (Fischer 1995: 156; emphasis: GF)

Looking at Mudrooroo's frame drama, which, for the most part, exhibits a highly theatrical comment on the German pre-text, the role of Sasportas is indeed one key issue in the debate among the actors. When playing Sasportas, both the old Aborigine, King George, and later on Peter, who takes over this part, enrich Müller's one-sided character with the individuality of their respective life-stories. In contrast to King George, who is constantly haunted by the traumatic experience of his time in prison, Peter is the urban career Aboriginal who has made it. Earlier on he also had to accept the role of the slave in the cage, a part so full of nightmarish memories that King George was unable to proceed. As it is, Peter, the bureucrat, now undergoes the mimetic theatrical experience of humiliation that has been the everyday reality of his older partner. This new experience favours a delayed process of identification, which through its theatrical enactment ensures a greater homogeneity within the group.

Though the *Aboriginal protesters* abounds with structural references to the work of Peter Weiss, Günter Grass, Jean Genet, Luigi Pirandello, and the

Berlin GRIPS Theatre's production of Leonie Ossowski's *Voll auf der Rolle* (cf. Fischer 1995: 143), the major impact of the frame recalls a Brechtian counter-play. From the point of view of post-colonial theory, however, it soon becomes obvious that Mudrooroo mounts a theatrical counter-discourse trying to subvert a canonical text. What might have looked like a structural exercise in syncretic performance, which fuses European and indigenous traditions (cf. Balme 1995: 31–35), leads to a downright dismissal of the established German text and its implicit ideological outlook. Confronting the black academic, Clint, on this issue, it is again the old Aborigine, King George, who has no doubt that his unwavering adherence to the mythological nexus of **the dreaming** compels him to reject Müller's play in favour of what he sees as true Aboriginal theatre:

> KING GEORGE: And yet you give us Müller, which is about victim. Worse victim, Man who lost his soul, heart and relations and spirit. You want that for us? You want that white way for us to walk along? In that university, you learn a little bit, then try to bring it over to us. Keep it there. We don't want it. We'll only chuck it out. We wanta keep seeing through black mind, through black heart, through black eyes. We got it all; what else we need. Their sickness; their sadness; their blandness. We are the aristocrats, the ones they chopped the heads off. They keep chopping our heads off every day; and they do this, why? They jealous. We own the land. So no more of this thing. We want a theatre of blackfella business. Proper theatre. (Mudrooroo 1993a: 100)

The Sydney production in January 1996 delivered the incompatibility between European text and Aboriginal context in two more ways. Not only were the actors dressed in historical white costumes of the 18th century and, except for Sasportas, in white half-masks during the Müller-inset, they also rendered a highly stylized version of the postmodern pre-text (cf. Michaelis 1996: 51), thereby setting it apart from the realist, sometimes drastic language of the cast. Both costume and diction thus foregrounded theatre in performance as mere presentation, which should be perceived as the antonym for a realistic representation of true Aboriginal concern.

Mudrooroo's post-textual criticism of Heiner Müller's *Der Auftrag* combines a number of serious issues which cannot be accepted by the Aboriginal community. To begin with, there is the assumption that – as Bob, the director of the play has it – "History belonged to the strongest" (Mudrooroo 1993a: 79). Hence, any historiographic record of the European centre can be deconstructed as a master narrative, which, even though it claims universal achievements apparently worthy of a global missionary export, tends to ignore the autonomy of the indigenous other. There is an obvious paradox between the British invasion of Australia in 1788 and the Enlightenment's political agenda put forward in the course of the French Revolution one year later. Bob sees this very clearly when he – still favouring Müller's play – declares:

> BOB: In 1788 the colony of Port Jackson came into being with the dumping of soldiers and convicts on our shores. In 1789 the French Revolution erupted with the threefold slogan of LIBERTY, EQUALITY AND FRATERNITY. It is what we were being deprived of. For us, LIBERTY came to mean SLAVERY; EQUALITY: SOCIAL DARWINISM; FRATERNITY: ALIENATION. The rich dark soil of our land became red with our blood. The invaders saw our land as empty. It became so: empty of dignity and humanity. (Mudrooroo 1993a: 78; emphasis: M)

In the course of the frame play, this antinomic debunking of the Enlightenment's political reality soon turns into a forthright disapproval of any political or, for that matter, cultural universalism which fails to consider the conditions of a different local experience. The way the Aboriginal actors see it, both the European export of political thought and the transplantation of culture lead to a final heteronomy of the other, to a colonial patronage, whose implications they also identify at the bottom of *Der Auftrag*. In addition, neither is Müller's understanding of violence as a historical agent supported by the actors, nor his seemingly Eurocentric construction of Black identity. Especially the female characters do not approve of Müller's portrayal of women as the sexualized body (cf. Mudrooroo 1993a: 86, 97, 99) and his tendency to invest a disenchanting historical analysis with feminised metaphors. A telling example of the latter can be found in Peter's lines, who in the role of Antoine exposes freedom's 'true' character: "Liberty leads the people to the barricades, and when the dead awaken she wears a uniform. I'll tell you a secret now: she too is only a whore" (Mudrooroo 1993a: 89). The playwright himself sees Müller's literary women as "evil, the seed-hungry, blood-hungry vampire, the femme fatale in search of the perpetually tumescent male and priestesses of man's severed head." (Mudrooroo 1993b: 24). Not surprisingly, feminism and post-colonialism combine in order to deconstruct the dramatic pre-text as a vehicle of imperial as well as patriarchal power. The construction of subjectivity, the identity formation of the Aboriginal self, be it female or male, ask for an authentic form and voice, which can only be found away from the restricting leadership of European emissaries. Yet, this authentic voice, which is to be promulgated in the Black theatre, is not exclusively based on Aboriginal thought. Provided that any process of transculturation still allows a marginalized group to select and modify specific material from the metropolitan culture, the play's final call for "Blackfella Liberty, Equality and sisterhood and brotherhood" (Mudrooroo 1993a: 121) clearly subscribes to an unforced appropriation within the interests of the periphery.

4. Theatricalism and the parody of cultural criticism

When during the early lines of David French's (*1939) comedy *Jitters*, the audience is startled by a man jumping up from his front row seat and shouting "All right, cast, we'll stop there." (French 1986: 12), they will begin to realize that what they have just seen was part of an inner play, *The care and treatment of roses*, which is being rehearsed on stage. *Jitters* opened at the Tarragon Theatre, Toronto, in 1979 and it has become an extremely popular play both within and outside Canada with more than a hundred professional productions to its credit.[5] Indebted to the structure of the comedy-of-the-stage,[6] the set of *Jitters* moves between the stage and the backstage of a small Toronto theatre with act I four days before the premiere, act II on the night *The care and treatment of roses* is going to open, and act III on the following afternoon. Comedy, farce and satire intermingle as soon as the actors rehearse the domestic drama by the fictitious author Robert Ross, who is also present. Ever so often the run-through of an act is interrupted by missing the cues, deficient props, nasty remarks on a colleague's role playing, rivalries, continual bickerings, petty jealousies, and the special requests of an oversensitive actor. It is not surprising, then, that at the end of act I the rehearsal ends in pandemonium. The major antagonists are Jessica Logan, a former Broadway diva, now working on her comeback, and Patrick Flanagan, an Irish-Canadian actor, who has toured the theatres of his country only to realize that his sarcastic wisecracks are a poor outlet for his anger over the lack of public recognition: "It's just I'd rather work in Canada. Where else can you be a top-notch actor all your life and still die broke and anonymous?" (French 1986: 39). While Jessica is anxiously awaiting the arrival of a New York producer, Bernie Feldman, who is supposed to be there for the opening of the play, Patrick will not be impressed by the idea that the whole production might move to Broadway:

> PATRICK: The critics there would laugh us out of town.
> JESSICA: They could do the same here, couldn't they?
> PATRICK: New York's tougher.
> JESSICA: That's never stopped anyone. We take risks all the time, don't we? New York's just a larger arena. Higher stakes.
> PATRICK: Well, I'm a Catholic and Catholics are against suicide. Besides, I don't think we should judge success by New York. No, really. I've never felt that or I'd be there, wouldn't I? (French 1986: 77-78)

---

[5] The number given here refers to the period up to the early nineties. See Albert-Reiner Glaap (1992: 230).

[6] Some critics have underlined the parallels between *Jitters* and Michael Frayn's farce *Noises off.* See, for instance, Alber-Reiner Glaap (1987; 1988).

The positions within this dialogue are clear. For Jessica, Broadway is the measure of all things, thereby implying a universal attraction and validity of the cultural standards set by the metropolis. Patrick, on the other hand, starts off with what seems to be the verbal gesture of a cultural cringe, but then adopts a more self-confident attitude, which questions the normative cultural power of the American centre. Judging from hindsight, one is tempted to analyse *Jitters* in terms of its almost seismographic potential to record an emergent development of the Canadian theatre which, at the end of the seventies, was trying to escape from the evaluative paternalism of Broadway or the West End. In 1981, Gina Mallet (1981: H3) used a common, yet fairly problematic metaphor to describe David French's central theme:

> What French describes is not so much neurosis as simply prolonged adolescence – a natural uncertainty and insecurity piled on top of the draining sense of anxiety that so often enervates Toronto theatre, and its ambivalent relationship with Broadway.

Given that irony and the ability to parody oneself frequently mark the end of adolescence, Mallet's analysis falls short of the play's actual achievement. Whereas the cultural anxiety, Mallet speaks of, is present all the time, thus adding to the ambiguity of the title, it does not rest there as the object of dramatic diagnosis, but is made the final target of the playwright's critical stance.

It is again the frame play that gives French the opportunity to highlight the interdependence between acting and the (anticipated) response of the theatre critics, whose influence surpasses their competence by far. Referring to a specific reviewer, Jessica, who happens to be the only one the critic does in fact run down, gives way to her anger. This time, however, not without a humorous diatribe against the stereotyped diction and sketchy nature of the review:

> JESSICA: I don't take it seriously, George, and I don't give a damn *what* he thinks. It still hurts. We spend weeks, months on a play to be carved up by someone on a free pass who rushes home to scribble off six or seven hundred words in sixty minutes that affects our livelihood and reputation. I don't know about you, but I can't even write a letter in that length of time. And oh, his writing style, let's not forget that. He writes like he needs a good enema. His sentences are so tight-assed, if he ever left out a period he'd run right into Classified Ads. (French 1986: 155; emphasis: DF)

At first glance, the second act is high farce. Set in the backstage area immediately before the performance of the inner drama, it focuses on the actors' strain, last minute revisions, and above all, the untimely logic of Murphy's law. As it is, the director's wife has an accident, the New York producer will be late, one of the actors, Tom, turns up dead drunk and another one almost misses his cue after being locked in the washroom. Yet, the performance of *The care and treatment of roses* is a success with the fictitious audience. When during the last act of *Jitters*, the cast assembles on the following afternoon, the talk is about Friedman's non-appearance and the mixed reviews of the show. Patrick's reading from a particular article, which – as Cynthia Zimmerman has pointed out – includes authentic quotes from French's own reviews (cf. 1982: 120), not only informs the audience about the contents of the whole inner play. It also paves the way for a witty and ironic juxtaposition of an actor's poor condition in the 'reality' of the frame play and the critic's later praise for his performative skills. Notwithstanding the absence of the New York producer, who thus symbolizes the irrelevance of an *a priori* interest in Broadway, it is the favourable review of Tom's acting which is the most indicative of the critic's qualification. Since the audience has seen Tom drunk and disorderly just a few minutes before the opening of the inner play, the following lines from the review will not miss their authorial target:

> PATRICK: Enter the son (Tom Kent), the catalyst, who sets off the powder keg of conflicts. From the moment Mr. Kent staggers onstage, hungover from the previous night, the stage is set for a classic battle of wills, refereed by the priest – a battle that rages almost unrelentingly until the final curtain ... Tom Kent in the pivotal role of the son, Jimmy, manages to strike the right balance between awkward youth and groping aspirations. A fine debut for a young actor in his first professional role. (French 1986: 143–144)

What is more, even Phil, who during rehearsals was hardly able to memorize the script and kept forgetting his cue, is suddenly cheered with "The most memorable performance of the night". And the review, this time read aloud by the director, George, substantiates its compliments:

> GEORGE: Mr. Mastorakis [Phil], vulnerable in an almost painfully childlike manner, fumbling for words that seem constantly to elude his grasp, makes the inner struggle seem all the more urgent and adds a dimension of humanity that endears him instantly to the audience. (French 1986: 144)

With the advantage of knowig the inner as well as the outer play, the audience will easily spot the blunder of the reviewer, who takes the consequences of intoxication and the botched job of one actor for tokens of artistic merit. If, in other words, personal deficits are reviewed as mimetic qualities, the ongoing paranoia about performative failure turns out to be nonessential. In David French's parody of theatre criticism, the power of the reviewers is measured in terms of their control of public response, whereas their evaluative competence is made the object of a satirical deconstruction situated in the witty interplay between the comedy's frame and inset.

5. Conclusion

The metatheatrical encounter between dramatic texts generates a specific kind of dialogue that is not so much the outcome of a more or less sophisticated intertextuality, but the result of a contextual need to address social, political as well as cultural issues within the design of genuine theatricalism. Thus, Timberlake Wertenbaker's play *Our country's good* focuses on the reformative effect of acting and the humanist potential of the theatre in order to protest against the close-fisted cultural policy of her day. Though set in Australia, her play is by no means to be confused with post-colonial rewriting processes, because the playwright's matter of concern does not extend to questions of canonical counter-discourse. This, however, is Mudrooroo's major idea of theatricalism. The final dismissal of the German text *Der Auftrag* in *The Aboriginal protesters* follows the combined effort of post-colonialism and feminism to deconstruct the European pre-text in favour of a more authentic and autonomous theatrical experience. While Wertenbaker and Mudrooroo use familiar dramas as insets, David French's comedy incorporates a fictional inner play. Against the background of a cultural inferiority complex in Canada, the playwright's approach to theatricalism works as a satire on the awkward fixation with Broadway and as a parody on the power of theatre criticism. Yet, the public appeal of all three plays is not only a matter of content. One of the most attractive potencies of the theatrical endeavour affects the audience, for it is in the course of the reception that the complex interplay between inner and outer drama comes into its own.

References

(1) Primary sources

Farquhar, George (1995): "The recruiting officer". *The recruiting officer and other plays*. Oxford: OUP, 159–242.

French, David (1986): *Jitters*. Vancouver: Talonbooks.

Keneally, Thomas (1987): *The playmaker*. London: Hodder & Stoughton.

Mudrooroo (1993a). "The Aboriginal protesters confront the Declaration of the Australian Republic on 26 January 2001 with the production of *The commission* by Heiner Müller". Gerhard Fischer, ed. *The Mudrooroo/Müller project: a theatrical casebook*. Kensington: New South Wales UP, 75–122.

Müller, Heiner (1991). *Germania Tod in Berlin [und] Der Auftrag*. Roland Clauß, ed. Stuttgart: Klett.

Wertenbaker, Timberlake (1996a): "Our country's good", *Plays 1*. London: faber & faber, 161–281.

(2) Secondary sources

Balme, Christopher (1995): *Theater im postkolonialen Zeitalter: Studien zum Theatersynkretismus im englischsprachigen Raum*. Tübingen: Niemeyer.

Boireau, Nicole, ed. (1997). *Drama on drama: dimensions of theatricality on the contemporary British stage*. Houndmills: Macmillan.

Cohn, Ruby (1991): *Retreats from realism in recent English drama*. Cambridge: CUP.

Davis, Jim (1993): "A play for England: The Royal Court adapts *The playmaker*". Peter Reynolds, ed. *Novel images: literature in performance*. London: Routledge, 175–190.

Fischer, Gerhard (1995): "Twoccing *Der Auftrag* to Black Australia: Heiner Müller *aboriginalised* by Mudrooroo". Gerhard Fischer, ed. *Heiner Müller: ConTEXTS and HISTORY: A collection of essays from The Sydney German Studies Symposium 1994 Heiner Müller/Theatre-history-performance*. Tübingen: Stauffenburg, 141–164.

Fischer, Gerhard (1998): "Performing multicultural and post-colonial identities: Heiner Müller *aboriginalized* by Mudrooroo (with a postcript on Mudrooroo's dilemmas". Wolfgang Klooß, ed. *Across the lines: intertextuality and transcultural communication in the new literatures in English*. Cross/Cultures 32, ASNEL Papers 3. Amsterdam/Atlanta, GA: Rodopi, 215–236.

Gilbert, Helen/Joanne Tompkins (1996): *Post-colonial drama. Theory, practice, politics*. London: Routledge.

Glaap, Albert-Reiner (1987): "Noises off and Jitters: two comedies of backstage life". *Canadian Drama/L'Art dramatique Canadien* 2, 210–215.

Glaap, Albert–Reiner (1988): "Was ist kanadisch am (Englisch-)Kanadischen Drama?". *Zeitschrift der Gesellschaft für Kanada-Studien* 2, 7–15.

Glaap, Albert–Reiner (1992): "Familiendrama, Romanze und Komödie: Zu den Dramen von David French". Albert–Reiner Glaap, ed. *Das englisch-kanadische Drama*. Düsseldof: Schwann, 229–241.

Hughes, Mary Ann (1998): "The complexity of Aboriginal identity: Mudrooroo and Sally Morgan". *Westerly* 1, 21–27.

Hughes, Robert (1987): *The fatal shore: a history of the transportation of convicts to Australia, 1787–1868*. London: Collins Harvill.

Humphrey, Richard (1990): "The stage in a state: public financing of the theatre in the first Thatcher decade – an historical review". *anglistik & englischunterricht* 41, 15–36.

Laurie, Victoria (1996): "Identity crisis". *Australian Magazine*, 28–31.

McDonough, Clara J. (1996): "Timberlake Wertenbaker". William W. Demastes, ed. *British playwrights, 1956–1995: a research and production sourcebook*. Ed. William W. Demastes. Westport: Greenwood Press, 406–415.

Mallet, Gina (1981): "David French's long journey comes full circle". *Toronto Star*, November 14, H3.

Michaelis, Rolf (1996): "Auferstehung der Lebenden". *Die Zeit* 4, 51.

Middeke, Martin (1997): "Drama and the desire for history: the plays of Timberlake Wertenbaker". Uwe Böker/Hans Sauer, eds. *Anglistentag 1996 Dresden. Proceedings.* Trier: Wissenschaftlicher Verlag Trier, 223–233.

Mudrooroo (1993b): "The aboriginalising of Heiner Müller". Gerhard Fischer, ed. *The Mudrooroo/Müller project: a theatrical casebook.* Kensington: New South Wales UP, 19–32.

Sakellaridou, Elizabeth (1993): "Feminist heterologies: contemporary British women playwrights and the rewrite of myth and history". Robert Clark/Piero Boitani, eds. *English studies in transition: papers from the ESSE Inaugural Conference.* London: Routledge, 306–319.

Tiffin, Helen (1987): "Post-colonial literatures and counter-discourse". *Kunapipi* 3, 17–34.

Vaßen, Florian (1991): "Wider das Vergessen: Heiner Müllers Theater der Erinnerung". Bernd Ruping/Florian Vaßen/Gerd Koch, eds. *Widerwort und Widerspiel.* Hannover: Bundesarbeitsgemeinschaft Spiel und Theater, 139–162.

Wertenbaker, Timberlake (1996b): "Preface to *Our country's good*". *Plays 1.* London: faber & faber, 163–164.

Wilson, Ann (1991): "*Our country's good*: theatre, colony and nation in Wertenbaker's adaptation of *The playmaker*". *Modern Drama* 1, 23–34.

Zimmerman, Cynthia (1982): "David French". Jeffrey M. Heath, ed. *Profiles in Canadian literature* 4. Toronto: Dundurn Press, 117–123.

Clausdirk Pollner *(Leipzig)*

'Braw pearls' - the New Testament in Scots

I. One of the well-known (and often-repeated) reasons for the rapid loss of prestige of the old Scottish national language – Scots – as a written medium has to do with the Reformation and the Bible. When the ideas of the reformation movement arrived in Scotland in the second half of the 16th century, the vernacular version of the Bible available was in English (*Geneva Bible*), not in Scots.

> In 1560 the Reformation took place in Scotland and the English Bible, translated in that same year by English refugees in Geneva, was, in default of a Scots translation which never existed, circulated throughout the land. Its language became familiar to the people as the language of solemnity and abstract thought, of theological and philosophical disputation, while Scots remained as the language of ordinary life, of the domestic, sentimental and comic, and from here we can trace the split mind that Scots have had about their native language ever since. (Murison 1977: 5)

According to McClure (1988: 15) it was the Scottish Reformers, who undermined the role of their own language by introducing and using an English Bible; not, he goes on, "deliberately, but simply lacking any sense that the distinctiveness of Scots was to be ... prized". It is in the second half of the 16th century, then, that Scots receives "the first of the great blows which halted its growth and ultimately led to its replacement by English" (Murison 1977: 5). Strictly speaking, however, to say that there was no Scots version of the Bible is not true, of course. There had been a Scots version of the New Testament (with a few fragments from the Old Testament) since circa 1520, undertaken by an Ayrshire Scot, Murdoch Nisbet. But this version remained in manuscript and was first printed, astonishingly, only at the beginning of the 20th century. What little we know about Nisbet is summarized in Royle (1984: 227):

> Nisbet was a native of Ayrshire who was forced to flee the country on account of his Lollardry, and it was probably during his period in exile that he completed his work on the Bible. He returned later to Scotland but was forced to hide in a vault in his house of Hardhill in Ayrshire. After his death Nisbet's Bible was passed on by successive generations, from father to son, until it came into the possession of Sir Alexander Boswell of Auchinleck.

The manuscript was re-discovered as late as 1893 and finally published for the *Scottish Text Society* between 1901 and 1905. "The announcement made eight years ago [i.e. 1893] that a manuscript of the New Testament, with sundry lessons from the Old Testament, in Scots, was among the Auchinleck MSS. ... came then with the surprise of a new and welcome discovery" (Law 1901: VIII). So, in all fairness to Murdoch Nisbet, it is not so much the absence of a Scots *Bible* that is to be blamed for so much that follows, but the absence of a printed version, without which it was impossible for abstract religious/biblical thought in Scots to be disseminated into the community.

II. Nisbet's rather tragic role is reflected by the fact that histories of the Scottish language and histories of Scottish literature largely ignore him or relegate him to footnotes. Smith (1902) quotes two brief excerpts from Nisbet's *New Testament*, without naming him in the list of contents. In a little note above the first excerpt we read "ascribed to Murdoch Nisbet" (Smith 1902: 101). Henderson (1910) has a section on the role of the Reformation in Scotland (10-14), but does not mention Nisbet at all. Westwood (1933: 58f.) devotes one page to him and his particular variety of Scots, including a twelve-line excerpt from Nisbet's version of the gospel of Luke. Wittig (1958: 158) just mentions Nisbet in passing, incidentally without even bothering to give his first name. Watson (1984: 91) at least furnishes his readers with some of the linguistically relevant background:

> The translation of the Bible into English ... had a profound effect on the development of Scots vernacular prose. Murdoch Nisbet is credited with a Scots version of Wycliffe's fourteenth-century New Testament translation, but the work remained in manuscript and was not printed until 1901, so by far the most potent influence on the northern reformers came from testaments published in English.

Lyall (1989: 177) covers the same ground when he points out that the prose style of Scottish reformers was influenced by English models "not least because [of] the absence of a Scots Bible". It is, in fact, the only "non-technical" (or "popular") history of Scots in my random sample that devotes a little more space to the Scottish Lollards and Nisbet in particular (Kay 1988: 63-64). Apart from quoting a short excerpt from Nisbet's text, Kay ventures a hypothesis: "Unfortunately the Nisbet version remained in manuscript form during the crucial period. If it had been printed it may have acted as a catalyst for a complete Scots Bible" (Kay 1988: 64). And it may have had an influence on the development of serious Scots prose.

III. We have to wait for over 450 years before we get "an entirely new translation" (Tulloch 1989: 73) of the *Bible* into Scots. This is William

Laughton Lorimer's *The New Testament in Scots*, first published as a hardcover edition in 1983 and an immediate success. Lorimer (1885-1967) was born near Dundee and worked for most of his life as an academic teacher of Classical Greek at Dundee and St Andrews. Lorimer had always been keenly interested in Scots, and he was an important contributor to the collections of the *Scottish national dictionary*. He was convinced that "if Scots was ever to be resuscitated and rehabilitated, two great works must first be produced: a good modern Scots dictionary, and a good modern Scots translation of the New Testament ..." (Lorimer 1983: XIV). We now have both: the *SND* and Lorimer's *New Testament*.

Nisbet's and Lorimer's versions could not be more different. Nisbet took as his source a Wycliffite version of the New Testament, possibly revised by John Purvey (cf. Tulloch 1989: 4-6), whereas Lorimer worked from the original Greek. What follows in this paper is, therefore, not a critique of two **translations** of the New Testament but a comparison of a few linguistic aspects of two very different **texts**. Impressionistically, one might say that Lorimer's version 'looks' and 'feels' more Scottish than Nisbet's. This is due to the fact that Nisbet does not so much translate as transcribe an English version literally, whereas Lorimer is much less constricted and at the same time more colloquial. He produces, in Tulloch's words, "a much more interesting narrative style" (Tulloch 1989: 74) than all the other versions of the *Bible* in Scots, including Smith's 19th century effort.

The second chapter of Matthew affords a good example of the different strategies in textual (surface-)cohesion which the two texts employ. In Nisbet's version, 17 out of 23 verses (usually but not in all cases coinciding with sentence units) take *and* as their initial element. (This count excludes sentence medial occurrences, since these are not textually cohesive.) *And* is certainly an element of cohesion; Halliday/Hasan (1976: 242) classify it as "simple additive". Its constant repetition, however, does not do much for an "interesting narrative style" (Tulloch 1989: 74). In Nisbet's case this impression is reinforced by the fact that the remaining six sentence-openers in Matthew 2 are of the conjunctive type as well: *tharfor* 'therefore', *bot* 'but', and *than* 'then', some used more than once. Lorimer, on the other hand, avoids conjunctions of addition in sentence initial position; the other types of conjunction – adversative, causal, temporal – are used sparingly: *sae* 'so', *syne* 'next, afterwards', *than* 'then', *efter* 'afterwards', *for sae* 'so that', *whan* 'when' and *but*. *Sae* occurs three times and once in the variant *for sae*; *than* is used twice, in one case following the subject: *Herod than* ...; and *but* is employed twice. *An* 'and' only occurs once – to open a stretch of direct speech by Herod. The textlinguistic/cohesive use of conjunctions, then, is applied very differently in the two specimen-texts: Lorimer tries to vary his use of conjunctive items, Nisbet is content with using the additive conjunction repeatedly. This pattern can be observed right through the four gospels.

The second chapter of Mark offers an even more obvious example. The chapter has 28 verses, again roughly corresponding to sentence units, apart from a few cases where a colon or semicolon divides a verse into two or more sentence units. Nisbet here opens his sentences 27 times with *ande/and*. In addition he uses *bot* 'but' (four times), *sa that* 'so that' (once), *for* (twice) and *als lang tyme as* 'as long as' (once). A more sophisticated means of textual cohesion occurs in this particular chapter between verses 25 and 26. Verse 26 is a question: *How he went into the hous of God ...?* The cohesive strategy employed here is one of ellipsis – the full form having been given in verse 25: *Redde ye neuer quhat Dauid did ...?* The question in 26 only makes sense – is cohesive – when the reader keeps *Redde ye neuer ...?* in mind. Again, additive conjunctions in sentence initial position are conspicuous by their absence in Lorimer's version of Mark 2. He structures the timing of the stories told in this chapter very carefully with *efter some days* 'after some days', *at that* 'then', *syne* 'then, next', *ae day efterhin* 'one day later', *ae day* 'one day', *ae Sabbath* 'one Sabbath'. In addition we find *whan* 'then, when' and *but*. At one point Lorimer begins a verse with *nou* 'now': *Nou, th' war some Doctors of the law sittin by* ...; this is a good example of his successful use of colloquialisms even in the narrative text. *Now* is here, of course, not a temporal item:

> If it [= *now*] is reduced [in its tonicity] it means the opening of a new stage in the communication; this may be a new incident in the story, a new point in the argument ... and so on. (Halliday/Hasan 1976: 268)

This is the kind of cohesive element that Lorimer employs in order to give his text a certain narrative immediacy – the introduction of items of spoken language into his narrative text. (Other occurrences of continuative *now* can be found in John 11 and Luke 19.)

As has already been mentioned, Lorimer's text seems to be more consciously Scottish than Nisbet's. Nisbet does not go out of his way in the process of scottifying his source:

> When English words used by Purvey are quite intelligible north of the Tweed, Nisbet is inclined to make no change. For example, the common Scottish words *speir*, for 'ask' or 'inquire', and *thole*, for 'suffer', do not once occur in the three gospels here printed. (Law 1901: XX)

Incidentally, Hudson (1985: 109) has this to say about Nisbet's alleged source: "I see no reason whatever to assign to Purvey any particular association with the Lollard Bible, or with any of the texts advocating vernacular scriptures." Her evidence and arguments are very persuasive (1985: 85-110).[1]

Lorimer, on the other hand, scottifies where he can; when Nisbet – in Luke 2: 36 – says of Anna that she was *of the lynage of Aser*, Lorimer has *o Clan Asher*. Nisbet goes on to characterize her: *scho had gaan furth in mony dais, and had leuet with hir housband VII yeris fra hir maidinhede*. Lorimer's version is more elaborate and informal, more 'chatty': *She wis a gey an eildit carlin, at hed mairrit in her quean-days, but hed tint her guidman efter seiven year an bidden a widow-wuman sinsyne*. In the same chapter – Luke 2 – Lorimer introduces a syntactic colloquialism, which follows a popular Scottish speech-cadence: the use of the same verb, once at the beginning of a sentence and then again at the end of the following sentence: *Nou, there wis wonnin in Jerusalem ... a man o the name o Simeon. A weill-daein ... man he wis*. Nisbet on the other hand has strict parallelism: *A man was in Jerusalem ... And this man was ...* To come back briefly to Anna of Clan Asher. She is, in Lorimer's words, a *widow-woman*, where, of course, *widow* would have sufficed. Nisbet has *wedo*. Lorimer is unco fond of compounds/phrases and the rhetorical figure of hendiadys – particularly when they alliterate or show internal rhyme: cf. e.g. *castin o' caivels* 'drawing lots', *tung-tackit* 'tongue-tied', *fair-forfluthert* 'very confused', *poke-pudding* 'dumpling, term of abuse', *windlestrae waggin i the wind* 'stalk of grass shaking in the wind'. In Nisbet's version, Jesus has dinner with *publicanis and synnaries* 'excommunicated persons and sinners', the latter term a variant of *synfulmen* 'sinners' in the same verse (Mark 2:16). Lorimer, on the other hand, has him eat with *tax-uplifters an outlans* 'tax/rent collectors and outcasts', and he refers back to them in the next sentence as *sic clamjamphrie* 'such riff-raff' – one of the glories of Scots vocabulary. In the Christmas story we read: *growin ey the langer, the stranger in spirit* 'growing taller and stronger'.

Nisbet's Mark 2:21 goes like this: *And na man sewis* 'sews' *a clout* 'patch' *of new clathe to ane ald clathe; ellis* 'or else' *he takis away the new clout fra the ald, and a maire breking* 'an even larger hole' *is made*. Lorimer's rendering is, again, more colloquial and 'more Scottish': *Naebodie platches* 'patches' *an auld dud* 'rag' *wi a bit onwaukit* 'unhardened, soft, new' *claith: an* 'if' *he dis, the new eik rives* 'also tears' *awa at the auld claith an maks the screid* 'gash' *waur nor* 'than' *before*. What does 'more Scottish' mean? It simply refers to the fact that Lorimer prefers items such as *platch, dud, onwaukit, rive, screid* over Nisbet's rather tamer *sew, clathe, breking*.

---

[1] I am grateful to Klaus Bitterling, Berlin, for drawing my attention to Hudson's research.

Lorimer's *New Testament* is full of these kinds of informal phrases and words. He produced – both in terms of narrative structure and vocabulary – what Law (1901: XX) may have had in mind when he comments on the 1520 transcription: "The language of Nisbet ... is not altogether such as we should have obtained from a Scot making his own independent translation." Lorimer provides exactly that.

References

(1) Primary sources

Law, Thomas Graves, ed. (1901, 1903, 1905): *The New Testament in Scots, By Murdoch Nisbet c. 1520.* 3 vols. Scottish Text Society.

Lorimer, William Laughton (1983): *The New Testament in Scots.* Edinburgh: Southside.

(2) Secondary sources

Halliday, M.A.K./Ruqaiya Hasan (1976): *Cohesion in English.* London: Longman.

Henderson, Thomas F. (^{3}1910): *Scottish vernacular literature.* Edinburgh: Grant.

Hudson, Anne (1985): *Lollards and their books.* London etc: Hambledon.

Kay, Billy (1988): *The Mither tongue.* London: Grafton.

Lyall, Roderick J. (1988): "Vernacular prose before the Reformation". Ronald D.S. Jack, ed. *The history of Scottish literature.* Vol.I: *Origins to 1660.* Aberdeen: AUP, 163-181.

McClure, J. Derrick (1988): *Why Scots matters.* Edinburgh: Saltire Society.

Murison, David (1977): *The Guid Scots tongue.* Edinburgh: Blackwood.

Royle, Trevor (1983): *The Macmillan companion to Scottish literature.* London: Macmillan.

Smith, Gregory (1902): *Specimens of Middle Scots.* Edinburgh: Blackwood.

Tulloch, Graham (1989): *A history of the Bible in Scots.* Aberdeen: AUP.

Watson, Roderick. (1984). *The literature of Scotland.* London: Macmillan.

Westwood, John D. (1933): "Scottish theological and proverbial literature". *Edinburgh essays in Scots literature.* Edinburgh: Oliver and Boyd. 56-77.

Wiechert, Paul (1908): *Über die Sprache der einzigen schottischen Bibel-übersetzung, on Murdoch Nisbet. I: Lautlehre.* Königsberg: Hartung. Diss. Univ. Königsberg.

Wittig, Kurt (1958): *The Scottish tradition in literature.* Edinburgh: Oliver and Boyd.

Josef Schmied *(Chemnitz)*

The domains of the Lampeter Corpus as a window to Early Modern English social history

1. The Lampeter Corpus domains as a basis for sociohistorical studies[1]

This contribution is based on the Lampeter Corpus, a corpus of Early Modern English texts from the Tract Collection in the Founders' Library at St David's University College, Lampeter (cf. Schmied 1994). This is a new standardsized historical corpus, available on a handy CD in SGML format; it contains around 1.12 million tokens and 43,500 types and takes up 7.5 MB of disk space net. The Lampeter Corpus is the only corpus that consists of complete texts and is available in Standard General Mark-up Language (SGML). This has advantages not only for reconstructing the original pamphlet but also for selecting pamphlets with common features for analysis (such as self-descriptions according to genre in title pages, for instance).

The time-span selected for the corpus was 1640 to 1740, as this appeared to be a highly interesting one in terms of both language change and historical developments. The main objective of its compilation was to fill a gap in the market of historical corpora,[2] since this period lacked a balanced corpus with complete texts for text-linguistic and stylistic analyses. Since the term *tract* was used for various short Early Modern English publications, the Lampeter Corpus consists of 120 texts from various text-types grouped together in the

---

[1] Current work using the corpus is made available on the net http://www.tuchemnitz. de/phil/english/real/lampeter/lamphome.htm). The project was initiated in 1991 and has been funded by the German Research Association (DFG) since 1994. Travel grants made available by the German Academic Exchange Service (DAAD) have made possible research co-operation with the English Department at Helsinki University and the Department of Linguistics & Modern English Language at Lancaster University on questions of corpus compilation and annotation (cf. Schmied 1996). I would like to thank them and the project team at Chemnitz, especially Claudia Claridge and Rainer Siemund, for many years of fruitful collaboration.

[2] The basic idea of the Early Modern English corpus-linguistic development is to use the Early Modern English part of the Helsinki Corpus as a spine corpus and create specialized corpora around it (cf. Rissanen 1991). Thus the Lampeter Corpus can be compared with compatible textbases of roughly the same period; it is complemented for instance, by the Hartlib papers and the Helsinki Corpus of Early Modern English Correspondence.

five 'domains' of politics, religion, economy, science and law, plus a miscellaneous category. Table 1 shows the construction of the corpus and the word counts per decade and domain.[3]

Table 1: The Lampeter Corpus: word counts per decade and domain

	Religion	Politics	Eco-nomics	Science	Law	Miscel-laneous	Totel/Decade
1640s	29,279	14,948	11,640	25,786	16,659	22,497	120,809
1650s	15,502	18,440	11,993	14,233	21,696	12,037	93,901
1660s	15,210	13,243	15,541	19,656	17,299	12,367	93,316
1670s	28,243	22,074	13,426	29,565	21,002	21,708	136,018
1680s	14,627	31,809	35,667	23,289	23,348	17,389	146,129
1690s	19,938	31,935	18,416	16,723	16,581	16,222	119,815
1700s	12,349	15,076	19,728	17,943	21,391	16,839	103,326
1710s	16,733	18,034	9,191	18,304	21,011	12,842	96,115
1720s	23,287	16,764	11,982	22,584	16,075	20,718	111,410
1730s	16,043	12,597	13,094	20,349	24,722	10,593	97,398
Total/Domain	191,211	194,920	160,678	208,432	199,784	163,212	1,118,237

One major problem for the compilers of the Lampeter Corpus was the sub-categorization into text-types or genres (cf. Schmied/Claridge 1997). In the end, the safest categorization we could find was that according to 'domain' and even there we found it necessary to add a miscellaneous category for interesting texts that could not clearly be attributed to any of the five domains of religion, politics, economics, law and science. These problems of classification can be illustrated by a particularly fascinating text in the collection on financing universities. In this text (MscB1658) all Christians are advised to buy their good life after death by bequeathing their money to a university because there the priests are trained for the propagation of the Christian faith. This text is thus a mixed case of economics, science and religion and had to be attributed to the miscellaneous domain. However, from a cultural point of view, this set-up offers a unique possibility of comparing the lexis not only of

---

[3] Thus, when we compare absolute figures, we have to bear in mind that the economics section, for instance, is 20% shorter than the science section or that the 1660s texts contain a fifth less material than the 1640s texts. Frequency studies based on the Lampeter Corpus can of course also be compared to (parts of) the LOB and Brown corpora of late 20th century English.

individual texts but also of groups of texts and for relating the findings to the sociohistorical background.

In the end, it was felt that the Tract Collection, as well as the Lampeter Corpus as a (carefully and still somewhat impressionistically chosen) cross-section of it, can be seen as a window into the social, political and cultural history of life in 17th and 18th century England (cf. also Claridge 2000). Through the tracts the public discourse at the time becomes available. It is clear that the nature of public discourse does not cover all sections of life, but it adds at least some interesting perspectives to the picture that we have from the great works of fiction writers and other public figures, since it includes views and exchanges from as wide a section of the (literate) population as possible.

2. Keywords as an objective way to a quantitative lexical description

An inductive approach to the specific lexicon of a particular domain is, of course, to calculate those words in one domain that are over- or underused in comparison to their occurrence in the entire corpus. Fortunately, WordSmith provides a tool that does just that. It identifies key words on a mechanical basis by using the Log Likelihood (or G^2) coefficient (Dunning 1993): in its 'keyness' tables, WordSmith indicates which items show a greater than expected (i.e. statistically significant) difference in frequency between a specific domain and the Lampeter Corpus as a whole and lists the lexical items according to the values of this G^2 coefficient.

Overall, the keyness of *god* and *church* for the religious texts seems clear. But it is not only the most significant single words that are important but also the fifty most signficant as a group. Here, scientific texts seem to be the most closely knit, with political and – not surprisingly – miscellaneous texts the least.

It has to be emphasised at the very beginning that it is, of course, problematic to do lexical studies on the basis of a 1.12 million word corpus, even if one only takes the top fifty words of each domain or century. Even then, the problem of skewing the results by individual high-frequency texts has to be borne in mind; again statistical evidence has to be used to measure this and confirm all the personal impressions. However, the Lampeter Corpus is the most extended database that we have for a single century in the development of English before the present one, so we can use it to explore the new opportunities of this approach as well as its limits.

3. Religion, the pervasive way of thinking

If we compare the frequency of words that we would associate with religion, like *God, pray* and even *religion*, across domains, we notice that they occur not only in the religious domain but also in all the others. A word like *religion* even occurs in the domains of law and science, which may seem strange from a modern perspective (Schmied 1999).

Table 2: Keywords in the domain RELIGION

N	Word	Dom. all	%	Lamp. all	%	
1	*GOD*	1886	.43%	1463	.12%	986.0
2	*CHURCH*	596	.29%	885	.07%	764.7
3	*CHRIST*	311	.15%	357	.03%	535.5
4	*TRUTH*	423	.21%	755	.06%	418.4
5	*YOU*	1068	.52%	3321	.28%	321.2
6	*RELIGION*	297	.14%	533	.04%	290.7
7	*CHRISTIAN*	170	.08%	231	.02%	241.7
8	*BISHOP*	151	.07%	208	.02%	211.0
9	*ANTICHRIST*	99	.05%	101		189.4
10	*POPE*	109	.05%	130	.01%	178.7
11	*SCRIPTURE*	109	.05%	136	.01%	170.1
12	*TEXT*	102	.05%	120	.01%	169.5
13	*WORD*	185	.09%	350	.03%	165.9
14	*CHRISTIANS*	114	.06%	154	.01%	162.5
15	*GOSPEL*	99	.05%	119		160.7
16	*SINNE*	82	.04%	84		155.8
17	*FAITH*	138	.07%	227	.02%	152.6
18	*BISHOPS*	104	.05%	147	.01%	140.1
19	*WORSHIP*	77	.04%	85		135.0
20	*APOSTLES*	74	.04%	80		133.3
21	*SPIRIT*	133	.06%	238	.02%	129.8
22	*HOLY*	101	.05%	149	.01%	128.9
23	*ROME*	102	.05%	157	.01%	123.1
24	*JESUS*	66	.03%	73		115.9
25	*ST*	140	.07%	278	.02%	115.4
26	*CONSCIENCE*	121	.06%	222	.02%	113.4
27	*COMMUNION*	67	.03%	77		113.2
28	*PAGE*	126	.06%	239	.02%	112.0
29	*YE*	67	.03%	79		110.2
30	*PAUL*	85	.04%	127	.01%	106.4
31	*IS*	2594	1.26%	12024	1.01%	105.5

Table 2 continued

N	Word	Dom. all	%	Lamp. all	%	
32	*GODS*	89	.04%	139	.01%	105.1
33	*SIN*	79	.04%	113		104.4
34	*DIVINE*	88	.04%	140	.01%	101.3
35	*THINGS*	280	.14%	815	.07%	101.3
36	*THY*	102	.05%	184	.02%	97.9
37	*US*	577	.28%	2115	.18%	95.5
38	*SERMON*	57	.03%	69		90.8
39	*UNTO*	230	.11%	649	.05%	90.4
40	*LP*	47	.02%	47		90.2
41	*APOSTLE*	50	.02%	56		86.1
42	*CLERGY*	84	.04%	146	.01%	85.1
43	*LOVE*	111	.05%	230	.02%	84.6
44	*THAT*	4126	2.00%	20439	1.71%	83.5
45	*SCHISMA*	43	.02%	44		80.5
46	*CHURCHES*	61	.03%	87		80.4
47	*REV*	42	.02%	42		80.3
48	*PSAL*	47	.02%	53		80.2
49	*SAVIOUR*	58	.03%	82		77.2
50	*DOCTRINE*	80	.04%	144	.01%	76,7

The results of for the religious texts (in Table 2) are obviously that *God*, *Church* and *Christ* are the (relatively) most distinctive words. In the list of the fifty most striking candidates we find some surprises, however, that tell us a lot about the position of religion and the nature of religious texts in the Lampeter century.

- From the present-day perspective, it may seem strange that words like *text*, *word* and *page* are among the top thirty in religious texts compared to the rest of the corpus. This shows that publishing and learning were clearly related to religion at a time when a university served primarily to educate the clergy and was dominated by the established church (see the illustrative example above).

- Secondly, it is also revealing that religious texts have by far the greatest number of archaic spellings[4] (like *sinne*) or formal, traditional words like *unto* and *thy*.

---

[4] This raises, of course, issues of regularization on a morphemic and orthographic level, but the Lampeter Corpus tries to record faithfully what was in the original, since it is intended to leave analyses open to as many researchers as possible.

- Generally, the second person pronoun *you* is obviously most important for religious discourse, both when the priest speaks to the congregation and when Christians talk to their God. It may be reassuring that the spirit of *love* and *community* also speaks from religious texts which can also be seen by the unusual relative frequency of *us*.

4. Politics, the new way of exchange

There can be no doubt that the Lampeter century was the formative period of the British political system, since it witnessed the establishment of a strong parliament and finally of the **constitutional** monarchy. The Lampeter Corpus does not concentrate on texts of political theory but it makes available the works of the pamphleteers, political activists deeply involved in the discourse of the current affairs of the day. They influenced the course of history since they formed public opinion – and this became increasingly important as the will of the absolute monarch became subjugated to the public discourse of the (still rather restricted) electorate.

The pronouns *us*, *our* and *we* are significantly more frequent in political texts (Table 3). This is, of course, hardly surprising, for the time when pamphleteers tried to gather their followers around themselves and emphasized the contrast between *we* and *they*. This is also indicated by the distinctive use of national words like *England* and *kingdom* (singular or plural).

Table 3: Keywords in the domain POLITICS

N	Word	Dom. all	%	Lamp. all	%	
1	*KING*	689	.33%	1488	.12%	484.6
2	*SCOTS*	102	.05%	106		189.4
3	*PARLIAMENT*	371	.18%	967	.08%	174.3
4	*CROWN*	166	.08%	281	.02%	173.7
5	*SCOTLAND*	166	.06%	150	.01%	171.6
6	*SPAIN*	147	.07%	240	.02%	161.8
7	*TREATY*	106	.05%	142	.01%	150.3
8	*FRANCE*	143	.07%	258	.02%	135.6
9	*SESSION*	80	.04%	92		133.8
10	*SPANIARDS*	88	.04%	114		129.3
11	*OUR*	1139	.55%	4490	.38%	128.7
12	*WE*	1118	.54%	4431	.37%	122.8
13	*TORIES*	61	.03%	62		114.6
14	*LORDS*	194	.09%	456	.04%	114.3

Table 3 continued

N	Word	Dom. all	%	Lamp. all	%	
15	*SCOT*	71	.03%	85		113.5
16	*LAWS*	226	.11%	585	.05%	107.5
17	*VOTE*	67	.03%	81		105.8
18	*ENGLAND*	331	.16%	1001	.08%	104.4
19	*WHIGS*	55	.03%	56		102.9
20	*MAJESTY*	175	.08%	418	.04%	99.5
21	*PRINCE*	137	.07%	289	.02%	99.5
22	*DARIEN*	52	.02%	52		98.8
23	*NATION*	229	.11%	622	.05%	96.8
24	*UNION*	64	.03%	81		96.0
25	*POWER*	298	.14%	899	.08%	94.6
26	*TYRANT*	60	.03%	73		93.9
27	*JUSTICE*	200	.10%	524	.04%	92.3
28	*HIS*	1791	.86%	8001	.67%	91.6
29	*US*	571	.27%	2115	.18%	86.6
30	*THEY*	1777	.85%	8053	.68%	80.9
31	*KINGDOMES*	53	.03%	66		80.5
32	*HIGHNESS*	64	.03%	94		80.2
33	*WAR*	136	.07%	326	.03%	76.5
34	*PEACE*	158	.08%	409	.03%	74.8
35	*INTEREST*	197	.09%	568	.05%	70.9
36	*EMPEROR*	59	.03%	90		70.2
37	*LAW*	328	.16%	1124	.09%	68.1
38	*RIGHTS*	71	.03%	127	.01%	67.4
39	*HANOVER*	38	.02%	41		66.4
40	*FRENCH*	124	.06%	309	.03%	63.9
41	*NATIONS*	111	.05%	263	.02%	63.8
42	*LIB*	63	.03%	111		61.0
43	*VIENNA*	33	.02%	34		60.0
44	*PRINCES*	80	.04%	166	.01%	59.3
45	*HORFILL*	135	.06%	361	.03%	58.9
46	*TROOPS*	47	.02%	69		58.4
47	*LOT*	41	.02%	54		57.9
48	*HESSIANS*	31	.01%	31		57.8
49	*ALLYANCE*	31	.01%	31		57.8
50	*AND*	8086	3.89%	42400	3.56%	55.5

The political issues of the day can clearly be seen from the most significant words. The contrast between *king* or *crown* and *parliament*, the preoccupation with *Scots* and *Scotland* through a *treaty* that led to the *Union* of *Parliaments* (in 1703) and the external contrasts or controversy with *Spain, France,* even *Vienna,* with the importance of *troops* of *Hessians.*

We have to point out, however, that even frequencies spread across thirty individual texts may skew the picture so that we have to bear in mind not only the relationship between the political domain texts as a whole and the Lampeter texts as a whole, but also between an individual text and the other texts of the domain and the corpus as a whole. Thus the absolute frequencies of *Hessians* and *Vienna* and their distribution across many texts has to be taken into account.

Although England as still preoccupied with its own development, including its relationship with Scotland (cf. PolB1689 and PolA1699) and Ireland (cf. PolA1720), and thus most Lampeter tracts show an insular outlook, some texts point to increasing wider involvement (again PolA1699).

5. Economy, the new global view

On first glancing at the economic texts we see a surprising similarity to the political texts: *Our* and *their, kingdom, England, Dutch, Holland* and *French* are among the most characteristic words again. In contrast to the political texts, however, the economic texts show a more 'global' outlook. The East India Company figures prominently in the corpus (EcB1641, EcB1676, EcB1681, EcA1697). The world-wide trade connections were established in this period and, although the prominence of *India* in those early days may seem surprising, the importance of the *East* for *plantations, shipping* and *exportation* seems clear. The new global outlook can be sensed in these beginnings.

Although 'economics' was not yet established as an academic discipline (e.g. Adam Smith's *Wealth of nations* appeared in 1776), the importance of solid finances was an obvious concern for the state and the private entre-preneur and the rise of the financial sector is symbolized by the foundation of the Bank of England in 1694.

Table 4: Keywords in the domain ECONOMICS

N	Word	Dom. all	%	Lamp. all	%	
1	*TRADE*	1027	.58%	1292	.11%	2011.0
2	*MONEY*	399	.22%	646	.05%	585.2
3	*INDIA*	222	.12%	262	.02%	460.3

Table 4 continued

N	Word	Dom. all	%	Lamp. all	%	
4	*COMMODITIES*	211	.12%	236	.02%	460.2
5	*STOCK*	208	.12%	259	.02%	408.8
6	*TRADES*	177	.10%	199	.02%	383.7
7	*OUR*	1170	.66%	4490	.38%	296.3
8	*PER*	279	.16%	570	.05%	295.2
9	*BANK*	131	.07%	146	.01%	285.5
10	*CENT*	124	.07%	136	.01%	274.1
11	*COMPANY*	219	.12%	415	.03%	258.9
12	*GOODS*	198	.11%	362	.03%	246.1
13	*PRICE*	145	.08%	209	.02%	242.7
14	*PLANTATIONS*	109	.06%	128	.01%	225.6
15	*SELL*	127	.07%	177	.01%	220.5
16	*CLOTH*	119	.07%	160	.01%	214.7
17	*WILL*	1048	.59%	4262	.36%	214.3
18	*MARKET*	115	.06%	150	.01%	214.2
19	*WARES*	90	.05%	98		199.4
20	*EAST*	192	.11%	402	.03%	194.9
21	*WOOLLEN*	83	.05%	85		194.0
22	*MERCHANTS*	114	.06%	163	.01%	192.0
23	*LAND*	226	.13%	551	.05%	176.9
24	*SHOP*	105	.06%	151	.01%	175.5
25	*IRON*	96	.05%	133	.01%	167.1
26	*KINGDOM*	233	.13%	598	.05%	165.4
27	*PAY*	175	.10%	389	.03%	160.9
28	*SHIPPING*	74	.04%	85		155.5
29	*CREDIT*	115	.06%	202	.02%	150.1
30	*MANUFACTURES*	94	.05%	143	.01%	146.9
31	*SILKS*	62	.03%	65		141.2
32	*SUGAR*	70	.04%	84		140.8
33	*TREASURE*	84	.05%	122	.01%	138.3
34	*DUTCH*	114	.06%	216	.02%	133.9
35	*LANDS*	100	.06%	178	.01%	128.0
36	*CHEAPER*	61	.03%	71		126.0
37	*ENGLAND*	305	.17%	1001	.08%	123.4
38	*THEIR*	1499	.84%	7353	.62.%	122.5
39	*HOLLAND*	92	.05%	161	.01%	120.3
40	*CHEAP*	65	.04%	85		199.6
41	*EXPORTATION*	51	.03%	52		118.4
42	*FISHERY*	50	.03%	50		118.0
43	*INTEREST*	200	.11%	568	.05%	114.7

Table 4 continued

N	Word	Dom. all	%	Lamp. all	%	
44	*BE*	2607	1.46%	13925	1.17%	114.4
45	*WOOLL*	53	.03%	59		113.8
46	*FRENCH*	133	.07%	309	.03%	112.9
47	*PROFIT*	82	.05%	138	.01%	112.7
48	*YEARLY*	65	.04%	91		111.0
49	*COMMODITY*	52	.03%	59		109.6
50	*COLONIES*	58	.03%	75		107.7

More down-to-earth, clearly economic terms are, of course, *trade(s)*, *commodities*, *stock*, *company* and *bank*. Other (less unique) economic words are specialised goods, such as *cloth* (or *wollen* and *wool* just off the list), *iron*, *sugar*, *silks* and *fishery*. These terms illustrate that current events or problems were of interest in the public debate of the day.

6. Science, the new view on the world

It is clear that scientific texts play a major role in public discourse in the age of the Royal Society (founded in 1662). Its president, Isaac Newton, however, not only revolutionized physics but also dabbled in alchemy. This shows that the Lampeter age marks the turning point from the old, Elizabethan and metaphysical world picture to the rationalistic and mechanical one in the new 'real' philosophy. Science in those days did not take a narrow view, "centring on natural and mechanical problems but [extended] through life sciences towards medicine and through chemistry and applied mathematics towards technology" (Hunter 1981: 32). All this is reflected in the Lampeter tracts, whose authors range from astrologers (in SciA1644) to modern authors like Hooke and Boyle.

At a first glance, science also seems to be preoccupied with travel; this can be seen from the most characteristic words such as *longitude*, *meridian*, *earth*, *water* and *globe* and even the *moon* and *mars*.

Table 5: Keywords in the domain SCIENCE

N	Word	Dom. all	%	Lamp. all	%	
1	*THE*	16615	7.50%	72609	6.09%	626.0
2	*LONGITUDE*	231	.10%	231	.02%	409.4
3	*MERIDIAN*	208	.09%	212	.02%	361.7
4	*EARTH*	283	.13%	420	.04%	319.7
5	*BLOUD*	198	.09%	218	.02%	318.4
6	*WATER*	259	.12%	366	.03%	312.1
7	*MOTION*	200	.09%	245	.02%	286.3
8	*DEGREES*	205	.09%	262	.02%	279.4
9	*GLOBE*	149	.07%	152	.01%	258.1
10	*MOON*	166	.07%	191	.02%	254.4
11	*POX*	146	.07%	149	.01%	252.8
12	*BEE*	189	.09%	255	.02%	241.0
13	*LATITUDE*	156	.07%	184	.02%	232.5
14	*SMALL*	287	.13%	546	.05%	221.0
15	*PHYSICK*	130	.06%	144	.01%	206.9
16	*OR*	2213	1.00%	8565	.72%	193.6
17	*SUN*	166	.07%	248	.02%	185.0
18	*HORIZON*	108	.05%	112		183.4
19	*PARTS*	265	.12%	549	.05%	174.3
20	*DISTANCE*	135	.06%	181	.02%	172.9
21	*STAR*	127	.06%	165	.01%	168.9
22	*CIRCLE*	100	.05%	108		162.8
23	*PHYSICIANS*	100	.05%	111		158.3
24	*STARS*	103	.05%	119		156.2
25	*WATERS*	103	.05%	124	.01%	149.3
26	*NORTH*	137	.06%	210	.02%	147.0
27	*LINE*	126	.06%	190	.02%	138.2
28	*BATH*	86	.04%	94		138.0
29	*POLE*	86	.04%	98		132.0
30	*SALT*	112	.05%	160	.01%	132.0
31	*MEDICINES*	79	.04%	83		131.7
32	*ZENITH*	73	.03%	73		127.6
33	*OBSERVATIONS*	102	.05%	139	.01%	127.5
34	*PLACE*	351	.16%	945	.08%	126.9
35	*SULPHUR*	74	.03%	76		126.1
36	*MARS*	76	.03%	86		117.3
37	*ECLIPTICK*	67	.03%	67		116.9
38	*WEST*	123	.06%	205	.02%	116.6
39	*EQUATOR*	67	.03%	68		115.2
40	*ARTERIES*	67	.03%	69		113.6

Table 5 continued

N	Word	Dom. all	%	Lamp. all	%	
41	*PORES*	64	.03%	64		111.5
42	*YEARE*	74	.03%	86		110.9
43	*DIFFERENCE*	115	.05%	194	.02%	106.9
44	*ISAAC*	62	.03%	66		101.5
45	*FIXT*	65	.03%	73		100.8
46	*CENTER*	68	.03%	80		100.1
47	*DISTEMPER*	69	.03%	83		99.4
48	*I*	2005	.90%	8445	.71%	98.0
49	*INOCULATION*	56	.03%	56		97.3
50	*SOUTH*	106	.05%	182	.02%	95.7

What is not quite so clear is why *the* and *I* seem so special here. *I*, in particular, seems to be in contrast with modern objective *observations*, which have to be totally independent of the individual observer. It has been shown, however, (e.g. in Claridge 1998) that the scientific subject is much more involved in those days, since this is seen to add authenticity to the investigation. Nevertheless, precision can be found in the language of measurements (e.g. the attention paid to *distance* and *difference*) and scale (e.g. *degrees*). On the grammatical level, this precision can be seen in heavy noun groups; that is why the article *the* and, later, the postmodifying preposition *of* occur in our lexical ranking list.

7. Law, fixing the world in discourse

Although in the legal domain some texts, such as court-room transcripts (Law B1678), statutes (LawA1643), petitions (LawB1661) and pleas (LawB1715), are clearly legal genres, many texts are rather **about** law and are more a fixing of events and states of general public interests. Thus texts in the legal domain can have an affinity to all domains of public life, such as politics (e.g. numerous high treason cases like LawA1723), religion, economics and even law (e.g. LawA1680 deals with the administration of law). This attempt at fixing matters in a world that was felt as changing more rapidly than before was taken to be achieved best in a certain formality and stylistic 'remoteness', which became a typical feature of the domain. This aim and this form made the domain 'naturally' conservative. It also made law probably the last sphere of life to give up the official use of a foreign language (with the abolition of

'Law French' in 1732), but French or traditional spellings (e.g. *generall*) can still be found in the Lampeter Corpus. This conservatism also has repercussions in the lexicon (e.g. *aforesaid* and *upon* are typical 'legalese' even today).

On this conservative basis, it is not really surprising that so many occurrences of *God* (though not in the top 50) can be found in political and legal texts, because, pragmatically speaking, the appeal to the highest authority gives a tract credibility and makes its argumentation even more convincing, at least in the 17th century. The reference to a higher authority seems only natural in the endeavour to find a standpoint in the rapidly changing world.

The vocabulary in the domain law, of course, reflects the proceedings in the *courts: prisoners, jury, judges, sheriff, petitioner, witnesses* and *lords* are clear cases at hand.

Table 6: Keywords in the domain LAW

N	Word	Dom. all	%	Lamp. all	%	
1	*SAID*	719	.34%	1577	.13%	483.2
2	*LAW*	553	.26%	1124	.09%	427.7
3	*COURT*	324	.15%	521	.04%	362.1
4	*JURY*	210	.10%	247	.02%	343.2
5	*WAS*	1503	.72%	5365	.45%	260.5
6	*LORDSHIP*	163	.08%	199	.02%	255.3
7	*GUILTY*	180	.09%	247	.02%	246.5
8	*SILVER*	206	.10%	317	.03%	243.9
9	*YOUR*	740	.35%	2240	.19%	228.6
10	*WILLIAM*	168	.08%	235	.02%	224.6
11	*PRISONER*	125	.06%	140	.01%	213.9
12	*JUDGES*	166	.08%	245	.02%	207.3
13	*SHERIFF*	104	.05%	106		194.8
14	*CASE*	384	.18%	974	.08%	188.9
15	*EVIDENCE*	152	.07%	236	.02%	177.3
16	*PETITIONER*	94	.04%	95		177.2
17	*EARL*	113	.05%	144	.01%	168.0
18	*JUSTICE*	243	.12%	524	.04%	167.7
19	*PARLIAMENT*	365	.17%	967	.08%	161.7
20	*HOUSE*	327	.16%	858	.07%	148.2
21	*INDICTED*	75	.04%	76		140.5
22	*ACTION*	145	.07%	260	.02%	136.9
23	*LORD*	333	.16%	914	.08%	134.7
24	*TREASON*	90	.04%	117		130.3
25	*VERDICT*	73	.03%	78		129.9
26	*SIR*	245	.12%	615	.05%	123.0

Table 6 continued

N	Word	Dom. all	%	Lamp. all	%	
27	*HORE*	63	.03%	63		119.0
28	*MARRIAGE*	103	.05%	161	.01%	118.4
29	*WITNESSES*	80	.04%	102		118.2
30	*JOHN*	146	.07%	292	.02%	115.0
31	*PARTY*	148	.07%	300	.03%	113.9
32	*JUDGMENT*	146	.07%	296	.02%	112.3
33	*LORDS*	190	.09%	456	.04%	105.2
34	*WITNESS*	74	.04%	99		103.2
35	*OFFICE*	114	.05%	210	.02%	102.8
36	*LIBEL*	56	.03%	59		100.4
37	*STATUTE*	93	.04%	152	.01%	100.2
38	*HE*	1618	.77%	7018	.59%	97.7
39	*SWORN*	70	.03%	96		94.6
40	*JURIES*	50	.02%	51		92.2
41	*COUNTY*	71	.03%	102		90.6
42	*REORT*	80	.04%	126	.01%	90.6
43	*COMMONS*	115	.05&	231	.02%	89.6
44	*PETITION*	70	.03%	101		88.8
45	*GOLD*	118	.06%	242	.02%	88.6
46	*INFORMATION*	71	.03%	104		88.4
47	*THREAD*	59	.03%	74		88.2
48	*LETTERS*	91	.04%	160	.01%	88.0
49	*AGAINST*	417	.20%	1418	.12%	86.8
50	*LACE*	52	.02%	61		83.4

Because of the direct speech in some documents, personal names occur relatively often. This personal touch is also seen in the address terms *your* and *he*, for instance. The main topics of the disputes can be inferred from the words *silver*, *gold* and *marriage*. Two words one might have expected in other categories show a certain overlap, *evidence* with science and *lace* with economics.

8. A mixed bag with a personal touch

Finally, a brief look at the problematic miscellaneous category. Here, the third person pronouns seem to be very prominent, especially in the female forms *her* and *she*. This is the case not only because there are manuals or texts that give practical advice, e.g. in *garden(s)* and household, but also because there are biographies of people of interest, even of swindlers (MscB1692) and adventurers (MscA1685). These elements of 'popular press' (in a positive sense) were considered important, since they add a personal touch; thus personal pronouns and personal names were used relatively frequently.

Table 7: Keywords in the domain MISCELLANEOUS

N	Word	Dom. all	%	Lamp. all	%	
1	*HER*	730	.43%	1571	.13%	789.7
2	*SHE*	450	.27%	874	.07%	565.9
3	*NAVIE*	118	.07%	123	.01%	293.0
4	*CAPTAIN*	143	.08%	195	.02%	275.4
5	*MASTER*	182	.11%	315	.03%	266.0
6	*BURRELL*	99	.06%	99		254.1
7	*HE*	1537	.91%	7018	.59%	244.3
8	*HIS*	1663	.98%	8001	.67%	206.0
9	*LADY*	93	.06%	118		191.8
10	*FLOWERS*	79	.05%	68		187.8
11	*GUSTAVUS*	81	.05%	94		181.7
12	*SHIPS*	193	.11%	459	.04%	175.9
13	*NIGHT*	128	.08%	252	.02%	156.4
14	*MR*	236	.14%	673	.06%	152.5
15	*HIM*	691	.41%	2947	.25%	145.0
16	*A*	3148	1.86%	17669	1.48%	143.1
17	*ORDNANCE*	55	.03%	57		135.5
18	*SHIP*	139	.08%	321	.03%	132.7
19	*CAME*	173	.10%	453	.04%	132.2
20	*FRIGATES*	47	.03%	47		118.8
21	*MY*	548	.32%	2333	.20%	115.6
22	*WING*	47	.03%	50		112.7
23	*CITY*	160	.09%	438	.04%	112.0
24	*GARDEN*	50	.03%	58		111.0
25	*PLANT*	55	.03%	80		97.1
26	*TOOK*	110	.07%	268	.02%	95.4
27	*MARCHED*	41	.02%	45		95.2
28	*WAS*	1053	.62%	5365	.45%	94.5
29	*TRUSTEES*	42	.02%	49		92.3
30	*WITH*	1298	.77%	6879	.58%	90.6
31	*COUNTRY*	147	.09%	430	.04%	89.5
32	*PLANTS*	57	.03%	92		89.2

Table 7 continued

N	Word	Dom. all	%	Lamp. all	%	
33	*FLOWER*	46	.03%	62		87.8
34	*SPILLER*	34	.02%	34		85.0
35	*TOWN*	84	.05%	187	.02%	84.5
36	*HORSE*	70	.04%	139	.01%	83.6
37	*GARDENS*	36	.02%	40		82.3
38	*JANE*	37	.02%	43		81.2
39	*THORN*	32	.02%	33		77.7
40	*WENHAM*	31	.02%	31		77.2
41	*VVE*	34	.02%	38		77.1
42	*MILE*	37	.02%	48		72.9
43	*BOAT*	35	.02%	43		72.7
44	*FIRE*	65	.04	137	.01%	70.9
45	*REGIMENTS*	31	.02%	35		69.4
46	*LITTLE*	231	.14%	889	.07%	68.9
47	*LONDON*	143	.08%	467	.04%	67.4
48	*BUGGS*	27	.02%	27		66.8
49	*REGIMENT*	29	.02%	33		64.3
50	*GROW*	62	.04%	135	.01%	64.2

Conclusion

I hope that our analysis of the domain-specific lexicon in the Lampeter Corpus has shown

- that the Lampeter Corpus can be used as a new database, although it is still not large enough for many purely lexical searches,
- that WordSmith can be used for inter-variety, text-type-specific comparisons, although a quantitative view has to be complemented by a close qualitative one, and
- that the Lampeter corpus really opens a window on Early Modern English social history, thus combining language and culture in a traditional and a modern way at the same time.

References

Claridge, Claudia (1998): "Early Modern English science: authorial and factual styles of writing". Paper delivered at ICAME 1998 (Belfast).

Claridge, Claudia (2000): *The way of words: multi-word verbs in Early Modern English. A study based on the Lampeter Corpus of Early Modern English tracts.* Ph.D. thesis Chemnitz 1999. Amsterdam: Rodopi.

Dunning, Ted (1993): "Accurate methods for the statistics of surprise and coincidence". *Computational Linguistics*, 61-74.

Hunter, Michael (1981): *Science and society in restoration England.* Cambridge: CUP.

Rissanen, Matti (1991): "The diachronic corpus as a window to the history of English". Jan Svartvik, ed. *Directions in corpus linguistics.* Berlin: Mouton de Gruyter, 185-209.

Schmied, Josef (1994): "The Lampeter Corpus of Early Modern English tracts". Merja Kytö/Matti Rissanen/Susan Wright, eds. *Corpora across the centuries.* Amsterdam: Rodopi, 81-89.

Schmied, Josef (1996): "Networking on corpora". Doris Feldmann/Fritz-Wilhelm Neumann/Thomas Rommel, eds. *Anglistik im Internet.* Heidelberg: Winter, 113-128.

Schmied, Josef (1999): "Lexical variation in the domains of the Lampeter Corpus of Early Modern English tracts". Paper presented at the colloquium The History of English as a History of Genres. Bochum. February 5/6, 1999.

Schmied, Josef/Claudia Claridge (1997): "Classifying text- and genre variation in the Lampeter Corpus of Early Modern English tracts". Merja Kytö/Matti Rissanen/ Raymond Hickey, eds. *Trancing the trail of time.* Amsterdam: Rodopi, 119-135.

Manfred Markus *(Innsbruck)*

ESP from a linguistic and didactic point of view: some suggestions

1. Introduction

Since the seventies, English for Specific Purposes (ESP) or 'Fachsprache Englisch' has been of increasing scholarly interest both in Britain/the US and in the German-speaking countries. New periodicals such as *English for Specific Purposes*, quite a number of special (English and/or German) dictionaries[1] and published analyses[2] bear testimony to the well-established status of this new branch of academic English studies.

There are good reasons for this growth: the readiness of linguists and lecturers in teaching methods to take into account the needs of the job market and of professional schools; the search for new academic fields in optimistically-founded universities and in the face of falling students numbers; the greater accessibility of ESP texts due to their machine-readability, etc. Yet, a cursory glance at the manifold publishing activities in ESP makes clear that scholars are bound to be confronted with two barriers: quantitative and qualitative.

In terms of quantity, the huge number of ESP words alone seems to be beyond human reach. According to an estimate done by Langenscheidt-Verlag (Voigt 1981: 26), English has more than 10 million specific words, as against just over a million common words, or some 40,000 which educated native speakers of English could claim to have at their disposal.

In addition, we are confronted with problems resulting from the quality of ESP words. A lexeme such as *minimum strain energy twisted-folded geometry* confronts us with special problems of both word formation and

---

[1] For example, Bucksch (1980) on building and architecture. For recent publications in general, see Lück (1997). – Some of them are now even available on the Internet, for example, an *English-German dictionary of common computing terms* (http://www.css. qmw.ac.uk/foreign/engl-germ.htm); also a (German) dictionary on biology: http://www. biologie.de/lexikon.html.

[2] A query in the MLA bibliography on CD-ROM from 1981 to 1998 delivered an output of 70 titles on English for Specific Purposes/ESP, most of them of a non-Anglo-American origin.

semantics and can obviously not be grasped without some knowledge of the matter at issue.[3]

In view of these problems, researchers are advised to approach ESP with an attitude of modesty. Indeed, ESP as a whole seems an inaccessible fortress, if not from a theoretical point of view,[4] at least for linguists and learners. A division of labour, which is absolutely necessary, appears feasible along the lines of the following parameters/criteria:

(1) domain: sciences vs. humanities, other academic disciplines (such as medicine, law, economics, etc.);

(2) text types: written vs. oral, with two long lists of subtypes (cf. Gläser 1990: 60-297);

(3) vertical stratification according to user groups: scholars, practitioners, sales persons;[5]

(4) language(s) concerned: one language or two or more (which can then be contrasted);

(5) level(s) of language system: syntax, morphemes, lexemes, word formation, stylistic features;

(6) textual purpose of ESP texts: descriptive, instructive, or directive;[6]

(7) scholarly purpose: descriptive, explanatory, or didactic.

While all these (and other) parameters allow for challenging scholarly issues, this paper suggests focussing on what is considered to be the main practical problem concerning ESP: how can we learn/teach ESP terms?[7]

The answers given to this question so far seem to be greatly influenced by two fallacies: one is that you learn ESP terminology automatically by doing, and that there is therefore no need to acquire *Sprachkenntnis* irrespective of *Sachkenntnis*. Naturally the two types of knowledge acquisition should go hand in hand, yet many cognitive impulses will come from the language side or will at least be helpful in the process of ESP acquisition.

The other fallacy is that we can leave the problem of ESP vocabulary to good and comprehensive dictionaries and data banks. It is true that in this

---

[3] Albrecht (1992: 76) has raised the general question of whether *Sprachkenntnis* and *Sachkenntnis* can be kept separate at all.

[4] A striking example of the dominant theoretical approach of many ESP studies is Jahr (1993).

[5] The threefold classification could be elaborated; cf. Hoffmann's five types of the vertical stratification of users (Hoffmann 1985: 64ff.), or Sager's six types (Sager et al. 1980: 183). The three types just mentioned are those given by Reinhardt (1983); they are referred to by Jahr (1993: 13). – On the whole question of vertical stratification, cf. also Gläser (1990: 10-14).

[6] Cf. Möhn/Pelka (1984: 45ff.), about these and other, less relevant functions of ESP texts.

[7] The fact that lexis is the most striking formal feature of ESP is also emphasized in *Lexikon der Germanistischen Linguistik* (= LGL; 1980: 284).

age of ours, when "the future for dictionaries must surely be electronic" (Summers 1988, 13f.), comprehensive ESP dictionaries have profited remarkably from the possibilities offered by the computer, and a great many dictionaries and data banks of this kind have become available.[8] In 1990, the renowned *Fraunhofer Gesellschaft* in Stuttgart published a comprehensive database dictionary in the area of building and architecture, which, however, is meant as a basis for automatic translation and is anything but learner-friendly.[9] Various university departments have also initiated ESP courses and/or project work, for example the universities of Bochum, Siegen (Beier/ Forner 1994), Graz and Salzburg[10] (to mention only a few).

Such initiatives are good for comprehensive and at best temporarily complete descriptions of wide ESP fields and for catching the latest trends. What learners need most, however, are **learning** dictionaries, methodologically governed by three main principles: bilingualism, a thematic arrangement of the material selected and strategies for motivating the learners. Such **learning** dictionaries hardly exist.

2. State of the art: shortage of learning dictionaries

For ESP learning purposes, a great many textbooks concerning the various branches are available. In the 1980's the Verlag Enzyklopädie in Leipzig started publishing an ESP series of this kind.[11] One advantage of the vocabulary given is the separate listing of internationalisms, i.e. those usually Greek- or Latin-based words that have likewise been borrowed by several European languages, such as *seminar, anatomy* and *function*, and have retained their (semantic) equivalence.[12]

But learning new vocabulary is, of course, only one of the various teaching/learning aims in these booklets; they also emphasize phonetics/

---

[8] In the history of lexicography, ESP dictionaries carry on the tradition of earlier English dictionaries, in particular of the early 18th century; cf. Landau (1989: 20).

[9] Most entries, often misleadingly, apply a one-to-one correspondence between English and German vocabulary.

[10] Apart from AREAS, detailed information is now available on the Internet; for the Salzburg project, for example, see http://www.sbg.ac.at/filcom/home.htm.

[11] As is well-known, many scholars associated with the University of Leipzig, such as Hoffmann, Gläser, and contributors of the present volume (Graustein/Thiele), were intensively committed to ESP long before western publishers and scholars. As the book *Englisch für Mediziner* (Sprigade/Adler/Mitchell 1986) reveals, other universities in the former GDR, in this case the Humboldt-University in Berlin, were also involved.

[12] For an exact definition and the theoretical status of internationalisms, see Schaeder (1994: 100-105).

speaking, word formation, grammar, translation and the reading of original texts.

Again more on the textbook side is the series of *Collins Cobuild English guides* (Harper Collins Publishers), based on the Birmingham University International Language Database. The booklets are mainly concerned with grammatical and stylistic problems, in the context of which important vocabulary is briefly listed.[13] For building and architecture, three textbooks have come to my attention: Kreiter et al. (1982), Wallnig/Everett (1984), and Killer (1984). They all no doubt have their strengths,[14] and as the repeated editions show, the latter two books have answered a demand of the market. But linguistically and didactically, they are reductionist or even naive.[15]

All textbooks, however, are meant to support language courses, thus presupposing the time and energy needed for course attendance. For effective vocabulary work, we need (learning) dictionaries.

1. Pons: The *Pons-Fachwörterbücher*, published by Klett Verlag für Wissen und Bildung since 1996, are dictionaries proper, to be more precise, English-German dictionaries with German-English index lists. The dictionary entries offer definitions in simple English, supplemented often by explanatory comments and quotations from authentic publications. At the back of the books, supplements give additional information in the form of tables.

As with all dictionaries compiled in alphabetical order, the approach is mainly a semasiological one: the user comes across a word and wants to know what it means. This approach is insufficient for answering onomasiological questions. For example, if users of the *Fachwörterbuch Touristik, Hotellerie, Gastronomie* are interested in the different types of 'Mehlspeisen' (in the Austrian sense), they do not get any specific information except the wrong reference to bread. This series, then, is not a collection of learning dictionaries.

2. Routledge/Langenscheidt: The same holds true for the collection of *Fachwörterbücher* published by Routledge/Langenscheidt. They are offered in bookform plus electronic Windows-versions, allowing quick keyword and fulltext queries and also hypertext functions. They are fairly comprehensive (the dictionary on medicine, for example, has 157,000 terms, that on chem-

---

[13] Cf., for example, vol. 5, which is dedicated to reporting (Thompson 1994: V).

[14] Kreiter et al. (1982) uses tapes and slides, and also gives a great many grammatical hints, e.g. p. 135 about the *for+N+to+inf*-construction. – Killer's book (1985) is nicely and richly illustrated by cartoon-like drawings.

[15] Wallnig, Everett and Killer were building professionals; Kreiter's (et al.) book is more ambitious in linguistic and didactic items, but there is no systematic linguistic approach and the book reveals an unbalanced emphasis on building concrete flats ('Plattenbauweise'), typical of the former East German building style.

istry 160,000) and prohibitively expensive, thus excluding most individual users both as learners and buyers.

3. Further series: Various other publishing houses have started initiatives with ESP dictionaries, such as Peter Collins Publishing (for example, Collin 1986), Verlag Franz Vahlen, Munich (for example, Köbler 1998), Beck'sche Verlagsbuchhandlung, with its *Dictionary of legal, commercial and political terms* (Dietl 1988), and Oldenbourg Verlag, with, for example, a book on *Professional English* (Guess 1994). Only the last mentioned publication, of the Oldenbourg Verlag, is of interest here, since it deviates from the mechanically alphabetical order of entries in favour of a thematic arrangement. It represents the core of scientific and technical English within an overall arrangement of 10 lexical fields as cover terms: knowledge, modality, number, time, space, change, relationship, substance, quality, and purpose. While neither this classification nor the hyponyms in these groups will finally stand their ground against serious philosophical argument, the arrangement is – though with a pragmatic fuzzy logic – based on cognitive notions and concepts.[16]

4. Die Blaue Eule: I myself have begun a series of English and German ESP learning dictionaries in the Verlag Die Blaue Eule (1994ff.). Of the over twenty books scheduled, the first three volumes (*Building and architecture, Conference German and English,* and *English linguistics*) have appeared. The concept behind this series and the method of compilation used in these booklets implicitly underpin this article.

To conclude this fragmentary survey: English-German lexicography has not cared much for special-field dictionaries.[17] Those that we have are not learner's dictionaries in the specific sense that their entries are complemented by further grammatical, contextual or illustrative information liable to satisfy the learners' interests. They are even less learning dictionaries ('Lernwörterbücher' in the sense of Zöfgen 1991), meant for users to enlarge and improve their active vocabulary command. The only exceptions in the more recent publishing history are the Oldenbourg dictionary series and my own in Die Blaue Eule.

The distinction between learner's and learning dictionaries is considerable. Learner's dictionaries, meant for decoding, i.e. for looking up given words, tend to be comprehensive; learning dictionaries are intended for encoding

---

[16] Various methodological aspects of the Oldenbourg books are in need of improvement. For example, the order within the cover concepts/terms is neither transparent nor convincing. And the books do not allow searches for German words, i.e. they overemphasize the English-speaking point of view.

[17] The attitude that has helped contribute to this situation comes out in Landau's casual remarks (1989: 21-22) concerning "amateurish" subject-field dictionaries.

and are bound to be selective (though the criteria for selection must vary, depending on the target group). Learner's dictionaries can be either mono-lingual or bilingual, even multilingual.[18] Learning dictionaries, at least in the domain of ESP, should be bilingual, since the learners, when they acquire elements of the foreign language, simultaneously learn to master the equi-valents in their mother tongue and also the things and structures referred to.[19] Learning dictionaries should also use a thematic, rather than alphabetic arrangement.

What, then, should be included in the entries of learning dictionaries? Apart from the support by the mother tongue (bilingualism) and the rigor-ously selective thematic arrangement, which is bound to be somewhat subjective, the decisive guiding rule concerning learning dictionaries is, as mentioned earlier, for dictionary compilers to give motivating information.

In theory, motivating factors are manifold. They can, for example, be based on references to local history, known to teacher(s) and/or learner(s).[20] In general terms, the motivating/elucidating force has three sources: it is based on form (for example, word formation); it stems from an aspect of content (mainly semantics), or it may come from the historical/cultural back-ground of a word. In the following, the role of these three aspects will be illustrated tentatively with a few examples, mainly from the field of building and architecture.[21]

3. Word formation

It seems much easier for EFL learners to grasp and remember the words of a language if the internal structure of these is somewhat transparent to them, for example, if some basic rules of word formation are known to them. On principle, these rules are the same in ESP as in the common standard, but some of the possibilities of common word formation seem to be differently and uniquely exploited in ESP.

The most important types of word formation are, in ESP as in everyday language, compounding and derivation. In everyday language, both in Eng-

---

[18] An example of a multilingual dictionary on conference language is *Conference terminology* (1976).

[19] We should not forget that the average ESP learners, whether students of medicine, business, or chemistry, or practitioners in any particular craft or branch of industry, are not language specialists from English departments.

[20] For a survey of the key elements of dictionaries, see Landau (1989: 88-115): grammatical information, pronunciation, synonyms and illustrations can be important motivating fac-tors, but they are beyond the scope of this paper.

[21] The text examples are mainly taken from Hardwick/Markus (1994).

lish and German, speakers shy away from extremely long compounds. But compounds with three or more (up to seven) elements are not unusual in German for specific purposes (cf. Beier 1980: 49) – such as *Wohnsiedlungsplan, Wohnbauförderung*, and *Sachverständigenausschuß*. The English equivalents (*housing project, building support grant*, and *committee of experts* respectively) suggest that the compounded words are sometimes fewer in number, that they are usually spelt separately, and that the compound is sometimes avoided altogether in favour of a phraseologism. Whichever of these patterns applies, English compounds are often more transparent on the syntactic surface (as with *housing project*), but semantically, as will soon be clear, more complex than their German equivalents. This difference justifies a contrastive appproach.

A striking difference between English and German consists in the fact that German more often prefers the nominal compound, consisting of two nouns, where English has *Adj+N, N+ gen. attr.*, or some other phraseologism. Thus, we have *residential area* vs. *Wohngebiet* or *consent to build* vs. *Bauerlaubnis*. Looking for adjectival compounds with adjectives ending in *-ic/-ical* and *-able/-ible* in the field of building and architecture, we find a great many words such as:

1

panoramic view	*Panoramablick, Rundblick*
plastic filler	*Spachtelmasse*
pneumatic caisson	*Druckluft-Senkkasten*
electric storage heater	*Elektro-Warmwasseraufbereiter*
septic tank	*Faulgrube*
acoustic insulation	*Schallisolierung*
magnetic catch	*Magnetschnäpper*
acrylic paint	*Akrylfarbe*
synthetic resin	*Kunstharzgrundanstrich*
domestic garbage	*Haushaltsmüll*
mastic asphalt	*Gußasphalt*
hydroelectric dam	*Wasserkraft-Talsperre*
bureaucratic delay	*Amtsschimmel*
hydroelectric power station	*Wasserkraftwerk*
practical completion	*Gebrauchsabnahmeschein*
tropical woods	*Tropenhölzer*

removable casement	*Abstellflügel*
transportable plant	*Mobilanlage*
submersible pump	*Tauchpumpe*[22]

The following examples are phrasal lexemes,[23] using an infinitive with *to* (a) and prepositional phrases with *to* or *on* (b) – as opposed to the complex lexemes or syntagmas of German;

2a
consent to build	*Bauerlaubnis*
right to vote	*Stimmrecht*

2b
delivery to site[24]	*frei Baustelle*
stairs to loft	*Dachbodentreppe*
cover plate to switch	*Schalterdeckel*
debate on procedure	*Geschäftsordnungsdebatte*

Both in English and German the strategy of coining complex terms is similar in that the language signs are abbreviative; but in English the reduction or ellipsis seems to take place at the cost of semantics, syntax basically being intact. Thus the first phrase, *consent to build*, though it embeds an infinitive clause (*to build*), does not mark the subject or object of this clause; and in the cases of 2b, the nouns *site*, *loft* and *switch* lack a determiner and are thus not referentially, i.e. semantically, identified. *To loft* and *to switch* could, from the merely syntactic point of view, be also interpreted as verbs; only the semantic deep structure disambiguates the syntactic ambiguity.

The tendency towards a kind of telegraphic style in English goes even a step further. In the context of window opening types, compound participles are used in English (like *bottom hung, horizontal pivot hung, horizontally sliding*), where German has nouns (*Kippflügel-, Schwingflügel-*) and a noun plus a postpositioned adjective (*Schiebefenster horizontal*).[25] In other words, German tends to be more explicit by using a noun (such as *Flügel*) when reference is made to a thing (such as a window), whereas English tells us what state that thing is in or what it does (it is *hung* or it *slides*), but you have to be an insider to know that all this refers to a window.

---

[22] Many more examples for English *Ad.+N* vs. German *N+N* can be found in the booklets on conference language and linguistic terminology in my ESP series (ESP2 and 3): cf. *Delegationsleiter(in)* vs. *head of delegation, Gegenpartei* vs. *opposing party, Berater-gremium* vs. *advisory group, Wortfeld* vs. *lexical field*, etc.

[23] For the terminology used here cf. Lipka 1990: 80.

[24] Actually, 'Lieferung zum Grundstück'.

[25] Postposition of the adjective attribute is occasionally found in German ESP (*Forelle blau*); cf. Markus (1997: 492).

These observations correspond to the hypothesis developed by Hawkins, to the effect that in many ways English does not 'give away' the meaning on the surface structure, but 'hides' it in the syntactic deep structure, more so at least than German (Hawkins 1986).

A few further points of word formation are apt to enhance this theory. The common suffix *-er* for all kinds of professionals (*worker, carpenter*, etc.) or for people doing something habitually (*smoker*) is also frequently used in ESP for tools and machines, like *lever, crawler loader* (*Laderaupe*), *dozer* (*Flachbagger*), *pile driver* (*Pfahlrammer*), *starter bar* (*Anschlußeisen*), etc. In German the suffix *-er* is likewise used for both people and things, but it is, as the examples just given suggest, used less frequently for tools and machines.

There is no time here to discuss other types of word formation beyond compounds and derivations – though some scholars have emphasized the particular role of blends, back-derivations (example: *to air-condition* from *air-conditioning*),[26] clippings or other abbreviative reductions in everyday ESP like *sledge* or *hammer* for *sledge hammer* (cf. LGL 1980: 285). It stands to reason that in applied contexts of technology and crafts, where "time is money", syntactic and semantic abbreviation, both in German and English, will be frequent: a car mechanic will not always take the time to ask for a *14-mm Schraubenschlüssel*, but clip the term to a mere *14-er Schlüssel* or even to the decisive *differentia specifica*: '14-er'.

4. Semantics

One of the main devices of coining new words in ESP, particularly in building and architecture, is by metaphor.[27] Metaphorization is of course a common linguistic phenomenon: one refers to some level of meaning, at least implicitly, by explicitly using a word of another level, usually of more visual character or of a more familiar field than that which one really has in mind. Thus, for example, we refer to a person's *getting rooted* or *getting settled*, without meaning this literally. The matter-of-fact, usually non-organic worlds of languages for specific purposes (LSP's) generally reveal quite a fondness for anthropomorphic metaphors and other metaphors of the organic/animate world, i.e. that of animals or plants.[28] To begin with, in building and architecture many things are referred to in terms of parts of the body. Thus, *wall footing* is the foundation of a wall, *face shovel* is a special type of excavator

---

[26] For these two types, see Hansen et al. (1982: 145, 137).

[27] Gläser (1979: 33) has pointed out the role of metaphorization for many types of ESP.

[28] Cf. Gläser (1979: 34), where these types are mentioned.

(namely a *Hochlöffelbagger*), and *grab* evokes the concept of grabbing animals, but, in the context of heavy building machines, means another special
type of excavator, namely *Schalengreifer*. As the latter example suggests, the
reference to the sphere of human beings or animals can be an indirect one: *to
grab* implies hands or feet.

Building professionals are likely to have visual minds. We should therefore expect a great many metaphors in the field of building and architecture,
more than average. Checking this in our dictionary, I have found more than
can be mentioned here. The general plan for a house to be built is the
masterplan (German: *Hauptbebauungsplan*), a *worm's eye view* is the view
of something from a low position on the ground (the German equivalent is
Froschperspektive), and *dovetailed* in the branch of carpentry means a special
technique of joining boards, which is common today and which German
speakers slightly more functionally call *genutet und gefedert*.

It has been rightly suggested that metaphorization thrives particularly
strongly in colloquial ESP (LGL 1980: 285; Beier 1980: 36). Electricians,
when referring to voltage, in English often use the informal term *juice*.[29] In
the same way many expressions for tools of craftsmen are subject to register
or dialectal variation – if we only think of the different names of the
bricklayer's main tool, the trowel, both in English and German.[30] Such
specific problems of dialectal use, however, are beyond the primary concern
of foreign language learners.

Apart form metaphors, building terminology often contains metonymy,
to be opposed to metaphor, but sometimes defined as a subtype of it. A metonymy refers to something in terms of something else which is causally or
empirically connected with what the speaker really has in mind (see Bussmann 1996: 305). As such, metonymy, too, is common in everyday language.
But there seems to be a preference for certain metonymous types in ESP, at
least in contrast to German.

The point may be illustrated by the following three contrastive examples,
where English and German have a different notion of the words as to the
semantic feature [±abstract].

3
roof structure   *Dachstuhl*
supporting   *(Holz-)Bohle*
central reservation (motorway) *Grünstreifen* (Autobahn)

Structure in English can be something abstract or concrete; in other words, it
is ambivalent as to the feature [abstract]. The German equivalent *Stuhl* in the

---

29 Another meaning of this in informal English is 'petrol'.
30 In German we have *Kelle, Truffel* (cf. Bucksch 1980).

context of *Dachstuhl*, on the other hand, is of course a metaphor evoking the concrete idea of support in the way of a chair. Similarly, *supporting*, in the second example, refers to the function of something rather than to a concrete object (as the German word *Bohle*). And *reservation*, in the third case, at first sight refers rather abstractly to an activity, and only by metonymous transfer to a relic area left to the American Indians or, as in our case, to a strip of land in the middle of a motorway. By the same token, a *vacancy* is not an equivalent to German *Vakanz* (the abstract state of something to be vacant), but a (concrete) job, position or room which is vacant.

Many other similar examples reveal that German often semantically pins things down to a more precise meaning, where English prefers a cover term (or hyperonym).[31] Thus, the term *hot water* in English includes both the substance of (hot) water and the supply of it; in German we (still) have *Warmwasser* for the liquid and *Warmwasserversorgung* for the facility offered by the pipe.[32] Similarly, the English word *alarm* levels the semantic distinction between the noise that you can hear (German: *Alarm*) and the expensive warning system that many house owners wouldn't be without these days (German: *Alarmsystem*). Finally, *finishes* (plural of the noun *finish*) levels the difference between what is being done to a wall, ceiling or floor in a house and the materials used in these working processes. Accordingly, *timber finishes* – surprisingly from the German point of view – means *Holzböden*.

The distinction between an action or job and its product, i.e. the result of the action, is generally less marked in English building vocabulary. The word *building* itself is a good case in point. *Building*, without attributive specification, refers to the product that you can see and that can burn down. But in the phrase *the building of conventional houses* the term is to be marked by the feature [+activity]. On the basis of this principle of semantic ambiguity many compounds with the determinant *building* – such as *building authority*, *building contract*, *building plot*, *building regulations* – are ambiguous as to whether *building* is an object or an activity. And in our dictionary dozens of other verbal nouns with *ing*-suffix – such as *timber boarding* for German *Bretterbelag* or *Verbretterung* – are unmarked as to the distinction of activity vs. product, so that either of the features or both of

---

[31] As to the general role of hierarchy in word fields, cf. Lipka (1990: 135).

[32] I think nowadays insiders and homeowners would often clip *Warmwasserversorgung* to a mere *Warmwasser*.

them may be relevant.[33]

Another semantic feature which seems to be less often marked in English than in German is that of [±person]. A case in point is the word *foaming agent* for German *Schäummittel*.[34] *Agent* in the building trade is also a synonym for the *contract manager* of a firm (German: *Bauführer*). The point takes us back to the many nouns in the building trade ending in -*er*, nouns that refer to either a person or a machine/tool.

5. The motivating role of history

As mentioned in the introduction above, ESP domains are likely to be different in their coding policy. Building and architecture, like seafaring, agriculture, cooking, hunting and fishing, many common crafts, and various academic fields, such as law, are traditional occupations which have developed their technical nomenclatures in different countries over centuries. Here, learning difficulties will mainly be due to the non-transparent historicity of many words, and a well-dosed amount of historical contextuality as well as some etymological transparency should be welcomed by learners. By contrast, there are a great many new branches whose history must be counted in decades or even years, as, for example, in the case of linguistics, computer studies, genetic engineering, space technology, and the sciences in general. In fields of this kind the special terms have often been imported with the new 'things'. Accordingly, we should here reckon with a greater number of borrowings and with those types of word formation which reveal little heed to a word's origin: abbreviations, clippings, blends. This trend will be particularly striking in branches affected by business, i.e. in domains subject to the rules of the market and to rapid change.

Between these extremes of traditional words and recent borrowings, there are a great many medium-age borrowings in ESP, assimilated, yet testimony to the Greek and, in particular, Latin and French influences on historical English. While a knowledge of any of these languages cannot, of course, be generally expected of ESP learners, teachers and learners could be concerned with the most frequent foreign morphemes. It does not take much effort, but

---

[33] Cf. *housing* + *N* (German: *Siedlungs-, Immobilien-, Wohnungs-, Wohn-*); *shopping centre* (*Einkaufs-/Ladenzentrum*); *detail drawing* (*Detailplan*); *drawing office* (*Zeichenbüro*); *working drawing* (*Ausführungszeichnung, Installationsplan*); *drawing paper*(*Zeichenpapier*); *living area* (*Wohnfläche*); *engineering* (*Ingenieurwesen*); *shopping arcade* (*Ladenpassage*); *bearing pressure* (*Auflagerdruck*); *bending moment* (*Biegemoment*), etc.

[34] Cf. also *detergent* vs. *Waschpulver*. English *walkman, diskman*, etc., which also reveal the transfer of the semantic feature [person] into the world of objects, but German has borrowed these words.

renders things more transparent to realize that Greek *dys-* (as a prefix) means 'deviation from a norm' (e.g. in *dysphasia*), whereas Latin *dis-* means 'apart'.

Above all, both teachers and learners should be aware of the fact that certain ESP domains favour certain loaning languages. In medicine, astronomy, geometry, physics, rhetorics and other fields Greek morphemes must be reckoned with (for historical reasons); French is bound to have left an influence in diplomacy, gastronomy, tourism, fashion, and various cultural branches inititated or encouraged by France's leading role in these fields in the 18th and 19th centuries.[35] Latin was the European *lingua franca* in academic activities until the later 17th century and therefore has had a particularly strong influence on the levels of research and academic teaching, at least in traditional subjects. Business, on the other hand, is a fairly young academic field and, as is well-known, strongly influenced by Anglo-American theory and practice.

Such remarks may sound trivial when theoretically stated, but imply a great amount of learning help when applied. In classical fields Greek/Latin internationalisms are bound to play a major role. Naturally this holds also true for morphemes.

Among the affixes, some of the foreign morphemes are certainly worth knowing, such as

4

a-/an- from Latin *a/ab* ('away from, without'): *asymmetric, anelectric*
sub- from Latin ('under'): *subway, substructure*
super- from Latin ('above, over'): *superstratum, superheat*
auto- from Greek ('by/of oneself' or 'itself'): *autointoxication, autodynamic, automotive*
bi- from Greek ('two'): *bifocal, bipolar*
hyper- from Greek ('exceeding the norm'): *hyperacid, hyperaccurate*
iso- from Greek ('equal'): *isosceles triangle*

All these prefixes have been said to be typical of, though not restricted to, ESP.[36] On the basis of my work in the field of building and architecture, I would like to add that they are not quite as frequent in building crafts as in the sciences (due, perhaps, to the lack of a classical education on the part of building practitioners). And looking at the examples just given, one will find that most of them do not come from building activities proper, but from subsections or marginal fields such as geometry, electrical engineering,

---

[35] Cf., for example, terms of theatre life (*theatre, role, character, part, protagonist*, etc.) – most of them are French by origin.
[36] Hansen et al. (1982: 72-84). I owe part of the preceding list to this source.

medicine,[37] etc. The same limited relevance can be attested to Latinate pre-fixes, such as *de-* (as in *deform*), and to suffixes, such as

5
nominal *-ant/-ent* (*coolant, disinfectant, attendant*)
nominal *-ee* (*trainee, nominee, escapee*)
verbal *-ize*[38] or *-ate*[39] (*to moisterize, to chlorinate*).

The nominal suffix *-ee*, which raises the question of its origin, deserves some special attention. It is usually interpreted as a marker of a person who is passively involved. Words like *employee, trainee*, etc. at first sight look like French feminine forms, but since this interpretation does not make much sense, the *-ee* is better explained as a mere spelling variant for original stressed /e:/ of the French participial ending *-é*. This participle was used not only in the context of the passive form (*il est traîné*), but also for the *passé composé* (*il est echappé*). Accordingly, an *escapee*, just as an *escapist*, is 'sb. who has escaped'. The English suffix *-ee*, then, is again a case of an ambiguous surface structure – here with either a passive or a perfective meaning.

The historicity of an ESP domain is not only a question of the particular lending languages looming large in the background. It also implies the specific rootedness of an ESP field. Building, for example, unlike modern sciences such as chemistry or computer sciences, is a very traditional and ubiquitous craft. Accordingly, its terminology tends to be very old and regional.

The often local quality of lexis in the language of building is the very opposite of what one has to expect in the language of sciences, which are basically international.[40] Building trade vocabulary reveals not only a local, but also a slangy touch. One only has to imagine the situation of bricklayers or other craftsmen on a building site. Unless we are talking about very big building projects, particularly abroad, craftsmen would be local people, and they would have less knowledge of 'hard' international terms, but rather use visual metaphors instead (like English: ?, German: *Speis* (Austrian *Malter*) for *mortar*). On the other hand architects, engineers and technical designers would naturally use more scientific, which means, a great number of inter-

---

[37] Medical terms have found their way into our dictionary in the section on building abroad, where preventive medical measures are of interest.

[38] From Latin *-isare*, as in *stabilisare*.

[39] From the participial ending *-atus*, which has given rise to many loan words (verbs, such as *to assimilate*, and adjectives, such as *appropriate*).

[40] Computer studies are a good example: most terms have simply been borrowed by German and other languages from English and have only slightly been integrated – cf. *CD-ROM, PC, portable printer* etc., which have been well established in German as *CD-Rom, (der) PC* and *portabler Printer*.

national terms. We have, in other words, to reckon with a marked vertical stratification in this field.

One decisive factor of this stratification is the different origin of the words used, thus their historical dimension. Many of the words of the architects are 'hard' words of Latin or French origin; cf.

6

industrial project	*Industriegebiet*
pedestrian zone	*Fußgängerzone*
structural alteration	*Umbau*
housing estate	*Wohnsiedlung*
feasibility study	*Durchführbarkeitsstudie*
final design	*endgültiger Entwurf*

The designers will also know a great many Latin terms, but, on the other hand, will also be familiar with geometrical terms, which, given the Greek history of geometry, will in many cases be of Greek etymology. Cf.

7

from Latin:

oblique angled	*schiefwinklig*

from Greek:

sepia print	*Sepiadruck*
cylinder	*Zylinder*
isoscele	*gleichschenklig*
scalene, with unequal sides	*ungleichseitig*
trapezium	*Trapez*

By contrast, the craftsmen will mainly use words of Germanic, Scandinavian or French origin. This is obvious with the terms for the craftsmen themselves. Cf.

8

carpenter	*Zimmermann*
electrician	*Elektriker*
floor layer	*Bodenleger*
foreman	*Vorarbeiter, Meister*
ganger	*Schachtmeister*
glazier	*Glaser*
ironmonger	*Beschlägespezialist*
joiner	*Schreiner*
labourer, unskilled worker	*Hilfsarbeiter*
painter	*Maler, Anstreicher*
paper-hanger	*Tapezierer*

| *plasterer* | *Verputzer, Stukkateur* |
| *roofer* | *Dachdecker* |

It should come as no surprise that as a rule the tools of craftsmen also have very old names, which, if of Romance origin, are at least very much integrated in English. Thus we have *bucket, hammer, trowel, axe, screwdriver, drill*, etc., on the one hand, and *pliers (Zange), forge (Esse), vice (Schraubstock), adhesive (Klebstoff)* etc., all from French, on the other. While there are no ready-made rules for the etymological attribution of these and other names for tools, there is at least a tendency for common and basic tools (and crafts) to be rooted in Britain's pre-Norman period, whereas tools and machines that were invented later and/or are products of the industrial age are likely to be of French etymology – like the word *machine* itself and many of its compounds, for example *planing machine* (German: *Hobelmaschine*, from French: *planer*), *veneering press (Furnierpresse)* and *to solder (löten*, from French: *souder)*.

History has also left its traces in the field of house painting, where we should not search for words in the 'drawer' of traditional Germanic terms if we are talking about modern applications of painting, i.e. those that we owe to chemistry. *Emulsion paint, enamel paint, lacquer, polyestyrene, synthetic resin primer (Kunstharzmennige)* are such terms for poisonous paints, to be contrasted with the terms of old applications that are used for what are now called environmental paints: *varnish (Firnis), lime wash (Kalkfarbe), (to) oil, stain (Beize)*, etc.

So while English draws on its etymological wealth and has freely borrowed from Greek, Latin, French and other languages, German LSP words are often transparent in their word formation.[41] Learners of ESP should be aware of this contrastive difference.

6. Summary and conclusion

The learner's acquisition of LSP vocabulary depends less on textbooks and comprehensive dictionaries, however good and useful they may be, than on well-constructed learning dictionaries which should be bilingual, arranged in cognitively convincing thematic groups, and enriched by informative details which can motivate the learners.

---

[41] Von Hahn (1983: 86f.) has argued that German LSP words often reflect the implicit hierarchical structure of compounds or derivations (e.g. *Anhängerbremskraftregler = Regler für die Bremskraft von Anhängern*). As opposed to this motivation of learners to be gleaned from word formation, learners of ESP have to reckon with more foreign etymological elements.

Since motivation is a complex field and naturally includes the personality of the teacher, the suggestions in this paper on how to endow dictionary entries with motivating pieces of information are tentative. They may be considered less so in view of the present picture of ESP dictionaries, which is desolate from the point of view of the German-speaking learner. There are both didactic and linguistic deficits.

Trying to indicate possible ways of improvement, I have focussed on three main chapters: word formation, semantics, and etymology. They may help to give ESP, in spite of its formidable extent and erratic quality, a degree of coherence and causality.

On the basis of what we have found on the three levels, one of the more complex questions can now be answered, namely why do we have relatively many semantic ambiguities in the surface structure of ESP?

The *-er* derivations discussed above are not so typical of ESP as a whole, since they are Germanic by origin. The main and all-pervasive feature of almost all ESP types, including building and architecture, is the Latin/French background of probably more than two thirds of all words. The fact is well-known, but the natural consequences for the vocabulary structure of ESP have obviously been overlooked.

It seems natural that native speakers of English, not understanding the Latinate words that were handed down to them, have tried to cover more things with them than for example the native speakers of German. In German LSP, the meaning of a word is, more often than not, fairly transparent, even to the less-educated competent speaker. In English, on the other hand, words are widely dissociated so that speakers would have a motivation to simplify things somewhat on a semantic level, leaving the distinction of some of the semantic features which count in the surface structure of German to disambiguation by syntax and context.

References

Albrecht, Jörn (1992): "Wortschatz versus Terminologie: Einzelsprachliche Charakteristika in der Fachterminologie". Albrecht, Jörn/Richard Baum, eds. *Fachsprache und Terminologie in Geschichte und Gegenwart*. Tübingen: Narr, 59-78.

Beier, Rudolf (1980): *Englische Fachsprache*. Stuttgart etc.: Kohlhammer.

Beier, Rudolf/Werner Forner (1994): "Zum Stand der Fachsprachenlehre am SISIB". Burkhard Schaeder, ed. Siegener Institut für Sprachen im Beruf (SISIB). *Fachsprachen und Fachkommunikation in Forschung, Lehre und beruflicher Praxis*. Essen: Blaue Eule, 149-164.

Bucksch, Herbert (1980): *Wörterbuch für Architektur, Hochbau und Baustoffe*, 2 vols. Wiesbaden etc: Bauverlag.

Bussmann, Hadumod (1996): *Routledge dictionary of language and linguistics.* Gregory P. Trauth/Kerstin Kazzazi, eds. London/New York: Routledge.

Collin, Peter H. (1986): *English business dictionary.* Teddington, Middlesex: Collins Publishing.

Conference Terminology (1976*): A manual for conference members and interpreters in English, Russian, French, Italian, Spanish, German, Hungarian.* Amsterdam etc: Elsevier Scientific Publishing Company.

Dietl, Clara-Erika (1988): *Wörterbuch für Recht, Wirtschaft und Politik.* 2 Teile. München: Beck'sche Verlagsbuchhandlung.

Gläser, Rosemarie (1979): *Fachstile des Englischen.* Leipzig: Enzyklopädie.

Gläser, Rosemarie (1990): *Fachtextsorten im Englischen.* Tübingen: Narr.

Guess, John C. (1994): *Professional English in science and technology. A learner's essential companion with German equivalents.* München etc.: Oldenbourg.

Hansen, Barbara/Klaus Hansen/Albrecht Neubert/Manfred Schentke (1982): *Englische Lexikologie. Einführung in Wortbildung und lexikalische Semantik.* Leipzig: Enzyklopädie.

Hardwick, Benjamin/Manfred Markus (1994): *Bauen und Architektur. Building and architecture. The main words in their fields. ESP 1.* Essen: Blaue Eule.

Hawkins, John A. (1986): *A comparative typology of English and German: unifying the contrasts.* London: Routledge.

Hoffmann, Lothar (1985): *Kommunikationsmittel Fachsprache.* Tübingen: Gunter Narr.

Jahr, Silke (1993): *Das Fachwort in der kognitiven und sprachlichen Repräsentation.* Essen: Blaue Eule.

Killer, W.K. ([5]1985): *Bautechnisches Englisch im Bild. Illustrated technical German for builders.* Wiesbaden/Berlin: Bauverlag.

Köbler, Gerhard (1998): *Rechtsenglisch. Deutsch-englisches und englisch-deutsches Rechtwörterbuch für jedermann.* München: Vahlen.

Kreiter, Wolfgang et al. (1982): *Englisch für das Bauwesen.* Leipzig: Enzyklopädie.

Landau, Sidney I. (1989): *Dictionaries. The art and craft of lexicography.* Cambridge: CUP.

Lipka, Leonhard (1990): *An outline of English lexicology. Lexical structure, word semantics, and word-formation.* Tübingen: Niemeyer.

LGL = Althaus, Hans Peter/Helmut Henne/Herbert Ernst Wiegand, eds. (1980): Lexikon der Germanistischen Linguistik. Tübingen: Niemeyer.

Lück, Erich (1997): "Neuerscheinungen auf dem Wörterbuchmarkt". *Lebende Sprachen* 42, 125-26.

Markus, Manfred (1995): *Conference English. Konferenzsprache Deutsch. ESP 2.* Essen: Blaue Eule.

Markus, Manfred (1999): *Linguistik Deutsch und Englisch. Linguistics German and English.* ESP 2. Essen: Blaue Eule.

Markus, Manfred (1997): "'The men present' vs 'the present case': word order rules concerning the position of the English adjective". *Anglia* 115, 487-506.

Möhn, Dieter/Roland Pelka (1984): *Fachsprachen. Eine Einführung.* Tübingen: Niemeyer.

Reinhardt, W. (1983): "Fachsprachliches Wortbildungsminimum und 'Fachlichkeit' von Texten". *Fachsprache* 5, 2-11.

Sager, John C./Davis Dungworth/Peter E. McDonald (1980): *English special languages. Principles and practice in science and technology.* Wiesbaden: Brandstetter.

Schaeder, Burkhard (1994): "Internationalismen – Gleiche Wortschätze in verschiedenen Sprachen". Burkhard Schaeder, ed. Siegener Institut für Sprachen im Beruf (SISIB). *Fachsprachen und Fachkommunikation in Forschung, Lehre und beruflicher Praxis.* Essen: Blaue Eule, 99-108.

Sprigade, Ragna/Christiane Adler/Renate Mitchell (1986): *Englisch für Mediziner.* Leipzig: Enzyklopädie.

Summers, Della (1988): "ELT dictionaries: past, present, and future". *English Today* 14, 10-16.

Thompson, Geoff (1994): *Collins Cobuild English guides 5: Reporting.* London: Harper Collins Publishers.

Voigt, Walter (1981): "Wörterbuch, Wörterbuchmacher, Wörterbuchprobleme. Ein Werkstattgespräch". *Wort und Sprache. Beiträge zu Problemen der Lexikographie und Sprachpraxis, veröffentlicht zum 125jährigen Bestehen des Langenscheidt-Verlags.* Berlin etc.: Langenscheidt, 24-33.

von Hahn, Walther (1983): *Fachkommunikation: Entwicklung, linguistische Konzepte, betriebliche Beispiele.* Berlin/New York: de Gruyter.

Wallnig, Günter/Harry Everett (⁷1984): *Englisch für Baufachleute. L'anglais dans le batiment.* 3 vols. Wiesbaden/Berlin: Bauverlag.

Zöfgen, Ekkehard (1991): "Bilingual learner's dictionaries". Franz Josef Hausmann/ Oskar Reichmann/ Edda Wiegand/L. Zgusta, eds. *Wörterbücher, dictionaries, dictionnaires (1989-1991): Ein internationales Handbuch zur Lexikographie.* Drei Teilbände. Berlin: de Gruyter, 1989, 1990, 1991. Art. 305.